Mastering Apex Programming

A developer's guide to learning advanced
techniques and best practices for building
robust Salesforce applications

Paul Battisson

BIRMINGHAM—MUMBAI

Mastering Apex Programming

Commissioning Editor: Richa Tripathi

Acquisition Editor: Denim Pinto

Senior Editor: Rohit Singh

Content Development Editor: Tiksha Lad

Technical Editor: Pradeep Sahu

Copy Editor: Safis Editing

Project Coordinator: Francy Puthiry

Proofreader: Safis Editing

Indexer: Tejal Daruwale Soni

Production Designer: Alishon Mendonsa

First published: November 2020

Production reference: 1191120

Published by Packt Publishing Ltd.
Livery Place
35 Livery Street
Birmingham
B3 2PB, UK.

ISBN 978-1-80020-092-0

www.packt.com

To Amanda, for all your love and support in all things.

– Paul Battisson

Packt.com

Subscribe to our online digital library for full access to over 7,000 books and videos, as well as industry leading tools to help you plan your personal development and advance your career. For more information, please visit our website.

Why subscribe?

- Spend less time learning and more time coding with practical eBooks and Videos from over 4,000 industry professionals

- Improve your learning with Skill Plans built especially for you

- Get a free eBook or video every month

- Fully searchable for easy access to vital information

- Copy and paste, print, and bookmark content

Did you know that Packt offers eBook versions of every book published, with PDF and ePub files available? You can upgrade to the eBook version at packt.com and as a print book customer, you are entitled to a discount on the eBook copy. Get in touch with us at customercare@packtpub.com for more details.

At www.packt.com, you can also read a collection of free technical articles, sign up for a range of free newsletters, and receive exclusive discounts and offers on Packt books and eBooks.

Foreword

The Salesforce platform is powerful, yet approachable. That is why I fell in love with it and teach it to this day at `MikeWheelerMediaPlus.com`. Simply put, Salesforce is the most attainable path to a cloud career.

Although much can be built in Salesforce with clicks instead of code, the ability to code will separate you from the crowd. This book unlocks that power and grants you extreme relevance in the marketplace.

Apex is the fundamental language of Salesforce. It drives the underpinnings of the platform. It is an efficient and elegant language. But as with all programming languages, it is not without its quirks.

In the pages ahead, *Paul Battisson* will share his own lessons learned from years of solving problems with Apex. It will serve you well as a reference and guide, illuminating the blind turns and challenging paths that lay before you as you strike out on your journey of finding the intersection of attainable and essential.

Mike Wheeler

Owner, Mike Wheeler Media, LLC

Contributors

About the author

Paul Battisson is a seven-time Salesforce MVP and has been a speaker at numerous global Salesforce events, including Dreamforce, London's Calling, and India Dreamin. He has been working with the Salesforce platform for over 11 years in a mix of both product development and consulting roles. Paul now helps lead a UK-based consulting partner, as well as blogs, has a YouTube channel, and leads a Salesforce Developer Group.

I would like to thank all who have listened to and supported me in writing this book. This includes the entire Cloud Galacticos team; Kerry Townsend for her support and ear; Carolina Ruiz for (once again) helping with my questions and ideas. I would also like to thank my family for their patience as I worked on the book, as well as Ian, Day, and James for listening to all of the book talk. A special thanks to Mike Gill for all his support, great advice, and fantastic feedback.

About the reviewer

Michael Gill is an experienced technical architect. His career in Salesforce and cloud technology now spans two decades; he started his career with Oracle NetSuite. For the past decade, he has been focused on the Salesforce platform and other leading cloud technologies.

He co-writes the hugely popular Salesforce Weekly blog dedicated to all things Salesforce. He was recognized as a Salesforce MVP for five consecutive years and was recently awarded the MVP Hall of Fame accolade.

He has previously reviewed *Learning Salesforce Visual Workflow and Salesforce CRM: The Definitive Admin Handbook* and the *Complete Lighting Development* video series.

Packt is searching for authors like you

If you're interested in becoming an author for Packt, please visit `authors.packtpub.com` and apply today. We have worked with thousands of developers and tech professionals, just like you, to help them share their insight with the global tech community. You can make a general application, apply for a specific hot topic that we are recruiting an author for, or submit your own idea.

Table of Contents

Preface

Section 1 – Triggers, Testing, and Security

1

Common Apex Mistakes

Technical Requirements	4	Retrieving configuration data in a bulkified way	8
Null pointer exceptions	4		
Exceptions on object instances	5	Bulkification – querying within loops	11
Exceptions when working with maps	6	Hardcoding	15
		Summary	18

2

Debugging Apex

Technical requirements	20	Apex Interactive Debugger	30
Debugging on Salesforce	20	ISV Customer Debugger	30
Prevention is better than a cure	20		
Log levels	21	Which tool to use?	30
SFDX and streaming logs	23	Summary	32
Debugging using the Apex Replay Debugger	26		

3
Triggers and Managing Trigger Execution

Technical Requirements   34   Trigger architecture   39

The Salesforce order of   Using trigger handler
execution   34   frameworks   41

An example scenario   35   Controlling trigger execution   49

The save order of execution   36   Summary   53

Clicks and code   38

4
Exceptions and Exception Handling

Technical Requirements   56   Catching errors   58

Understanding the different   Using the finally block   60
types of exceptions   56   Exception logging   62

Expected exceptions   56   Capturing state   66

Unexpected exceptions   56   Using custom exception types   69

Unknown exceptions   57   Summary   70

5
Testing Apex Code

Technical Requirements   72   with
                                                   static resources   81
Understanding the importance
of testing   72   Using Test.startTest and Test.stopTest
                                                   to demarcate the code under test 85
Using a test data factory to
create data   73   Using assertions to validate behavior 86

Loading test data using Test.   Writing a test for any bug that occurs 86
loadData   79   Summary   87

Testing RESTful web services

6
Secure Apex Programming

How permissions and sharing work on Salesforce 90
Sharing and performance 91

Enforcing sharing 92
Sharing records using Apex 95
Enforcing object and field permissions 98

Understanding Apex class security 102
Enforcing permissions and security within SOQL 103
Avoiding SOQL injection vulnerabilities 104
Summary 106

Section 2 – Asynchronous Apex and Apex REST

7
Utilizing Future Methods

Technical Requirements 112
When to use a future method 112
Mixed DML 112
Other use cases for future methods 113

Defining future methods 114
Passing state and coordinating data 116

Calling future methods 119
Monitoring execution of future method invocations 120

Testing future methods 121
Summary 124

8
Working with Batch Apex

Technical Requirements 126
When to use Batch Apex 126
Large data volumes 126
Complex logical manipulation processes 127

High-volume web service callouts 127
Asynchronous queue processing 128

Defining a Batch Apex class 130
The base interface 130

Invoking Batch Apex 137

Using Database.executeBatch 138

Monitoring Batch Apex 146

Exception handling and platform events 148

Testing Batch Apex 149

Summary 150

9
Working with Queueable Apex

What is Queueable Apex? 152

Queueable versus future 154
Queueable versus Batch 155

When to use Queueable Apex 156

Extensive or complex processes 156
Callouts 157
Chained processes 157

Defining Queueable Apex implementations 158

Allowing callouts 160

Invoking Queueable Apex 160

Enqueuing child/chained jobs 161

Testing Queueable Apex 162
Summary 163

10
Scheduling Apex Jobs

Technical Requirements 166

When to use Scheduled Apex jobs 166

One-off executions 166
Repeating jobs 167

Defining a schedulable Apex class 167

Scheduling an Apex class 168

Using the Apex Scheduler 168
Using the System.schedule method 171

System.schedule versus System.scheduleBatch for Batch Apex classes 174
Suicidal scheduling 176
Monitoring a scheduled job 176
Scheduled job limits 178

Testing scheduled jobs and Apex scheduling 179
Summary 182

11

Using Platform Events

Technical Requirements 184

An overview of event-driven architecture and the event bus 184

Exploring event-driven architecture 185
The event bus 185
When to use platform events 186
Defining and publishing a platform event 188
Using Apex 191
Using Process Builder to publish events 193
Publishing platform events through Flow 195
Using the REST API 198

Subscribing to and handling platform events 200

Handling platform events using Apex triggers 200
Subscribing to platform events in Process Builder 203
Change Data Capture and platform events 209

Testing platform events 210
Testing whether platform events are publishing 210
Testing the consumption of platform events 212

A discussion of the CometD protocol and handling events externally 216
Summary 217

12

Apex REST and Custom Web Services

Technical requirements 220
An overview of REST 220
HTTP methods 221
REST and Apex – when to use custom endpoints 222
Custom logic or complex endpoints 223

Defining endpoints 224
A more detailed example 226

Dynamic parsing using custom metadata 232
Testing endpoints using

Workbench 235
Exposing endpoints 237
Public APIs and Sites pages 238

An alternative using URL Rewriter and Visualforce pages 240
Handling request body data 243
Handling JSON 246
Handling XML 248

Testing Apex REST code 249
Summary 256

Section 3 – Apex Performance

13

Performance and the Salesforce Governor Limits

The Salesforce application request lifecycle 262

Multi-tenancy and performance 264

Governor limits and why we

should embrace them 266

Thinking about performance 268

Summary 270

14

Performance Profiling

Technical Requirements 272

Measure twice, cut once 272

The OODA methodology 273

Observe 274

Decide 274

Act 275

Profiling Apex performance 281

A utility class to profile Apex 283

Profiling Lightning Web Components performance 293

Summary 294

15

Improving Apex Performance

Technical Requirements 298

Improving CPU time 298

Faster for loops 299

Using maps to remove and reduce looping 302

Reducing the use of expensive operations 304

Reducing heap size usage 306

Batched for loops 307

Using scoping 307

Removing unwanted items 308

Improving query selectivity 310

Number of queries 314

Retrieving child records with a sub query 314

Cache results 315

Platform Cache 315

Understanding when to make some of these improvements 320

Summary 321

Chapter 13, Performance and the Salesforce Governor Limits, covers the Salesforce governor limits at a high level and how we should think about performance management in regard to Salesforce and Apex.

Chapter 14, Performance Profiling, details how to profile the performance of applications on Salesforce and correctly analyze the results.

Chapter 15, Improving Apex Performance, goes through specific examples of how to improve the performance of your Apex code.

Chapter 16, Performance and Application Architectures, finishes the book with a discussion on the impact different architectures can have upon application performance.

To get the most out of this book

It is assumed you have working experience of Apex, which you need in order to read this book. You can run all code in a developer edition org.

If you are using the digital version of this book, we advise you to type the code yourself or access the code via the GitHub repository (link available in the next section). Doing so will help you avoid any potential errors related to the copying and pasting of code.

Download the example code files

You can download the example code files for this book from GitHub at `https://github.com/PacktPublishing/Mastering-Apex-Programming`. In case there's an update to the code, it will be updated on the existing GitHub repository.

We also have other code bundles from our rich catalog of books and videos available at `https://github.com/PacktPublishing/`. Check them out!

Download the color images

We also provide a PDF file that has color images of the screenshots/diagrams used in this book. You can download it here:

`https://static.packt-cdn.com/downloads/9781800200920_ColorImages.pdf`

Conventions used

There are a number of text conventions used throughout this book.

`Code in text`: Indicates code words in text, database table names, folder names, filenames, file extensions, pathnames, dummy URLs, user input, and Twitter handles. Here is an example: "In the following screenshot, you can see how I have entered this URL with the `ACME123` resource identifier, and run a `GET` request to retrieve the hospital record with `Hospital_Ref_Code__c` set to `ACME123`."

A block of code is set as follows:

```
Dom.Document doc = new Dom.Document();
doc.load(data.toString());
Dom.XMLNode req = doc.getRootElement();
```

When we wish to draw your attention to a particular part of a code block, the relevant lines or items are set in bold:

```
public with sharing class ProfilingUtility {
    private static Map<String, Integer> recordings;
}
```

Bold: Indicates a new term, an important word, or words that you see onscreen. For example, words in menus or dialog boxes appear in the text like this. Here is an example: "However, you can click the **Show Raw Response** link and the raw response from the request will be shown."

> **Tips or important notes**
> Appear like this.

Get in touch

Feedback from our readers is always welcome.

General feedback: If you have questions about any aspect of this book, mention the book title in the subject of your message and email us at `customercare@packtpub.com`.

Errata: Although we have taken every care to ensure the accuracy of our content, mistakes do happen. If you have found a mistake in this book, we would be grateful if you would report this to us. Please visit `www.packtpub.com/support/errata`, selecting your book, clicking on the Errata Submission Form link, and entering the details.

Piracy: If you come across any illegal copies of our works in any form on the Internet, we would be grateful if you would provide us with the location address or website name. Please contact us at `copyright@packt.com` with a link to the material.

If you are interested in becoming an author: If there is a topic that you have expertise in and you are interested in either writing or contributing to a book, please visit authors.packtpub.com.

Reviews

Please leave a review. Once you have read and used this book, why not leave a review on the site that you purchased it from? Potential readers can then see and use your unbiased opinion to make purchase decisions, we at Packt can understand what you think about our products, and our authors can see your feedback on their book. Thank you!

For more information about Packt, please visit packt.com.

Section 1 – Triggers, Testing, and Security

In this section, we will begin by reviewing common mistakes made by developers in their Apex code and how to avoid them. This will lead us into a discussion around debugging Apex when we find an error. Following this, we will discuss how to work with Salesforce triggers effectively and how to improve our Apex testing, as well as understand how to improve security within our code.

This section covers the following chapters:

- *Chapter 1, Common Apex Mistakes*
- *Chapter 2, Debugging Apex*
- *Chapter 3, Triggers and Managing Trigger Execution*
- *Chapter 4, Exceptions and Exception Handling*
- *Chapter 5, Testing Apex Code*
- *Chapter 6, Secure Apex Programming*

1
Common Apex Mistakes

In this chapter, we will cover common mistakes made when developing in Apex and the appropriate defensive programming techniques to avoid them. Before we begin to move into more advanced topics within the Apex language, it is important that we first of all ensure a common grounding in removing any common errors within our code. For some of you, this material may simply be a refresher or a reiteration of some practices; however, these mistakes form the basis of many of the common exceptions and errors that I have seen in my time working with the Salesforce platform. By the end of this chapter, you will hopefully be more aware of when these mistakes may occur within your code and be able to develop in a defensive style to avoid them.

In this chapter, we will cover the following topics:

- Null pointer exceptions
- Bulkification of Apex code to avoid Governor Limits
- Hardcoding references to specific object instances
- Patterns to deal with managing data across a transaction

Technical Requirements

The code for the chapter can be found here, `https://github.com/PacktPublishing/Mastering-Apex-Programming/tree/Chapter-1`.

Null pointer exceptions

Almost every developer working with the Salesforce platform has encountered the dreaded phrase *Attempt to de-reference a null object*. At its heart, this is one of the simplest errors to both generate and handle effectively, but its error message can cause great confusion for new and experienced developers alike, as it is often unclear how the exception is occurring.

Let's start by discussing in the abstract form how the error is generated. This is definitely a runtime error, caused by the system attempting to read data from memory where the memory is blank. Apex is built on top of the Java language and uses the **Java Virtual Machine** (**JVM**) runtime under the hood. What follows is a highly simplified discussion of how Java manages memory, which will help us to understand what is happening under the hood.

Whenever an object is instantiated in Java, it is created and managed on the heap, which is a block of memory used to dynamically hold data for objects and classes at runtime. A separate set of memory, called the stack, stores references to these objects and instances. So, in simplistic terms, when you instantiate an instance called `paul` of a `Person` class, that instance is stored on the heap and a reference to this heap memory is stored on the stack, with the label `paul`. Apex is built on Java and compiles down to Java bytecode (this started after an update from Salesforce in 2012), and, although Apex does not utilize a full version of the JVM, it uses the JVM as the basis for its operations, including garbage and memory management.

With this in mind, we are now better able to understand how the two most common types of `NullPointerException` within Apex occur: when working with specific object instances and when referencing values on maps.

Exceptions on object instances

Let's imagine I have the following code within my environment:

```
public class Person {
    public String name;
}


Person paul;
```

In this code, we have a `Person` class defined, with a single publicly accessible member variable. We have then declared a variable, `paul`, using this new data type. In memory, Salesforce now has a label on the stack called `paul` that is not pointing to any address on the heap, as `paul` currently has the value of `null`.

If I now attempt to run `System.debug(paul.name);`, we will get a `NullPointerException` exception with the message *Attempt to de-reference a null object*. What is happening is that the system is trying to use the `paul` variable to retrieve the object instance and then access the `name` property of that instance. Because the instance is `null`, the reference to this memory does not exist, and so `NullPointerException` is thrown; that is, we have nothing to point with.

With this understanding of how memory management is working under the hood (in an approximate fashion) and how we are generating these errors, it is therefore pretty easy to see how we code against them—avoid calling methods and accessing variables and properties on an object that has not been instantiated. This can be done by ensuring we always call a constructor when initializing a variable, as shown in the following code snippet:

```
Person paul = new Person();
```

In general, when developing, we should pay attention to any public methods or variables that return complex types or data from a complex type. A common practice is simply to instantiate new instances of the underlying object in the constructor of data that may be returned before being populated.

Exceptions when working with maps

Another common way in which this exception presents itself is when working with collections and data retrieved from collections—most notably, maps. As an example, we may have some data in a map for us to use in processing unrelated records. Let's say we have a Map<String, Contact> contactsByBadgeId instance that allows us to use a contact's unique badge ID string to retrieve their contact record for processing. Let's try to run the following:

```
String badBadgeId = 'THIS ID DOES NOT EXIST';
String ownerName = contactsByBadgeId.get(badBadgeId).FirstName;
```

Assuming that the map will not have the key that badBadgeId is holding, the get method on the map will return null and our attempt to access the FirstName property will be met with NullPointerException being thrown.

The simplest and most effective way to manage this is to wrap our method in a simple if block, as follows:

```
String badBadgeId = 'THIS ID DOES NOT EXIST';
if(contactsByBadgeId.containsKey(badBadgeId)) {
    String ownerName = contactsByBadgeId.get(badBadgeId).
    FirstName;
}
```

By adding this wrapper, we have proactively filtered out any bad keys for the map by removing the error.

As an alternative, we could loop through a list of badge IDs, like this:

```
for(String badgeId : badgeIdList) {
    String ownerName = contactsByBadgeId.get(badBadgeId).
    FirstName;
}
```

We could also use the methods available to set collections to both potentially reduce our loop size and avoid the issue, as follows:

```
Set<String> badgeIdSet = new Set<String>(badgeIdList).
retainAll(contactsByBadgeId.keySet());
for(String badgeId : badgeIdSet) {
    String ownerName = contactsByBadgeId.get(badBadgeId).
    FirstName;
}
```

In the preceding example, we have filtered down the items to be iterated through to only those in the `keySet` instance of the map. This may not be possible in many instances, as we may be looping through a collection of a non-primitive type or a type that does not match our `keySet`. In these cases, our `if` statement is the best solution.

In general, most `NullPointerException` instances occur when a premature assumption about the availability of data has been made—for example, that the object has been instantiated or that our map contains the key we are looking for. Trying to recognize these assumptions will assist in avoiding these exceptions, going forward. With this in mind, let's now look at how we can effectively bulkify our Apex code.

Winter' 21 Safe Navigation Operator

In Winter 21, which will be released after this book is published, Salesforce will introduce the safe navigation operator to help avoid NullPointerException problems. This operator will allow you to write code such as contactsByBadgeId.get(badBadgeId)?.FirstName, which will return Null if badBadgeId is not in the map, avoiding NullPointerException. This will be an extremely useful method that you should consider using as part of your practice to help avoid NullPointerException errors.

safe navigation operator

NullPointerException

contactsByBadgeId.get(badBadgeId)?.FirstName

Null

badBadgeId

NullPointerException

NullPointerException

Retrieving configuration data in a bulkified way

No book on Apex is complete without some discussion around bulkification. Bulkification is a requirement in Salesforce due to the Governor Limits that are imposed on developers because of the multi-tenant nature of the platform. Many developers that are new to the platform see the Governor Limits as a hindrance rather than an assistance. We will cover this in more detail in *Chapter 13, Performance and the Salesforce Governor Limits*. However, a common mistake that developers make on the platform is to not bulkify their code appropriately—particularly, triggers. It is also common for intermediate to advanced developers to not bulkify their non-trigger code appropriately either. We will discuss bulkification of triggers more explicitly in *Chapter 3, Triggers and Managing Trigger Execution*, and will cover querying and **Data Manipulation Language** (**DML**) within loops later in this chapter. Firstly, however, I want to discuss bulkifying the retrieval of data that is not typically stored in a custom or standard object—configuration data.

Hot and cold data

I want to begin this section with a discussion on hot and cold data within the system, as well as the implications this has on bulkification. For all of the data within our system, let's assume that the data starts off with a temperature of 0 (our scale should not matter, but let's assume we are using °C, where 0 is freezing and 100 is boiling). Every time that our data is written to, its temperature increases by one degree, and if an entire day goes without it being updated, it drops a degree and decreases by one. If we were to run this thought experiment across our data, we would then obtain a scale for each data type we are retrieving, where the data would range from very cold (that is, hardly ever written to) through to extremely hot (edited multiple times a day).

For most objects in Salesforce, the temperature graph of the data would appear in a long-tailed distribution manner—that is, an initial peak of activity as a record is created and then updated, until it reaches a stage in its life cycle where it is no longer viewed and only really included for auditing and reporting purposes. Think of an opportunity record, for example: a lot of initial activity until it is closed, won, or lost, and then it is used mainly for reporting. When working with these records in Apex, we will need to ensure we query for them to get the latest version for accurate and up-to-date data. As we are in most cases not writing Apex to work on "cold" instances of this data, we need to be aware of the fact that these records may change during the scope of a transaction due to an update we are making. Our normal bulkification practices, discussed next, will help us manage this.

What about data that is truly cold—that is, created for all intents and purposes but never updated? Think of a custom metadata record that holds some configuration used in an Apex process. Such information is created and then only updated when the process itself changes. For such data, we actively want to avoid querying multiple times during a transaction yet ensure that it can be made available across the entire transaction as needed. As Salesforce applications have grown and more custom configuration has been added to make the applications more dynamic and easier to update, more organizations have deployed custom metadata, custom settings, and custom configuration objects (although these are now largely superseded by custom metadata and custom settings). How do we as developers manage retrieval of this data in a manner that is bulkified and that allows us to reuse this data across a transaction?

Retrieving and sharing data throughout a transaction

For this use case, a developer can either use the singleton pattern or make appropriate use of static variables to manage the retrieval of this data. We could implement a singleton utility class, as follows:

```
public class ExampleSingleton {

    private static ExampleSingleton instance;

    private Example__mdt metadata;

    public static ExampleSingleton getInstance() {
        if(instance == null) {
            instance = new ExampleSingleton();
        }
        return instance;
    }

    private ExampleSingleton() {
    }

    public Example__mdt getMetadata() {
        if(metadata == null) {
            metadata = [SELECT Id FROM Example__mdt LIMIT 1];
        }
        return metadata;
```

```
        }

    }
```

Our `private static` member variable—`instance`—holds the unique instance of the `ExampleSingleton` class for the transaction. The `getInstance` method is the only way of either instantiating or retrieving the instance for use, and we have ensured this by making the default constructor private. We can use this instance to retrieve our `Example__mdt` record, using the `getMetadata` method on our returned instance. The actual instance of the `Example__mdt` record is stored as a private member for the class and is state abstracted away from the change.

The benefit of such an approach is that we can both encapsulate our data and its workings and ensure that we are only ever retrieving the information from the database once. This singleton could be used to hold many different types of data as needed so that the entire transaction can scale in its usage of such data in a common way.

Alternatively, we could implement a static class such as the following one:

```
public class ExampleStatic {
    private static Example__mdt metadata;

    public static Example__mdt getExampleMetadata() {
        if (metadata == null) {
            metadata = [SELECT Id FROM Example__mdt LIMIT 1];
        }
        return metadata;
    }

    private ExampleStatic() {
    }
}
```

Again, we have ensured that our metadata will only be loaded once across the transaction and have a smaller code footprint to manage. Note that this is not a true static class, as these are not available in Apex. However, there is a close enough analogy to this in the language that we can consider as a static class (it cannot be externally instantiated due to its private constructor).

For cold data such as custom metadata, custom settings, or any custom configuration in objects, the use of a singleton or a static class can greatly improve bulkification. I have seen instances in production where the same set of metadata records was retrieved multiple times during a transaction as the code began to interact by recursively firing triggers through a combination of updates.

Singleton versus static class

It is a fair question to ask right now whether a singleton or a static class instance should be used in utility classes. The answer (as with all good questions) is *it depends*. While both have similar functionality from our perspective in terms of retrieving data only once, singletons can be passed around as object instances for use across the application. They can also extend other classes and implement interfaces with the full range of Apex's **object-oriented** (**OO**) features. While static classes cannot do this, they are more useful in lightweight implementations where the OO features of the language are not required.

Bulkification – querying within loops

Another common mistake seen in Apex is querying for data within loops. This is different than repeated querying for data, as discussed previously, but instead it focuses on performing a query with a (potentially) unique outcome for each iteration of a loop. This is particularly true within triggers.

When working with a trigger, you should always prepare your code to handle a batch of 200 records at once. This is true regardless of whether or not you believe the tool will only pass records to the trigger individually; all that is required is for an enterprising administrator to create a flow that manipulates multiple records that fire your trigger, and you will have issues.

Consider the following code block, wherein we are looping through each contact we have been provided in a contact trigger and retrieving the related account record, including some information:

```
trigger ContactTrigger on Contact (before insert, after insert)
{
    switch on Trigger.operationType {
        when BEFORE_INSERT {
            for(Contact con : Trigger.new) {
                Account acc = [SELECT UpsellOpportunity__c
                FROM Account WHERE Id = :con.AccountId];
                con.Contact_for_Upsell__c = acc.
```

```
                    UpsellOpportunity__c != 'No';
            }
        }
        when AFTER_INSERT {
            //after insert code
        }
    }
}
```

This simple trigger will set the `Contact_for_Upsell__c` field to `true` if the account is marked as having any upsell opportunity.

There are a couple of fairly obvious problems with the way we are querying here. Firstly, this is not bulkified—if we have 200 records passed into the trigger (over 100 records, in fact), we will break the governor limit for **Salesforce Object Query Language** (SOQL) queries and receive an exception that we cannot handle. Secondly, this setup is also inefficient as it may retrieve the same account record from the database twice.

A better way to manage this would be to gather all of the account IDs in a set and then query once. Not only will this avoid the governor limit—it will also avoid us querying for duplicate results. An updated version of the code to do this is shown here:

```
trigger ContactTrigger on Contact (before insert, after insert)
{
    switch on Trigger.operationType {
        when BEFORE_INSERT {

            Set<Id> accountIds = new Set<Id>();

            for(Contact con : Trigger.new) {
                accountIds.add(con.AccountId);
            }

            Map<Id, Account> accountMap = new Map<Id,
            Account>([SELECT UpsellOpportunity__c
            FROM Account WHERE Id in :accountIds]);

            for(Contact con : Trigger.new) {
                con.Contact_for_Upsell__c = accountMap.
                get(con.AccountId).UpsellOpportunity__c
```

```
                != 'No';
        }
    }
    when AFTER_INSERT {
        //after insert code
    }
  }
}
```

In this code, we declare a `Set<Id>` called `accountIds` to hold the account ID for each contact without duplicates. We then query our accounts into a `Map<Id, Account>` so that when looping through each contact for a second time we can set the value correctly.

Some of you may now be wondering if we have merely moved our performance issue from having too many queries to having multiple loops through all the data. In *Chapter 14, Performance Profiling*, when we talk about performance profiling, we will cover the use of big-O notation in detail when discussing scaling. However, to touch on the subject of scaling here, it is worth doing some rudimentary analysis. Looping through these records (maximum 200) will be extremely quick on the **central processing unit** (**CPU**) and is an inexpensive operation. It is also an operation that scales linearly as the number of records within the trigger grows. In our original trigger, for each new record we had the following:

- One loop iteration
- One query

This is scaled linearly at a rate of 1x for both resources—that is, doubling the items doubled the resources being utilized, until a point of failure with a governor limit (in this instance, queries). In our new trigger structure, we have the following for each record:

- Two loop iterations (one for each `for` loop)
- Zero additional queries

Our new resource usage scales linearly for loop iterations but is constant for queries, which are a more limited resource. As we will see later, this is the type of optimization we want within our code. It is therefore imperative that whenever we are looping through records and wish to query related data, we do so in a bulkified manner that, wherever possible, performs a single query for the entire loop.

Bulkification – DML within loops

Similar to the issue of querying in loops is that of performing DML within loops. The limit for DML statements is higher than that of SOQL queries at the time of writing and so is unlikely to present itself as early; however, it follows the same root cause and also the solution.

Take the following code example, in which we are now in the after `insert` context for our trigger:

```
trigger ContactTrigger on Contact (before insert) {
    switch on Trigger.operationType {
        when BEFORE_INSERT {
            //previous trigger code
        }
        when AFTER_INSERT {
            for(Contact con : Trigger.new) {
            if(con.Contact_for_Upsell__c) {
                Task t = new Task();
                t.Subject = 'Discuss opportunities with new
                contact';
                t.OwnerId = con.OwnerId;
                t.WhoId = con.Id;
                insert t;
            }
            }
        }
    }
}
```

Here, we are creating a task for the owner of any new contact that is marked for upsell to contact them and discuss potential opportunities. In our worst-case bulk scenario here, we have 200 contacts that all have the `Contact_for_Upsell__c` checkbox checked. This will lead to each iteration firing a DML statement that will cause a governor limit exception on record 151. Again, using our rudimentary analysis, we can see that for each additional record on the trigger, we have an additional DML statement that scales linearly until we breach our limit.

Instead, whenever making DML statements (particularly in triggers), we should ensure that we are using the bulk format and passing lists of records to be manipulated into the statement. For example, the trigger code should be written as follows:

```
trigger ContactTrigger on Contact (before insert) {
    switch on Trigger.operationType {
        when BEFORE_INSERT {
            //previous trigger code
        }
        when AFTER_INSERT {
            List<Task> tasks = new List<Task>();
            for(Contact con : Trigger.new) {
                if(con.Contact_for_Upsell__c) {
                    Task t = new Task();
                    t.Subject = 'Discuss opportunities with new
                    contact';
                    t.OwnerId = con.OwnerId;
                    t.WhoId = con.Id;
                    tasks.add(t);
                }
            }
            insert tasks;
        }
    }
}
```

This new code has a constant usage of DML statements, one for the entire operation, and can happily scale up to 200 records.

Hardcoding

The final common mistake I want to discuss here is that of hardcoding within Apex—particularly, hardcoding any type of unique identifier such as an ID or a name. For IDs, it is probably quite obvious for most developers as it is well established that between different environments, including sandbox and production environments, IDs can and should differ. If you are creating a sandbox from a production environment, then at the time of creation, the IDs are synchronized for any data that is copied down to the sandbox environment. Following this, IDs do not remain synchronized between the two and are generated when a record is created within that environment.

Despite this, many developers, particularly those working within a single environment such as consultants or in-house developers, will hardcode certain IDs if needed. For example, consider the following code:

```
for(Account acc : Trigger.new) {
    if(acc.OwnerId = 'SOME_USER_ID') {
        break;
    }
    //do something otherwise
}
```

This code is designed to skip updates on account records within our trigger context owned by a particular user, most commonly an **application programming interface (API)** user or an integration user. This pattern enables a developer to filter these records out so that if an update is coming via an integration, actions are skipped and the integration can update records unimpeded.

Should this user ID change, then we will get an error or issue here, so it is wise to remove this hardcoded value. Given that the ID for the user should be copied from production to any sandboxes, you may ask why this is needed. Firstly, there is no guarantee that the user will not be changed for the integration, going forward. Secondly, for development purposes, when initially writing this code, the user will not likely exist in the production organization (org), and so, in your first deployment, you will have to tweak the code to be environment-specific. Thirdly, this also limits your ability to test the code effectively, going forward. We will see how shortly.

As an update to this code, some may recommend making the following change (note that this is precisely the instance where we would extract this query to a utility class; however, we are inlining the query here for ease of display and reading):

```
for(Account acc : Trigger.new) {
    User apiUser = [SELECT Id FROM User WHERE Username = 'my.
    api@user.com'];
    if(acc.OwnerId = apiuser.Id) {
        break;
    }
    //do something otherwise
}
```

This code improves upon our previous code in that we are no longer hardcoding the user record ID, although we are still hardcoding the name. Again, should this change over time, then we should still have an issue, such as when we are working in a sandbox environment and the sandbox name is appended to the username. In this instance, the code would not be executable, including in a test context, without updating the record to be correct. This could be done manually every time a new sandbox is created, or through the code in the test. This means that our test is now bound to this user, which is not a good practice for tests, should the user change again.

In this instance, we should remove the name string to a custom setting for flexibility and improved testability. If we were to define a custom setting that held the value (for example, `Integration_Settings__c`), then we could easily retrieve the custom setting and the username for a query at runtime without the query, as follows:

```
for(Account acc : Trigger.new) {
    Integration_Settings__c setting = Integration_Settings__c.
    getInstance();
    User apiUser = [SELECT Id FROM User WHERE Username =
    setting.Api_Username__c];
    if(acc.OwnerId = apiuser.Id) {
        break;
    }
    //do something otherwise
}
```

Such a pattern allows us many benefits, as follows:

- Firstly, we can now apply different settings across the org and profiles, should we so desire. This can be increasingly useful in orgs where multiple business units operate.

- Secondly, for testing, we can create a user within our test data and assign their username to the setting for the test within Apex. This allows our tests to run independently of the actual org configuration and makes processes such as **continuous integration** (**CI**) simpler.

- Finally, we could extract both of these lines (the retrieval of the custom setting and the user query) to a utility class to abstract away, for the entire transaction to use as needed.

Summary

In this chapter, we reviewed some of the common Apex mistakes made by developers and how to resolve them. For many of you, the topics presented within this chapter will be familiar, although are hopefully a worthwhile refresher, with maybe some additional understanding or thoughts.

We begin this book with this chapter, as it is imperative we consider how to remove these common mistakes before we look at how to extend our knowledge around the rest of the platform's features. We also tried to cover in greater detail than is typical the reasoning behind some of these errors, either from the perspective of the underlying machine, as with the `NullPointerException` discussion we started with, or via the impact upon developer and deployment productivity, such as our final discussion on hardcoding.

To master any language means beginning by removing the minor common niggles that can cause issues and easily resolving bugs. Hopefully, through having a deeper or broader understanding of these issues and how they arise, you can more readily spot and rectify them in advance. That is not to say you will stop making them: I find these bugs and issues in my own code regularly, but I am able to recognize them in advance as I begin to develop, to stop them as routine and habit take hold.

Now that we have discussed these common problems and how to resolve them, we will move on to move detailed and prescriptive debugging in the next chapter.

2
Debugging Apex

In this chapter, I want to discuss the process of debugging your Apex code and finding errors. In the previous chapter, we saw how we can prevent common Apex mistakes, but there will still be instances and examples where we have errors or issues that we will need to debug within our solution. The focus here is on the process of debugging and using the tools provided to their maximum, rather than debugging a particular problem itself. Code bugs come in all shapes and sizes, and if the Salesforce Developer Community forums and Salesforce StackExchange are any indication, a never-ending book of fixing particular errors could be written. By focusing on improving and streamlining your debugging process, you should be able to find and resolve any issues more rapidly in the future.

We will cover the following topics in this chapter:

- An overview of debugging on Salesforce
- Using log levels when generating debug logs
- The use of **Salesforce Developer Experience (SFDX)** in debugging
- Streaming logs for near real-time capture
- Using the Apex Replay Debugger
- Using the Apex Interactive Debugger

Technical requirements

In order to follow along with the processes shown in this chapter, you should have **Visual Studio Code** (**VS Code**) and the SFDX **Command-Line Interface** (**CLI**) installed on your machine. You can get these set up by working through the Trailhead module *Quick Start: Visual Studio Code for Salesforce Development.*

Debugging on Salesforce

Debugging on Salesforce is different than debugging on most other platforms, as Apex code can only be run on the Salesforce servers. If you were building an application for deployment on Heroku, for example, you could still develop and test that application locally before deploying it to the cloud. With Apex code, however, there is no way of running the code locally to ensure that it operates as expected before deploying to the Salesforce servers for compilation and execution. This adds additional challenges for developers in terms of productivity and ease of debugging.

Debugging an issue can be a slow and repetitive process as each edit, save, and then execution action of the code takes multiple saves and potentially multiple page interactions to replicate the behavior. As an example, you may have to save the code (with some amendments or extended debugging statements), then navigate to a page within Salesforce to change or create one or more records, then view the debug logs for this interaction to make an update, and repeat the loop again.

This cycle can quickly drain the will of even the most dedicated Salesforce developer. So how do we reduce the cycle as quickly as possible and improve our ability to debug problems?

Prevention is better than a cure

All problems are best dealt with before they actually occur and become a problem. This may sound overly simplistic or even stupid, but it is extremely true when it comes to software development. Bugs cause side effects, both on data by inhibiting it from moving through its intended life cycle, and on the reputation of the system and its developers. Anything we can do to avoid a bug being found in the wild will help us to limit and mitigate this. We won't stop all bugs, but any bugs we can stop will be a help.

The first thing I wish to advocate, therefore, is extremely thorough Apex testing. Some of you may have just groaned audibly, but I will ask you to bear with me while I explain why for me this is the first step in debugging. And if you know and have taken a **Test-Driven Development** (**TDD**) approach here, you may just be laughing.

Firstly, tests can assist in pre-empting bugs. We will discuss in *Chapter 5*, *Testing Apex Code*, why testing is so important, but it's sufficient to say that as you write tests, you find ways of checking and validating any assumptions you have built into your code and ensuring that when these assumptions fail your code does not. If you thoroughly test your Apex code, you will certainly find bugs early and fix them before they make their way to the end user.

Tests are not just about pre-empting bugs though. As a best practice, whenever a bug is submitted my way, I will almost always write a unit test for it first to verify it is reproducible. I use the phrase *almost always* because there are a number of occasions where tests will not cover it, for example, a simple user error. For almost every bug though, I will write a unit test to verify it before I can then start on fixing it. I want to create a unit test that fails in exactly the way the user is describing. This has two powerful side effects:

- My debug cycle time has just been reduced. I can now replicate the error more rapidly in code than I could through the UI and never have to leave my IDE to do so.

- We will now know for sure when we have fixed the bug as the test will pass.

Log levels

Now that we have a simple way of replicating the issue that can speed up our debugging, the next step for us is to ensure we have the correct level of logging. Salesforce debug logs have a limit of 20MB, which is a large amount of data for a purely text-based output and can end up with you viewing what amounts to a lot of noise about the transaction. Setting up our log levels correctly is going to help us immensely in weeding out the issue without too much additional data to scroll and read through.

We can set the granularity of our debug logs to a series of different levels across a number of categories. The categories and a brief description of what information they contain is provided in the following table:

Category	Description
Database	Information relating to SOQL, SOSL, DML and any other database–related activity.
Workflow	Information around workflow rules, processes, and flows, including and actions taken.
NBA	Information relating to Einstein Next Best Action, including strategy and execution details.
Validation	Validation rule related, information including the rule name and whether it evaluated true or false.
Callout	External web service related callout information. Includes Salesforce Connect.
Apex Code	Apex code execution information that may include log messages from database actions, inline queries, trigger execution and test method execution.
Apex Profiling	Limit usage profiling
Visualforce	Viewstate serialization and deserialization, formula evaluation and other Visualforce related events.
System	Calls to system methods, including System.debug

Table 2.1 – Debug log categories

For each category, we can also define a log level from one of the following options:

- NONE
- ERROR
- WARN
- INFO
- DEBUG
- FINE
- FINER
- FINEST

This can give us over 100 million different combinations of log categories and levels that we can generate. I would hazard a guess that most developers have only ever used one.

Therefore, before we start debugging, it is worthwhile us reviewing what levels of information we want on our debug logs to avoid as much noise as possible. For most debugging work, I typically switch to something like the following:

- NONE: NBA, Validation, Workflow, Callout, Visualforce, Wave

- INFO: Database, Apex Profiling

- DEBUG: System

- FINE: Apex Code

Your needs will vary and so you should tweak and update as needed. If, for example, you were working on an issue involving a governor limit being breached, the **Apex Profiling** category would be important to include more detail on.

A pre-filtered log will now allow us to start to interrogate the important parts of the log more readily and understand what is happening within our code. It will also become invaluable, as we will stop having to visit Salesforce to view our logs each time, either via the Developer Console or through the UI.

For most developers, this is the standard practice—to view the logs in a static format after the transaction has finished executing, and view through the browser.

What if instead of having to switch windows and mental contexts and wait for the logs to generate, we could see them in real time? We can achieve this using a combination of SFDX and the terminal.

SFDX and streaming logs

One of the biggest changes for Salesforce developers over the past few years has been the launch of the **Salesforce Developer Experience**, **SFDX**. SFDX is a set of tools that aims to streamline the entire development life cycle, and has vastly improved the lives of most Salesforce developers.

One of the most useful aspects of SFDX is the CLI that is the core of SFDX from a developer's perspective. By integrating SFDX with the CLI, Salesforce has enabled developers to obtain the power of the command line in their development, and most importantly for us, in debugging. For this section of the book, I am assuming you are using the VS Code editor and that SFDX CLI is installed on your machine. If you have not got these installed, I recommend heading over to the Trailhead modules that cover them (at the time of writing, *Quick Start: Visual Studio Code for Salesforce Development* should be enough to get the basics set up and running). We will use VS Code and its project format as our baseline as it is the most common setup for developers; however, the steps we describe should work in any SFDX project.

> **Comfortable with the command line**
>
> For those who are not as comfortable with the command line, or even just wanting a refresher, I recommend undertaking the *Command-Line Interface* Trailhead module. Salesforce developer evangelist Peter Chittum wrote this trail after giving a talk with similar content at multiple conferences, which was extremely well received. It covers the basics of the CLI very well and should help anybody, who looks at a terminal and wonders what it is, develop a much better understanding of how it can be used.

Open your project folder in a terminal window. You can either use the built-in window provided by VS Code or an independent terminal window. In that window, run the following command:

```
sfdx force:apex:log:tail --color
```

SFDX will now start outputting the debug logs from your org for your user line by line into the terminal window. The additional `--color` option will also ensure that colors are added to the output to make it easier to differentiate the different output types visually. If you run a test class, for example, you will see a set of statements shown in the window, with highlighting for certain statements and lines, as shown in the following screenshot:

Figure 2.1 – A window with a debug log stream

This is useful, we can now inspect our debug logs as they come through in the terminal window to review the information within to find our bug. We can still improve this, however.

Head to the **Setup** area of your org and open the **Debug Logs** window where you would normally find and review all your logs. In this section, press the **New** button and then choose **New Debug Level**. From here, we can define our debug level as we previously discussed to make it more relevant for our debugging session. The following screenshot shows the level I was referring to earlier:

Figure 2.2 – Creating a custom debug level

If you then save this and cancel the creation of a new trace flag, you can head back to the terminal window and re-run our command from before, but with an additional option to use this debug level instead. For example, my command would now be the following:

```
sfdx force:apex:log:tail --color -d DEV_DEBUG
```

For a very rough comparison, the information from the screenshot in *Figure 2.1* can now be shown in a much smaller number of lines, as we can see in the following *Figure 2.3*:

```
10:22:33.123 (351668925)|USER_DEBUG|[46]|DEBUG|AFTER UPDATE START
10:22:33.123 (352137249)|METHOD_ENTRY|[50]|01p3z000005niTu|TaskTriggerHandler.isContactId(Id)
10:22:33.123 (352218722)|METHOD_EXIT|[50]|01p3z000005niTu|TaskTriggerHandler.isContactId(Id)
10:22:33.123 (352275753)|METHOD_ENTRY|[55]|01p3z000005niTu|TaskTriggerHandler.retrieveContacts(Set<Id>)
10:22:33.123 (352648049)|SOQL_EXECUTE_BEGIN|[21]|Aggregations:0|SELECT Id, No_of_Open_Tasks__c FROM Contact WHERE Id = :tmpVar1
10:22:33.123 (355951320)|SOQL_EXECUTE_END|[21]|Rows:1
```

Figure 2.3 – Reduce debug log through improved log-level filtering

Finally, we can use the command-line tools to filter this even further if we so wished. For example, if we wanted to only display our `System.debug` statements (those marked `USER_DEBUG`), we could do this using the `grep` command as follows:

```
sfdx force:apex:log:tail --color -d DEV_DEBUG | grep USER_DEBUG
```

> **Note**
>
> For Windows users, the equivalent command is `findstr`. However, in Windows 10 you also have the option of a Linux command line, which I would recommend using.

This will then further filter any lines we receive and only output our debug statements, as shown in the following *Figure 2.4*:

```
[paulbattisson@Pauls-MacBook-Pro-2 ApexBookDev % sfdx force:apex:log:tail --color -d DEV_DEBUG | grep USER_DEBUG
10:34:21.119 (275721610)|USER_DEBUG|[25]|DEBUG|AFTER INSERT START
10:34:21.119 (305124607)|USER_DEBUG|[42]|DEBUG|AFTER INSERT END
10:34:21.119 (333029563)|USER_DEBUG|[46]|DEBUG|AFTER UPDATE START
10:34:21.119 (365713440)|USER_DEBUG|[68]|DEBUG|AFTER UPDATE END
```

Figure 2.4 – Using the grep command to further filter debug statements

For most situations and most developers, applying these tools will help you to streamline your debugging process and receive information on what the code is doing in near real time.

Debugging using the Apex Replay Debugger

The Apex Replay Debugger is a tool that allows a developer to replay a set of code that has been run to debug it at particular breakpoints. You can gain a deeper insight into the code as it runs and can inspect any variables for their values within VS Code. The Replay Debugger allows you to have up to five breakpoints within your code, so it has to be used with this in mind.

To use the Replay Debugger, perform the following steps:

1. Open your org and ensure that your user has no debug logs turned on for your user.

2. Once you have done this, return to your VS Code project and apply a set of checkpoints to your code. This is done by clicking on the gutter of the file (this is the area to the left of the line numbers).

3. A red dot will appear signifying a breakpoint has been created, as is shown for the singleton instance we discussed previously, and shown in the following screenshot. Note that there is a difference in terminology between VS Code, which uses the term *breakpoint*, and the Replay Debugger, which uses *checkpoint*. Any breakpoints added in VS Code are treated as checkpoints by the Replay Debugger:

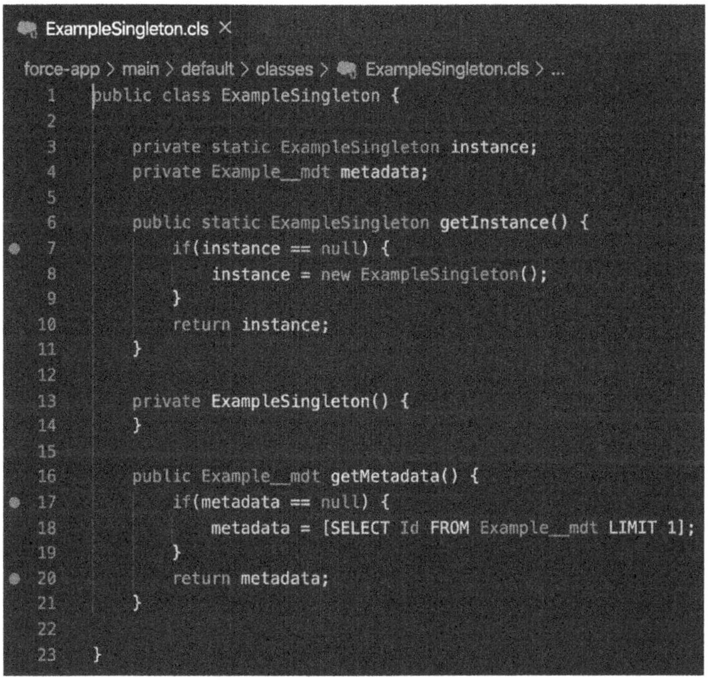

Figure 2.5 – Breakpoints set on a class

4. You must then update the org to use these checkpoints by opening the VS Code command palette (⌘+ ⇧+ P on Mac or *Ctrl* + ⇧ + *P* on Windows) and type SFDX: Update Checkpoints in Org, selecting this option when it appears. These new checkpoints will then be deployed to your Salesforce org for use.

5. Next, reopen the command palette and enter SFDX: Turn On Apex Debug Log for Replay Debugger, which will start the required logging. Once this command has succeeded, you should then invoke that code through your test or another means. For the following examples, I executed the following code:

```
ExampleSingleton es = ExampleSingleton.getInstance();
Example__mdt meta = es.getMetadata();
```

6. We must next retrieve our Apex logs using the command palette command SFDX: Get Apex Debug Logs, which will show a list of available debug logs. Select the latest log, as shown in the following screenshot:

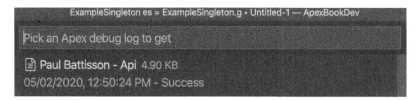

Figure 2.6 – Selecting the latest Apex debug log

This will download the log to your local machine, for use within the debugger, to the tools/debug/logs folder within your SFDX project (you can see this on the left-hand file browser in VS Code).

7. We can now open the Apex Replay Debugger and step through this log file. If you use the command palette command SFDX: Launch Apex Replay Debugger with Current File, you will be prompted to choose a log file. Select the file we have just downloaded, and you will have a screen similar to the following:

Figure 2.7 – Apex Replay Debugger window ready to replay the debug log

8. Press *F5* or the continue button (|▷) and the debugger will take you to the next breakpoint. On the left of the screen, you can see any variables and their current values (shown in the section labeled **1** in the following *Figure 2.8*). As the code goes through its execution, this will update so you can see the values of different variables throughout the transaction.

    In the section marked **2** in *Figure 2.8*, you can see the call stack as well as the breakpoints that are enabled. Finally, in the main window (labeled **3** in *Figure 2.8*), you can see the code under execution is highlighted, and if you hover over variables, you can see their current value displayed:

Figure 2.8 – The Apex Replay Debugger window

The Apex Replay Debugger is an extremely useful tool for debugging your code when you need to review what values were present for different variables throughout the life cycle of a transaction and can save you wiring a lot of debug statements, which you will later need to remove. Once you are done with the debugger, ensure to end the debugger session using the command palette SFDX: Turn Off Apex Debug Log for Apex Replay Debugger.

Apex Interactive Debugger

The Apex Interactive Debugger is a feature available to those with either Performance or Unlimited edition organizations for free, or as a paid add-on for those using other editions. It is designed to operate in the same way as the Apex Replay Debugger, but in real time rather than on a debug log. Due to it being a paid feature, we are not able to cover it in detail.

At a high level, it operates in the same way as the Replay Debugger we just discussed, but in real time. That is, there is no need to retrieve a log file, as the debugger will stop at the correct breakpoints as you hit them within the code. This can be extremely useful as you are developing to step through the code. Should you have an interest in this tool, your Salesforce Account Executive can assist.

ISV Customer Debugger

If you have the Apex Interactive Debugger and operate as an (**Independent Software Vendor**) **ISV**, Salesforce allows you to log in to the sandboxes of your subscribers and debug their org in a similar fashion to obtain more information. This ability is available in a special version of the tool called the ISV Customer Debugger.

The customer debugger enables Salesforce ISV partners to debug issues within a customer sandbox to help resolve problems faster. It is only possible within a subscriber's sandbox org and not within a production instance.

The use of this tool is out of scope for this book due to restrictions on obtaining access. If you are a developer within an ISV, you should investigate with your team whether you have access to this tool and how you can appropriately utilize it in debugging customer issues.

Which tool to use?

We have now seen a number of options to debug our code and improve our workflow away from the standard workflow for most developers, which are usually as follows:

1. Perform action in Salesforce UI.

2. Review debug log.

3. Update code.

4. Repeat.

Hopefully, it has now become clearer that replicating any issue in Apex code through a unit test will speed up our debug cycle immensely as it allows us to utilize the debugging tools available to us in VS Code and SFDX without a need to return to the browser repeatedly. I often find as well that the process of methodically writing a unit test to reproduce the error can make my brain get a small "aha" moment, allowing me to fix the issue straight away. If this doesn't happen though, we are left with two main improved ways of debugging:

- Filtered log levels and streaming of logs to the terminal for inspection
- Using the Apex Replay Debugger

A sensible question is, therefore, which one should you use?

Firstly, the biggest factor in this is your personal preference. If after using both, you find you prefer the Replay Debugger, then use that. If streaming logs is more comfortable and useful for you, do that. I personally aim to use the log streaming setup as a first pass for my debugging. I find that this is the quickest feedback cycle I can have for my debugging, as the logs arrive in near real time and I can filter them in my command line to display only the relevant information. It allows me to quickly change my debug statements, deploy the update, rerun the test, and see the output instantly.

If after a period (normally 20-30 minutes) I find I am still no closer to finding the error in this manner, I will switch to the Apex Replay Debugger. At this point, it seems likely that the error is not going to be quick to resolve and using the debugger will allow me to more methodically step through the code to review what data the variables are holding for me, and to inspect how the code operates.

My advice is to spend time working with both as you are debugging your code and see which one fits more naturally to you.

> **Note**
>
> Also, do not underestimate the power of simply *rubber ducking* your code – that is, explaining it out loud to an inanimate object such as a rubber duck. I have a plush toy puppy on my desk that I use to talk through my code with on occasions when I am trying to understand why something is not working in the way I imagine. He has resolved more issues than I can remember.

Summary

In this chapter, we discussed how we can best work to debug our Apex code when we have a bug or issue. We started by noting some of the differences between debugging Apex compared to other languages and platforms due to its cloud-centric execution model.

We then discussed the standard debugging life cycle for most developers, which involves a lot of switching between windows to get static debug logs to inspect. We looked at how we can improve this debug cycle, by first reproducing the bug in a test to (a) reduce our replication time and (b) provide us with a concrete way of ensuring that the bug has been fixed.

Following this, we discussed how we can aid ourselves by improving the way in which we configure the debug log filters within Salesforce to get access to the most relevant information. We then discussed the use of the SFDX CLI to stream these logs to the terminal and then further filter them using the tools provided by the command line. This provided us with a nice tight feedback loop for debugging our code.

The Apex Replay Debugger was then introduced and discussed as an alternative for when we need to step through code in a series of breakpoints to analyze what has occurred in a more granular fashion. This tool allows developers to generate detailed log files and replay them within the VS Code Salesforce plugins to inspect the variable values, call stack, and other information relating to the execution of some code. We saw how to set these breakpoints, generate the log, and then inspect that log using the Replay Debugger.

After a small discussion on the other paid options Salesforce provides for ISVs and large enterprises, we finished the chapter with a discussion of when to use streaming logs and when to use the Replay Debugger. As discussed, the primary determining factor will be down to preference, as different developers will find each tool easier or harder to use for them personally. I highly encourage you to go away and play with both to find the workflow that is most productive for you.

In the next chapter, we are going to look at how we can write effective trigger code within our system. As we will see, the Salesforce Save Order of Execution is a complex multi-step process that can lead to errors if not handled appropriately. We will focus on writing trigger code that is easy to test and helps us avoid errors; however, with our new knowledge of debugging, we will be better equipped to deal with any errors should they arise in the future.

3
Triggers and Managing Trigger Execution

In this chapter, I want to discuss Apex triggers and correctly managing and developing a structured execution framework for using triggers within Apex.

Triggers are where most developers start working in Apex on the Salesforce platform, and I would personally estimate that's where the majority of Apex bugs are found. I think there are a few reasons for this:

- Triggers demand bulkification, and a small resource leak can easily break a Governor Limit.

- Triggers often fire off other save processes that themselves may fail or over-consume resources.

- Triggers can be impacted by administrative changes more than other areas of code (validation, processes, flows, and so on).

- Where the triggers are the first thing many developers touch, they are the most prone to bugs due to inexperience.

In this chapter, we will cover the following topics:

- How triggers operate
- The Salesforce save order of execution
- Best practices for developing and architecting triggers
- How we can control trigger execution, should we need to

With this knowledge, we will be able to develop more robust and scalable applications that can handle both more complex logic and higher data volumes.

Technical Requirements

The code for the chapter can be found here: `https://github.com/PacktPublishing/Mastering-Apex-Programming/tree/Chapter-3`

The Salesforce order of execution

Let's start this chapter by covering the Salesforce save order of execution. It is my opinion that the save order of execution should be one of the first things taught to every administrator or developer working on the platform. This ensures they are aware of the implications of actions they make when building automation through either clicks or code. Why is this?

Think of the save order of execution as being similar to a nuclear reactor. Nuclear reactors use fission to create energy, a process which involves firing a neutron at an isotope, with it then splitting and releasing some energy and other small isotopes. The reason I'm using this as a comparison is that it is a stable system that is designed to function in a certain way. As long as the process is controlled, we get the right amount of fission, and energy is released. If it goes wrong, though, too much energy is released, and this can cause a meltdown. If it is completely uncontrolled, we have a nuclear explosion:

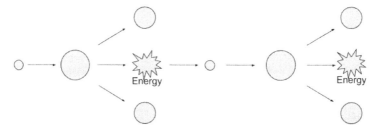

Figure 3.1 – A stable nuclear fission process has just the right amount of energy as a side effect. Too much and the results can cause a chain reaction

Triggers act in a similar manner (albeit with far less danger to life). When we save a record, we fire a trigger with the intention of performing some action. That trigger may have a set of side effects that we expect to occur when it comes to updating and creating records. If this is controlled and operates as anticipated, then we are fine. However, as systems grow more complex and have a greater number of code paths, the likelihood of an error occurring increases. Let's have a look at the following diagram:

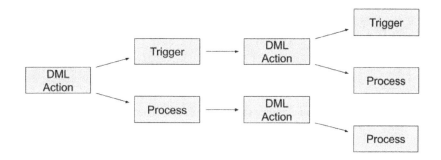

Figure 3.2 – Potentially unintended consequences of a DML action

Here, we can see how a DML action can have unintended consequences as triggers and processes that fire other DML actions interact.

An example scenario

Consider the following scenario: we have a system in place that helps us keep track of the number of open and completed tasks against an account. This is done via a trigger on the task object that, when a task is created or closed, sums the total number of tasks against the related record of an account, opportunity, contact, or other account-related record.

We also have a trigger on some of these related records to roll up the total to the account record when the relationship is a lookup and not a master detail. This allows us to report at, a granular level, how many open and closed tasks we have against our associated contacts and opportunities, as well as on the account record itself and against the account overall.

This system works fine until a new requirement comes in. When a lead is converted into an account, a contact, and an opportunity, a default task should be created on all these records. We now have a potentially expensive situation. We've converted a lead, which creates three tasks. The task trigger then fires an update on the contact, the opportunity, and the account.

Both the contact and opportunity then fire another update on the account. Our single operation here has resulted in five different updates. Our account, contact, and opportunity may each have a number of other different processes and workflows firing. If we have 20 leads converted en masse here, we could end up with over 100 DML actions and a governor limit exception:

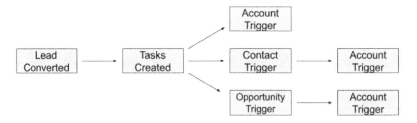

Figure 3.3 – In our example scenario, we've run five separate triggers,
leading to Governor Limit issues at scale

While this example has been simplified, it illustrates how rapidly a small change can escalate the usage of resources throughout the save order of execution. As developers, we must be extremely aware of this in our coding and testing to avoid such situations where possible.

The save order of execution

It is worth briefly discussing the save order of execution and which steps within this process can cause side effects or additional save operations. As you begin to develop more complex systems and solutions, this series of steps and the order in which they fire will be of an increasing concern to you as you decide how best to implement them.

> **Note**
>
> If you are looking to pass either the Platform Developer II exam or move on to being certified as a Salesforce Technical Architect, you will need to learn the save order of execution for the examinations. While I do not personally believe you need to remember it from memory (or think it is a great use of time to memorize it), whenever I am designing a solution, I refer to the save order of execution to verify that it will execute as I anticipate it to with no side effects.
>
> One way of managing this is through the use of a flow document, which swim lanes the various processes to see how they interact. Each step of the order of execution is given an independent swim lane for its actions, which can then refer to other flows for the order of execution for other objects. The steps of the order that have no action can either have the lane left blank, collapsed, or removed as necessary. Documenting in this way not only provides a good way of organizing your thoughts on paper but also serves as a useful artifact post-delivery.

At a high-level, the save order of execution is as follows:

1. Load records

2. Base validation (standard UI) and foreign keys

3. Before update flows

4. Before triggers

5. System validation rerun

6. Duplicate rules

7. Database save – no commit

8. After triggers

9. Assignment rules

10. Auto-response rules

11. Workflow rules

12. Processes and flows via a flow trigger workflow

13. Escalation rules

14. Entitlement rules

15. Roll up summaries and cross-object workflows

16. Criteria-based sharing

17. DML commit to database

18. Post-commit logic

This is a simplified version of the save order of execution, without the full descriptions of each step. You can find the full version in the Salesforce documentation (`https://developer.salesforce.com/docs/atlas.en-us.apexcode.meta/apexcode/apex_triggers_order_of_execution.htm`) and other sources. The key here is to highlight the steps where additional DML could occur:

- Before update flows

- Before triggers

- After triggers

- Workflow rules

- Processes and flows via a flow trigger workflow

- Roll up summaries and cross-object workflows

Some of these steps are pre-controlled by Salesforce. For example, the workflow rule updates for the fields will fire the before and after update triggers once and only once. Salesforce will also avoid step 9 onward in a recursive save, including rollup summaries on grandparent records.

For the others, however, we need to be aware of the effects the save process will have on our resources. We should always be prepared for bulk operations on our system. However, as we saw in our illustrative example, a relatively small change in data volumes can lead to far more increased resource usage than expected.

Clicks and code

Before we start looking at architectural patterns and solutions to these problems, we should discuss the proverbial elephant in the room: clicks and code or clicks versus code. One of the most powerful features of the Salesforce platform is the fact that there is a wealth of low or no-code tools that can be used to get a solution up and running in a relatively short amount of time. These tools stretch from formula fields through to powerful point and click tools such as flow.

Firstly, I would like to advocate that when building using click-based tools, a number of best practices are followed that will make these solutions more scalable and manageable over time. Most importantly, we should follow these two best practices:

- Use a single Process Builder process per object
- Implement bulk patterns within Flow

Process Builder processes do not have a defined order of execution; that is, if you have two processes defined per object, then you cannot guarantee the order in which they will run. For Flow, care should be taken to retrieve records once and then loop through them rather than repeatedly retrieving records through multiple loops (this is equivalent to not performing SOQL within a loop).

It is my personal opinion that, as complexity grows within a system and the use of triggers for an object becomes required to perform certain functionality, all processes and automated flows for that object should be migrated to trigger-based code where possible, rather than having overlapping triggers and processes/flows. This is not to say you cannot have both within an organization for a single object, just that this will dramatically increase your complexity and surface for potential failures and bugs.

One of the primary reasons behind this is testability. Flows and processes are not bound by the same testing requirements that developers are under. If a robust testing framework is in place against your code base (more on this in the next chapter), a greater degree of confidence can be placed in all edge cases and behavior being vetted. With declarative tools, testing is only available through manual means and will not necessarily be vetted through all edge and bulk use cases. Apex tests will still execute any Flows or Process Builder processes that are part of the save order of execution, although it is not currently a common practice to write bespoke unit tests for these.

Within most development teams, the concept of technical debt payoff is common, although less so across the Salesforce space. Within some large organizations I have worked with, time was dedicated during each development cycle to review certain existing code and to make sure that when it was updated, any technical debt was removed. This is of particular importance when we consider the support for API versions provided by Salesforce and that work should be undertaken to try and minimize the variation between different API versions of code within a code base.

Care must also be taken when working with a combination of automation tools and code to correctly anticipate governor limit usage and minimize this where possible. As an example, if we have both a trigger and a process on an object making updates, we should consider whether we can merge the two to avoid repeated DML or updates. Reviewing our save order of execution, we can see that updating a record in both an after update trigger and a process will cause the save order of execution to fire twice. This will not only use up a set of governor resources in a possibly unnecessary manner, but also slow down the user experience for our end users as the order of execution runs repeatedly.

Due to this, I advocate that, when working with multiple automation tools in an environment, an attempt is made to try and merge to a single tool per object – most likely an Apex trigger if they are in use (as this is most likely to be due to there being requirements that cannot be met by Process Builder or Flow). The important thing to note here is *per object*. If you are running some code on the account object that alters related contacts, then consider managing both object's automation with code. If no code is present, then continue using the point and click automation tools.

Trigger architecture

In the same way it is a best practice to have only a single Process Builder process per object, it is also a best practice to have only a single trigger per object. With multiple triggers, we cannot guarantee their order of execution, which may lead to unintended consequences. With a single trigger, however, we can control the order in which the updates are made as the code will run sequentially within the trigger.

A good question I was once asked when teaching a class on Apex was, *why one Trigger per object, rather than one Trigger per context per object?* That is, why is the suggestion to have an `AccountTrigger` and not a series of triggers on the `Account` object, where each manages a single context; `AccountBeforeInsertTrigger`, `AccountAfterUpdateTrigger`, and so on? This can be seen in the following diagram:

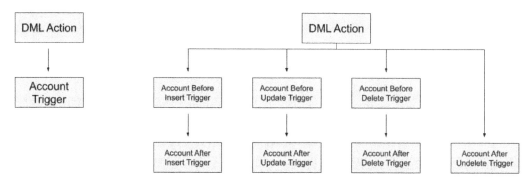

Figure 3.4 – A single trigger per object versus a single trigger per object per context

It is worth mentioning that this is a very valid architecture, although not one I have seen out in the wild within a Salesforce implementation. Such a design would maintain an order of execution and ensure we had predictability regarding the way our code executed. It does, however, come with a few flaws, which makes it less than optimal as a long-term solution.

The main issue is concerned with maintainability and ease of use. Why would we necessarily want multiple triggers to be defined instead of a single trigger that can cover all bases?

Let's consider that, for both the single trigger per object and single trigger per context architectures, we want to use Apex classes to group functionality outside of the trigger for both reuse and improved testability. One limitation of Apex triggers is that they do not allow the definition of functions within the trigger itself, so the code becomes a long sequence and can become difficult to both read and maintain. The use of Apex methods to extract common functionality for reuse and to improve testing is the most common way of handling this issue.

Both our trigger architectures could use the same Apex classes to extract this code, with the only primary difference being that for the single trigger option, we would have some routing logic, whereas in our multiple trigger structure, we would not. Within our Apex classes, we would then be working to ensure that we were not repeating ourselves and would extract common functionality, whatever the context, into a method that could be reused. For example, we may extract a query into a single method for reuse if we are retrieving the same data in both the `before insert` and `before update` contexts.

Therefore, the primary difference is that we have potentially got some decision-making logic within our single trigger to determine which context we are operating in, whereas within our individual context triggers, we can simply call the methods. If we were to extract this decision-making logic to the shared trigger utility class itself and have our single trigger call that, then the architectures would look almost identical, except the multiple trigger setup now has more files to manage.

Due to this, for ease of management and deployment, it is recommended that we stick to a single trigger per object rather than a trigger per object per context, and have the utility class manage the routing for each execution context in a repeatable manner. This is known as the trigger handler pattern, and we will discuss this next. You should also consider testing requirements.

Before we continue, I would also like to point out that due to the standardization across the Salesforce ecosystem regarding the use of trigger handler patterns, it is also a good idea to stick to the single trigger per object pattern with a handler for maintainability. If you are a consultant, it will make your code be more manageable by other parties in the future. For ISV developers and developers working on an internal environment, the use of a standardized pattern will make it much easier to onboard new developers and maintain a consistent architecture across the organization.

Using trigger handler frameworks

Trigger handler frameworks are a well-established architectural pattern across the entire Salesforce ecosystem for good reason. For one, they provide a standardized way of separating out your code for a trigger in a way that makes maintaining and testing the code simpler.

At its core, a trigger handler framework should do three things:

- Provide a simple and repeatable way of creating and managing trigger code.
- Provide a repeatable and abstracted way of handling how to switch trigger contexts.
- Allow the handler code to be tested without the need to execute the trigger.

Many frameworks also provide additional logic handling and management, but for the most basic handlers, these three functions should be provided. In this section, we'll learn how to build a simple framework to meet these needs.

> **Note**
>
> In this section, we are going to draft a simple framework to meet these requirements. In practice, I recommend using a framework such as the one provided by Kevin O'Hara, which is widely used and contains a deeper set of functionality. You can find Kevin's framework at `https://github.com/kevinohara80/sfdc-trigger-framework`. This code is completely open source and has been widely used with success. We should be happy to stand on the shoulders of giants and use a tried and tested solution where possible.

Let's start by thinking about how we would structure a single trigger handler class for the `Account` object. It would look something like this:

```
public class AccountTriggerHandler {

    public void handleBeforeInsert() {
        //Execute our before insert logic
    }

    public void handleAfterInsert() {
        //Execute out after insert logic
    }

    public void handleBeforeUpdate() {
        //Execute our before insert logic
    }

    public void handleAfterUpdate() {
        //Execute out after insert logic
    }

    public void handleBeforeDelete() {
        //Execute our before insert logic
    }

    public void handleAfterDelete() {
```

```
          //Execute out after insert logic
    }

    public void handleAfterUndelete() {
          //Execute out after insert logic
    }
}
```

Our account trigger would then call each of these methods independently:

```
Trigger AccountTrigger on Account(before insert, after insert,
before update, after update, before delete, after delete, after
undelete) {
    AccountTriggerHandler handler = new
    AccountTriggerHandler();

    switch on Trigger.operationType {
        when BEFORE_INSERT {
            handler.handleBeforeInsert();
        }
        when AFTER_INSERT {
            handler.handleAfterInsert();
        }
        when BEFORE_UPDATE {
            handler.handleBeforeUpdate();
        }
        when AFTER_UPDATE {
            handler.handleAfterUpdate();
        }
        when BEFORE_DELETE {
            handler.handleBeforeDelete();
        }
        when AFTER_DELETE {
            handler.handleAfterDelete();
        }
        when AFTER_UNDELETE {
```

```
            handler.handleAfterUndelete();
        }
    }

}
```

This would be a fine implementation for a single trigger and handler. If we wanted this to become a repeatable way to have the same logic, we need to abstract away the structure in our `AccountTriggerHandler` class to a class that `AccountTriggerHandler` can inherit from. Therefore, we need to define a generic `TriggerHandler` that is either an interface that `AccountTriggerHandler` implements or a virtual class that `AccountTrigggerHandler` extends.

> **Note**
>
> This section assumes you have some familiarity with the object-oriented properties of Apex and how to use them appropriately. If not, then you may wish to review the *Apex Developer's Guide* first before proceeding.

We are going to use a virtual class to extend rather than an interface for a number of reasons. Firstly, an interface requires an implementation, whereas a virtual class can provide a default implementation for one of our methods, namely the case where we take no action for that trigger context. Secondly, an interface's methods are always `public` in scope, which works fine for the example we have here, but as we will see, we can improve our code by correctly encapsulating our methods within the class.

Let's start by creating a generic `TriggerHandler` class that we can extend. Right now, our class looks like this:

```
public virtual class TriggerHandler {
    public virtual void handleBeforeInsert() {}
    public virtual void handleAfterInsert() {}
    public virtual void handleBeforeUpdate() {}
    public virtual void handleAfterUpdate() {}
    public virtual void handleBeforeDelete() {}
    public virtual void handleAfterDelete() {}
    public virtual void handleAfterUndelete() {}
}
```

Our `AccountTriggerHandler` will be updated to the following:

```
public class AccountTriggerHandler extends TriggerHandler {

    public override void handleBeforeInsert() {
        //Execute our before insert logic
    }

    public override void handleAfterInsert() {
        //Execute out after insert logic
    }

    public override void handleBeforeUpdate() {
        //Execute our before insert logic
    }

    public override void handleAfterUpdate() {
        //Execute out after insert logic
    }

    public override void handleBeforeDelete() {
        //Execute our before insert logic
    }

    public override void handleAfterDelete() {
        //Execute out after insert logic
    }

    public override void handleAfterUndelete() {
        //Execute out after insert logic
    }
}
```

If we were not performing any actions for one of these contexts, we could simply leave out the previous method override. We will keep them in our examples here for completeness, but it is worth noting that they are no longer required in all instances.

The next improvement we can make is to extract the repeated logic that we have within every trigger to execute the correct context method. This logic will need to be copied into every trigger, so this is a good candidate for our handler class. If we do this, we can change the scope of our `virtual` methods to `protected`:

```
public virtual class TriggerHandler {
    protected virtual void handleBeforeInsert() {}
    protected virtual void handleAfterInsert() {}
    protected virtual void handleBeforeUpdate() {}
    protected virtual void handleAfterUpdate() {}
    protected virtual void handleBeforeDelete() {}
    protected virtual void handleAfterDelete() {}
    protected virtual void handleAfterUndelete() {}

    public void execute() {
        switch on Trigger.operationType {
            when BEFORE_INSERT {
                this.handleBeforeInsert ();
            }
            when AFTER_INSERT {
                this.handleAfterInsert ();
            }
            when BEFORE_UPDATE {
                this.handleBeforeUpdate();
            }
            when AFTER_UPDATE {
                this.handleAfterUpdate();
            }
            when BEFORE_DELETE {
                this.handleBeforeDelete();
            }
            when AFTER_DELETE {
                this.handleAfterDelete();
            }
            when AFTER_UNDELETE {
                this.handleAfterUndelete();
```

```
            }
         }
      }
   }
```

We can then update our `AccountTrigger` to the following:

```
Trigger AccountTrigger on Account (before insert, after insert,
before update, after update, before delete, after delete, after
undelete) {
    AccountTriggerHandler handler = new
    AccountTriggerHandler();
    handler.execute();
}
```

This setup provides us with a framework that meets criteria 1 and 2 from before. How do we deal with criteria number 3, which is testability? We have two options here: either we mark our methods as `@TestVisible` so that we can execute them in tests, or we abstract the context for our handler to a separate variable and `enum` that we then make test visible and use to control our flow. Let's look at how we might implement this second method.

Firstly, within our `TriggerHandler`, we define a variable that is marked as `@TestVisible`. This holds our trigger context and has a new `enum` data type:

```
@TestVisible
private Context triggerContext;
@TestVisible
private enum Context {
   BEFORE_INSERT, BEFORE_UPDATE, BEFORE_DELETE,
   AFTER_INSERT, AFTER_UPDATE, AFTER_DELETE,
   AFTER_UNDELETE
}
```

We then define a new `setContext` method. This sets our `triggerContext` variable to one of the `enum` values that's dependent on the trigger context:

```
private void setContext() {
    if(this.triggerContext == null) {
        switch on Trigger.operationType {
            when BEFORE_INSERT {
```

```
                    this.triggerContext = Context.BEFORE_
                    INSERT;
            }
            when AFTER_INSERT {
                    this.triggerContext = Context.AFTER_
                    INSERT;
            }
            when BEFORE_UPDATE {
                    this.triggerContext = Context.BEFORE_
                    UPDATE;
            }
            when AFTER_UPDATE {
                    this.triggerContext = Context.AFTER_
                    UPDATE;
            }
            when BEFORE_DELETE {
                    this.triggerContext = Context.BEFORE_
                    DELETE;
            }
            when AFTER_DELETE {
                    this.triggerContext = Context.AFTER_
                    DELETE;
            }
            when AFTER_UNDELETE {
                    this.triggerContext = Context.AFTER_
                    UNDELETE;
            }
        }
    }
}
```

Finally, we update our execute method so that it uses this new `setContext` method and run our appropriate handler method:

```
public void execute() {
    setContext();
    switch on this.triggerContext {
        when BEFORE_INSERT {
            this.beforeInsert();
```

```
        }
        when AFTER_INSERT {
            this.afterInsert();
        }
        when BEFORE_UPDATE {
            this.beforeUpdate();
        }
        when AFTER_UPDATE {
            this.afterUpdate();
        }
        when BEFORE_DELETE {
            this.beforeDelete();
        }
        when AFTER_DELETE {
            this.afterDelete();
        }
        when AFTER_UNDELETE {
            this.afterUndelete();
        }
    }
}
```

With this new structure, we can set the trigger's context within a test method by calling the appropriate handler method for testing, without the need for DML.

This is a bare-bones handler implementation and is designed to illustrate how we should be maximizing our code reuse within Apex, particularly within our trigger structure. By having such a framework in place with a single trigger for the object, we can ensure that our code is executing logic in the order we expect and avoid any unintended side effects.

Controlling trigger execution

Even with our framework in place, there will still be instances where an update may occur that leads to our trigger running again. For example, if we create a child record in an after update trigger that is used in a rollup summary, this can cause our original after update trigger to fire again, which may not be desired or efficient. In many scenarios, we do not know whether we will be performing DML at the start of the trigger's execution; this only becomes clearer as we execute our code. This can consume additional resources and execute code that is not needed.

> **Important note**
>
> It should be noted that not all recursive scenarios are bad or need to be avoided; we just want to ensure that we are only performing them where necessary. We may want to set the maximum number of times the trigger can be executed. Similarly, there may be instances where we want to bypass a trigger altogether if we are performing some DML where we wish to bypass the execution; for example, when creating records via an API call. If you are using the documentation method I described previously, you can detect these situations and scenarios for management with ease.

We can define two scenarios where we may want to manage our trigger's execution to halt it, when we have reached a maximum number of executions recursively, or when we wish to bypass the trigger altogether. This is a form of circuit breaker, as shown in the following diagram:

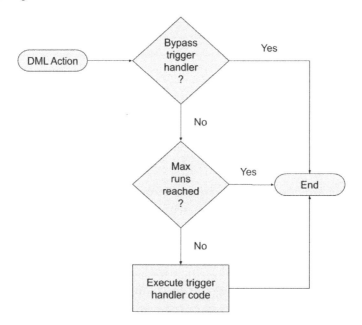

Figure 3.5 – Bypassing or skipping a trigger handler if it's been marked for bypass or if it has been executed a set number of times already

Recalling our singleton class from *Chapter 1, Common Apex Mistakes*, one way of managing this is through the use of a singleton to coordinate execution in tandem with our handler classes. We can create a `TriggerExecutionMediator` as follows. (The naming here is based upon the Gang of Four patterns that we are creating an interpretation of. Note that we are not creating an exact implementation of the mediator pattern but a close analogy for Apex.)

Firstly, we define our class using the singleton pattern we have seen previously. We also define member variables to hold the data we will use to coordinate our logic:

```
public class TriggerExecutionMediator {
    private static TriggerExecutionMediator instance;
    private Set<String> bypass;
    private Map<String, Integer> maxCounts;
    private Map<String, Integer> currentCounts;
    public static TriggerExecutionMediator getInstance() {
        if(instance == null) {
            instance = new TriggerExecutionMediator();
        }
        return instance;
    }
}
```

We then add a method called addBypass, which enables us to mark a particular handler for bypassing. This method adds the handler to the bypass set of strings we defined previously. We also define clearBypass methods to remove a handler from this set and stop it being bypassed, as well as a shouldBypass utility method that returns a Boolean value indicating whether the code should be bypassed or not:

```
public void addBypass(String handlerName) {
    bypass.add(handlerName);
}
public void clearBypass(String handlerName) {
    bypass.remove(handlerName);
}
public Boolean shouldBypass(String handlerName) {
    return bypass.contains(handlerName);
}
```

To avoid our handler being executed more times than is desired, we define some setMaxCount methods. This allows us to set the maximum number of times a handler should execute, as well as set the current execution count for that handler to 0:

```
public void setMaxCount(String handlerName, Integer max) {
maxCounts.put(handlerName, max);
    currentCounts.put(handlerName, 0);
}
```

When then utilize the data we have just captured in the `shouldExecute` method, which returns a boolean value indicating whether we should execute this handler based on whether it has a maximum count set and whether we have surpassed that:

```
public Boolean shouldExecute(String handlerName) {
    //return true if no max set
    if(!maxCounts.containsKey(handlerName)) {
        return true;
    }
    //if max not yet reached, increment count and return true
    if(currentCounts.get(handlerName) != maxCounts.
get(handlerName)){
        currentCounts.put(handlerName, currentCounts.
        get(handlerName)+1);
        return true;
    }
    //otherwise return false
    return false
}
```

We also need to update our `TriggerHandler` to execute the code:

```
public void execute() {
    String className = String.valueOf(this).split(':')[0];
    if(TriggerExecutionMediator.getInstance().
shouldBypass(className)){
        return;
    }

    if(!TriggerExecutionMediator.getInstance().
shouldExecute(className)) {
        return;
    }
    //Continue on with the same code as before
}
```

This additional code will then short-circuit our trigger execution and avoid execution when it's not required. Then, within our Apex code, elsewhere in the system, we can tell `AccountTriggerHandler` to be bypassed by calling the following code:

```
TriggerExecutionMediator.getInstance().
addBypass('AccountTriggerHandler');
```

Similarly, we can set the maximum execution count for a trigger by calling the following code:

```
TriggerExecutionMediator.getInstance().
setMaxCount('AccountTriggerHandler', 3);
```

This limits the amount of times the trigger can be recursively called within a single execution context.

> **Important note**
>
> Care should be taken here as such a maximum is set across all trigger contexts in that execution. For example, if we set the maximum to 2 and had both a before and after trigger, this maximum would be consumed by one `update` DML statement as the `shouldExecute` method is called twice. An alternative to the preceding code is to have a maximum execution per trigger handler per context. Should you find yourself in such a situation, then you may wish to update the code as required. Again, other frameworks have this already built out, and this example is just an illustration.

Summary

In this chapter, we took a deep dive into how Apex triggers function and how to improve our triggers through the use of trigger handlers.

We started by discussing the Salesforce save Order of Execution, how it operates, and the side effects that it can have when it is not properly accounted for when it comes to designing and developing solutions. As we discussed, not correctly accounting for the way in which it fires different actions can lead to recursion and overuse of resources, including unintended side effects and governor limit breaches in the most extreme scenarios.

With this knowledge, we reviewed how we should correctly architect our triggers for scalability and built out a basic trigger handler pattern to enable us to manage and maintain our code. This handler met our three criteria and allowed us to separate the execution of the code for our triggers from the actual trigger itself, thus making it easier to maintain and test.

Finally, we looked at how we could manage trigger execution through the use of a bypass and max counters. We looked at some example code that allows us to handle this appropriately and short-circuit the system when required. With all this knowledge, we should now be able to develop robust and flexible triggers that can effectively scale across the system.

Now that we have a thorough understanding of how our trigger code should operate, along with what we learned in the previous chapters on avoiding common mistakes and effectively debugging our Apex code, we should have a more robust code base with fewer errors. However, exceptions will still occur, and we need to ensure we handle them appropriately. This is what we will focus on in the next chapter.

4
Exceptions and Exception Handling

So far, we have spent a large amount of time discussing the causes of errors and how to develop solutions with Apex in a more defensive manner, to avoid them. In *Chapter 1, Common Apex Mistakes*, we discussed some common Apex mistakes that can lead to errors and how they can be proactively avoided. In *Chapter 2, Debugging Apex*, we looked at how we can debug and troubleshoot errors to find and eliminate them from code quickly and repeatably. In *Chapter 3, Triggers and Managing Trigger Execution*, we focused on triggers and used trigger handler and execution management to effectively control our triggers and avoid some of the common issues that occur within trigger development.

Sadly, it is a fact that no matter how well we develop code, we will at some point have an exception occur within our code. One of the nuances with Salesforce as a platform is that this can happen many months or even years after the code has been deployed, having worked successfully for that period. Configuration changes such as adding required fields or validation rules can stop your code from executing as anticipated and lead to failures that were never envisioned. So, in this chapter, we will see how to overcome these or avoid them.

In this chapter, we will cover the following topics:

- The different types of exception that we may encounter within Apex
- How we catch exceptions within our code
- Logging exceptions to ensure that no information is lost
- Using custom exceptions

Technical Requirements

The code for the chapter can be found here: `https://github.com/PacktPublishing/Mastering-Apex-Programming`

Understanding the different types of exceptions

Broadly speaking, I like to divide exceptions into three types: expected exceptions, unexpected exceptions, and unknown exceptions. Let's look at what is meant by each of these types.

Expected exceptions

Expected exceptions are ones that we anticipate occurring and want to handle appropriately. An example would be some validation logic in code or a required field for a process to occur. When developing the code, you are aware of these items and the exceptions that they will throw and will want to inform the user appropriately. If they press the **Send Invoice** button and there is no email address, they should be informed.

Unexpected exceptions

Your code has been working for a period of time without any hiccups, then suddenly someone changes the system and does not verify the impacts of the change.

At the time of writing this, I have just been dealing with a bug in a system relating to a code-based process that was originally implemented by another vendor 4 years ago. This code has run seamlessly since then and started failing due to a change made by an administrator who did not consider the impact. This exception was unexpected by the system as it involved a fundamental change in the business process that the developer could not have anticipated happening.

These exceptions can often lead to error messages that may not be usable for the user and so we have to tread a balance between providing enough information to let them know a failure has happened and hiding other information so as to not confuse the user. The information provided will still be of use to the developer, however, when they come to fix it.

Unknown exceptions

Unknown exceptions are the most interesting and rarest type of exceptions on the Salesforce platform and are commonly called *GACKs*. These are errors internal to Salesforce, such as the one shown in the following screenshot:

An internal server error has occurred

An error has occurred while processing your request. The salesforce.com support team has been notified of the problem. If you believe you have additional information that may be of help in reproducing or correcting the error, please contact Salesforce Support. Please indicate the URL of the page you were requesting, any error id shown on this page as well as any other related information. We apologize for the inconvenience.

Thank you again for your patience and assistance. And thanks for using salesforce.com!

Error ID: 607895028-150984 (-1198114167)

Figure 4.1 – A Salesforce internal server error or GACK

These internal errors are the underlying infrastructure. They cannot be caught or handled by a developer and cannot be debugged without the help of Salesforce support. They are identifiable by the long numeric ID that is provided.

When these exceptions arise, they are typically completely unknown to the developer and require support from Salesforce in order to manage them.

> **Dealing with a GACK**
>
> Should you encounter a GACK, you should raise a case with Salesforce including the error ID along with a description of how you can reproduce it. It is also a wise idea to review what your work is doing in general and review the Salesforce Stack Exchange and developer community. It is rarer nowadays to come across a GACK that is completely new. While the error message ID you will receive is unique, this can be a quick way of seeing whether you are doing something strange. For example, I recently found a known issue reference to using duplicate rules and Process Builder together by taking a step back and searching to see if anybody else had encountered similar issues.

In this chapter, we are going to focus on handling expected and unexpected exceptions appropriately. Sadly, we cannot currently handle unknown exceptions and have to rely on Salesforce support to assist us when these issues arise.

To begin this, we need to catch errors to be able to identify them as expected or unexpected. Let's see how this happens in the sections ahead.

Catching errors

The first step in correctly managing any exception is to begin by catching it correctly. Apex allows developers to do this using the `try-catch-finally` syntax, shown as follows:

```
try {
    //Run some code
} catch(ExceptionType ex) {
    //Handle the exception appropriately
} finally {
    //Perform some final clean up code
}
```

A `try` statement must have a `catch` or `finally` block associated with it in order for the code to compile correctly.

In the `catch` statement, we can specify a type of exception that we want to handle, for example:

```
try {
    Account acc = null;
    acc.Name = 'Test'; //This will throw a
                       //NullPointerException - see Chapter 1
} catch(NullPointerException ex) {
    //Handle the exception
}
```

Note that if in this code we had a `QueryException` thrown instead of a `NullPointerException`, the `catch` block would not have caught this exception. This is important for us to be aware of, as it presents us with the following two options for our `catch` blocks:

- Using multiple `catch` blocks for different exception types
- Using a single generic `catch` block

The correct answer here depends upon the code we are wrapping in our `try` block, the types of exceptions we expect to occur, and how we intend to handle the different exception types.

For example, if we were wrapping some code that performed a query and then a DML statement, we could reasonably expect the types of error that would occur to be either a `QueryException` or a `DMLException`. We could therefore structure our code as follows:

```
try {
    //Execute our code
} catch(DMLException dmlEx) {
    //Handle DML Exception
} catch(QueryException qryEx) {
    //Handle Query Exception
}
```

This would only make sense, however, if we were planning on handling the two different exception types in different ways, such as displaying different error messages to the user, as we see here:

```
try {
    //Execute our code
} catch(DMLException dmlEx) {
    displayMessage = Label.No_Matching_Records;
} catch(QueryException qryEx) {
    displayMessage = Label.Unable_To_Save_Records;
}
```

If instead, we plan on handling these different exception types in the same way, for example, with a generic error message, it would be better for us to simply have a single generic **catch** block as shown in the following code snippet:

```
try {
    //Execute our code
} catch(Exception ex) {
    //Handle Exception in a common way
}
```

I have found it is best practice to combine these methods to allow us both to handle specific exceptions and ensure that no other exceptions are left uncaught.

We may get exceptions that we do not anticipate as our system grows more complex or changes are made by administrators and other developers. We should therefore combine our previous examples to obtain something like the following code:

```
try {
    //Execute our code
} catch(DMLException dmlEx) {
    //Handle DML Exception
} catch(QueryException qryEx) {
    //Handle Query Exception
} catch(Exception ex) {
    //Handle any other exception types
}
```

What about the `finally` block? We now understand how we can appropriately capture errors, but how should the `finally` block be correctly incorporated into our handling? Let's understand this next.

Using the finally block

The `finally` block in Apex executes after your `catch` block has executed, when an exception occurs. It will not execute if either the exception is unhandled or no exception occurs. The primary use case of the `finally` block is to ensure that any changes we do not want to persist are rolled back or that the code can continue past the error. It can also be used to end the transaction should a piece of code fail and you wish to end the process.

In the following example code, we are creating a `Savepoint` before inserting a new account and then attempting to insert a new related contact:

```
Savepoint entryState = new Database.setSavepoint();

try {
    insert acc; //insert our populated account variable
} catch(DMLException accEx) {
    //handle the DML Exception
} finally {
    return; //Stop execution
}
```

```
con.AccountId = acc.Id;

try {
    insert con;
} catch(DMLException conEx) {
    //Handle the DML Exception
} finally {
    Database.rollback(entryState);
}
```

If the contact insertion fails, then we wish to roll the database back to before the account insertion. This is typical when we are developing RESTful APIs where we want to allow the external system to retry when a failure occurs with no leftover side effects.

The preceding code snippet highlights a number of things:

1. Should the first insertion on the account error, then we will try and stop the execution of the rest of the code through the use of the `return` statement in the `finally` block.

2. We can see the use of the `rollback` functionality in the second `finally` block, rolling the database back to its initial form.

3. You may be wondering why we are handling the exceptions in the `catch` block and not managing the `return` statements within this same block. This is an idiosyncrasy of the way in which the `finally` statement works—it will always run after the `catch` statement. As such, it is the correct place to handle both rollbacks and returns to short-circuit code as we are guaranteed its execution. This also enables us to have multiple `catch` blocks handling the different exception types appropriately before a single return.

We can also use the `finally` block to assist us in capturing detailed exception logs as a developer. When handling exceptions, we need to not only be aware of how we notify the user in the correct manner, when the user should be notified, but also how we log these exceptions for our own inspection and notification. Let's now look at a basic exception logging framework.

Exception logging

As discussed in *Chapter 2*, *Debugging Apex*, gathering information and debugging exceptions in Apex can be difficult. By default, Apex comes with no long-term persistent logging or exception handling framework. As a developer or administrator, you will receive emails when certain exceptions occur within the system, however, they often lack any context or the detailed information needed to rectify the error correctly.

In this section, we are going to construct a very basic error logging framework to enable you to persist exceptions and errors to the database in order to obtain additional information. We are also going to discuss some ways of capturing application state for review to help in this.

Of primary importance with this framework will be logging our exceptions in a persistent manner for us to inspect at a later date.

For this reason, we will create a custom object, Log__c, which will hold the details of the exception (or any other logs) that we want to persist and review. You can see in the following screenshot the structure for the custom object has been defined:

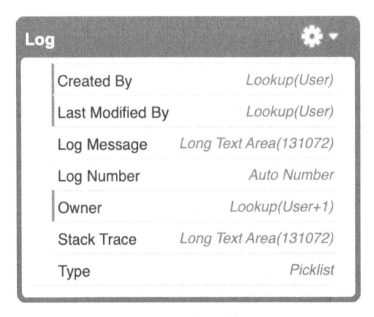

Figure 4.2 – Log object definition

We have defined two Long Text Area instances with the maximum number of characters to allow us to store the greatest amount of debug information possible. In practice, you may want to restrict this length to the default value or a preset number, dependent on how your organization is currently using resources.

Let's now start defining our new `Logger` class. We have two main use cases for this utility:

- To persist/log an exception or message straight away to the database
- To capture a set of logs or exceptions and then persist them at once

Let's start by dealing with the first use case.

This can be managed through the use of a `static` method, which will take in a set of parameters to populate our `Log__c` instance:

```
public with sharing class Logger {

    public static void log(String stackTrace, String
    logMessage, String logType) {
        Log__c log = new Log__c();
        log.Stack_Trace__c = stackTrace;
        log.Log_Message__c = logMessage;
        log.Type__c = logType;
        insert log;
    }

}
```

The `logType` parameter is for our `Type__c` picklist and can have the values of `Log` or `Exception`. This simple class would now allow us to log any information we wanted in our `catch` block should an error occur, for example:

```
try {
    Account a = null;
    a.Name; //This will throw a NullPointerException
} catch(NullPointerException ex) {
    Logger.log(ex.getStackTraceString(), 'This was an expected
    exception', 'Exception');
}
```

This structure can be useful when dealing with a single `catch` block where we have no rollback or cleanup required and simply want to log an exception. However, we ended the *Using the finally block* section by saying we were going to use the `finally` block to capture more detailed logs. Where does the `finally` block fit in?

So far, we have only seen a single use case for our utility to log a single exception straight away. You will notice that we have two types of Log__c record, Log and Exception. In the code, we may want to output logs irrespective of any exceptions occurring, to monitor system health and operation. This is where we need to meet our second use case and where the finally block will assist.

Firstly, let's update our Logger class to allow us to add logs to be kept in memory but not persisted:

```
private static List<Log__c> currentLogs;


public static void addLog(String stackTrace, String logMessage,
String logType) {
    if(currentLogs == null) {
        currentLogs = new List<Log__c>();
    }
    Log__c log = new Log__c();
    log.Stack_Trace__c = stackTrace;
    log.Log_Message__c = logMessage;
    log.Type__c = logType;
    currentLogs.add(log);
}
```

Throughout our code, we can now start generating logs that we wish to persist. We need to also add a method to persist these captured logs to the database. Refer to the following code:

```
public static void persistLogs() {
    if(currentLogs != null && currentLogs.size() > 0) {
        insert currentLogs;
        currentLogs = new List<Log__c>();
    }
}
```

We can now use these methods in a variety of ways. Firstly, within a code path, we can log multiple pieces of information; for example, earlier we had code that was using a savepoint to roll back on an error.

Let's imagine this was part of a RESTful endpoint we had developed. We could now use our `Logger` class in tandem with this code as follows:

```
Savepoint entryState = new Database.setSavepoint();
Logger.addLog(null, 'Savepoint created before processing
request with body:\n' + req.getBody(), 'Log');


try {
    insert acc; //insert our populated account variable
} catch(DMLException accEx) {
    //handle the DML Exception
    Logger.addLog(accEx.getStackTraceString(), 'Error in
    saving account:\n' + acc, 'Exception');
} finally {
    Logger.persistLogs();
    return; //Stop execution
}


con.AccountId = acc.Id;

try {
    insert con;
} catch(DMLException conEx) {
    //Handle the DML Exception
    Logger.addLog(conEx.getStackTraceString(), 'Error in
    saving contact:\n' + con, 'Exception');
} finally {
    Logger.addLog(null, 'Rolling back to savepoint', 'Log');
    Database.rollback(entryState);
    Logger.persistLogs();
}


Logger.persistLogs();
```

This code allows us to generate a set of logs that will be persisted to the database whether or not exceptions occur. We could remove the last call to `Logger.persistLogs()` and it would have the effect of only saving the logs in the case of an exception.

We have to be careful with heap size usage here as we hold logs for storage in memory throughout our transaction. This can be overcome by either making regular calls to `persistLogs()` or through careful management of the data we are persisting. Note that if we make regular calls to `persistLogs()`, we will be increasing our consumption of DML statements. In *Section 3*, *Apex Performance*, we will see that we will often have to balance out *Governor Limit* usage for optimal performance, but there is no free lunch.

A typical addition to this setup is to create a workflow rule to send an email to an administrator or developer when a new `Log__c` record of type `Exception` is created to proactively notify them. This can also be useful in helping to reach out to users or other system administrators when an issue has occurred, to help them correct any data entry issues and avoid exceptions happening again. One missing piece of the puzzle for this, however, is the state of the application when the exception is raised. This state, what our variables were at the time the exception occurred, is extremely useful in reviewing why an exception occurred and how to resolve it. This is effectively what we were doing in *Chapter 2*, *Debugging Apex*, with the use of the Apex Interactive Debugger. We cannot debug every session in real time, however. So, in order to proactively debug our solution, it would be useful to capture the application state when an exception occurs. In the next section, we will be doing this.

Capturing state

In order to capture the state of our class at a point in time, we will need to take the specific instance of the class and find a way of representing it that is both human-readable and simple to obtain. The prime way of doing this in Apex is with JSON, by serializing the class instance. We can then store this JSON as a file attached to the `Log__c` record to allow us to view it later.

In order to ensure we comply with the *Heap Size* governor limit, we should make this method single-use only and persist any other logs separately. Our method to do this would look as follows:

```
public static void logWithState(String stackTrace, String
logMessage, String logType, Object instance) {
    Log__c log = new Log__c();
    log.Stack_Trace__c = stackTrace;
    log.Log_Message__c = logMessage;
    log.Type__c = logType;
    insert log;


    ContentVersion cv = new ContentVersion();
```

```
    cv.VersionData = Blob.valueOf(JSON.
    serializePretty(instance));
    cv.Title = 'Log of state at ' + Datetime.now();
    cv.PathOnClient = 'Log of state at ' + Datetime.now();
    insert cv;


    ContentDocumentLink cdl = new ContentDocumentLink();
    cdl.ContentDocumentId = [SELECT ContentDocumentId FROM
    ContentVersion WHERE Id = :cv.Id].ContentDocumentId;
    cdl.LinkedEntityId = log.Id;
    cdl.ShareType = 'V';


    insert cdl;
}
```

This new method takes in an additional parameter, which is the instance we are storing the state of. We pass in the generic `Object` data type here so that we can handle any Apex class we pass in. The method generates the log in the same way and then creates a `ContentVersion` record, which will be the file that holds the data. We use the built-in Apex JSON serialization methods to create a readable version of the object and insert the `ContentVersion` record. Finally, we also need to create a `ContentDocumentLink` record to link the `ContentVersion` record to the `Log__c` record.

Let's now test this using the following code and see what the output is. We can create a `Person` class, which is easy to work with for testing:

```
public class Person {
    public String name {get; set;}
    public Integer age {get; set;}
    private String hiddenData = 'some hidden data';


    public Person(String name, Integer age) {
        this.name = name;
        this.age = age;
    }


    public void logMe() {
        Logger.logWithState(null, 'Logging out my person',
        'Log', this);
```

```
      }
 }
```

We can then run the following code to create an instance of our `Person` class and show how we can capture its state:

```
Person p = new Person('Mary', 24);
p.logMe();
```

If you run this code and view your `Log__c` records, then you should see something like the following screenshot:

Figure 4.3 – Generated log record and attached state data

You can download the attached file and it will contain data like the following:

```
{
    "name" : "Mary",
    "hiddenData" : "some hidden data",
    "age" : 24
}
```

As we can see, the file contains a useful representation of the state of our data, which we can use in debugging. We could also output additional information into the `Log Message` field of our `Log__c` record to give us the state of any other data in memory at the time.

So far, we have dealt with the standard exception types within Salesforce and handling them. To finish the chapter, I want to discuss custom exception types and how we can utilize them to improve our debugging and throw exceptions that we require when the system may not throw one by default.

Let's understand these in the next section.

Using custom exception types

Salesforce allows developers to extend the standard Apex `Exception` class to build custom exceptions that can provide bespoke errors and messages. To create a custom exception class, simply extend the standard `Exception` class as follows:

```
public with sharing class CustomisedException extends Exception
{

}
```

We can throw an exception of our new type using the `throw` keyword:

```
throw new CustomisedException('This is the exception message`);
```

Custom exception classes allow us a greater degree of control over the messages that are displayed within exceptions that are thrown and can also allow us to take action in throwing an exception when one would not typically be thrown or be thrown incorrectly.

Consider the following code, which is making a callout to a RESTful web service and receives a status code back that is not a `200 OK` code. Apex code will not error here (nor should it by default), however, we need to ensure that some sort of exception is provided to inform the user that the web service is unavailable (in the case of 5XX error codes) or that the administrator needs to take some action (in the case of 4XX error codes). We can do this using our `CustomisedException` class to provide more granular information:

```
HttpResponse resp = http.send(req);
Integer code = resp.getStatusCode();

//Handle 4XX errors
if(400 <= code && code < 500) {
    throw new CustomisedException('Callout returned status of
' + code + ', there is an issue with the client callout');
}
```

```
//Handle 5XX errors
else if(500 <= code && code < 600) [
    throw new CustomisedException('Callout returned status of
' + code + ', there is an issue with the server');
}


//Continue otherwise
```

This code provides us with more detailed information about the callout problem and would not have typically been handled within our Apex without this logic. As we can see, using custom exceptions can allow us a much greater degree of control and assist in presenting relevant error information to the end user.

Summary

In this chapter, we have seen how we can best handle those situations where an error occurs to ensure that we capture the most relevant information and inform the user appropriately.

We started by discussing the different types of exceptions that we could anticipate within our solutions and the ways in which we may want to respond to them. We covered how to correctly capture errors and use the `finally` block to roll back any changes or work that we did not want to persist.

Following this, we constructed a simple logging utility to allow us to capture and persist errors and logs to the database for review by an administrator or developer at a later point. We reviewed the different use cases for the logging utility as well as how we could capture and persist the state of an Apex class to this for review and to enhance our debugging capabilities.

In the last section of the chapter, we looked at how we can use custom exception types to provide varied exception outputs to the system in order to give more detailed information as well as throw exceptions where Apex may not normally do so.

Now that we understand how exceptions are handled and managed, we will look at Apex testing. Writing test code for your Apex code is not only a deployment requirement but a useful way of removing errors and bugs from your solution early. In the next chapter, we will see how we should test Apex code and the different ways of generating test data for consistency and performance.

5
Testing Apex Code

In the chapters so far, we have discussed a number of ways in which we can efficiently stop, debug, and capture errors within our applications to make them more robust and scalable. In this chapter, we will discuss Apex testing, which is a key part of any application's development as it is the earliest opportunity that a developer gets to capture errors and avoid exceptions occurring in an ongoing manner.

In this chapter, we will discuss the following topics:

- Understanding the importance of testing as a practice when developing Apex code
- The Test Data Factory pattern and the benefits of this pattern in developing test data
- Loading in test data using the `Test.loadData` method and the benefits this provides
- Using static resources to simplify testing web service callouts
- Testing best practices

Technical Requirements

The code for the chapter can be found here: `https://github.com/ PacktPublishing/Mastering-Apex-Programming/tree/Chapter-5`

Understanding the importance of testing

Through the years that I have been working in Salesforce, I have too often encountered the following scenarios:

- Developer receives problem
- Developer writes code
- Developer tests through the **user interface (UI)**
- They then declare the work as finished and hand over to testing team or customer for review
- Developer writes test methods to achieve 75% code coverage
- And then, developer deploys the code

The fact that the developer has declared the work as finished before the testing is complete is incorrect and should be discouraged as a practice. As a general rule, code without tests is not finished. A more correct order here would be the following:

- Developer receives problem
- Developer writes code
- Developer writes test methods to achieve at least 95% code coverage
- Developer tests through the UI
- They then declare the work as finished and hand over to testing team or customer for review
- Developer deploys code

Tests should be written as early as possible to validate any inbuilt assumptions, ensure that the code is functioning correctly, test bulk use cases, and ensure that the code is ready for deployment as soon as possible. I have stated here that at least 95% coverage should be aimed for to ensure that all your code paths are executed. In truth, wherever possible, you should cover 100% of your code for completeness.

> **Tip**
> I have worked with developers before who have stated that they found the request to test 100% of their code overly onerous because of the way in which it required data to be constructed for testing to occur. If you are finding your code difficult to test, it is typically a code smell that prompts you to refactor your code as it is not following best practices. I have often found that code that follows standard object-oriented practices, such as the SOLID and DRY principles, is much easier to test than code that does not.

As we discussed in *Chapter 2, Debugging Apex*, one of the key constraints on developers is the time that it takes to test code through the UI due to Salesforce being completely cloud-based. Code-based tests can be run from an **integrated development environment** (**IDE**) on your local machine and, if correctly written, will execute faster than UI-based testing. Any future changes can then have these tests rerun quickly to validate functionality has not been broken.

Tests are also extremely important in both the debugging and patching of code. Whenever a new bug comes in, a developer should write a test that replicates the bug before attempting to fix it. This provides a repeatable way to test that an issue exists and confirm that it has been fixed.

In general, code without tests lacks the same level of scrutiny as code that has been tested correctly and thoroughly. We want our tests to be like this:

- Quick to run
- Independent of each other
- To contain at least one assertion
- Independent of organization data

In order for a test to be independent of organization data and quick to run, we need to be able to create test data in a fast and repeatable manner. Let's see how a test data factory can help us in this.

Using a test data factory to create data

The factory pattern is a common object-oriented pattern from the famous *Gang of Four Design Patterns* book. A test data factory is a tweaked implementation of this pattern that enables the creation of data for use in testing, in a simple and repeatable manner.

Our test data factory will make it easier for us to create test data in a repeatable way by abstracting away the logic to create record instances into a single location, *the test data factory*. This will make it much easier for us to update the code in future should an update be required—for example, a new required field is added to the object.

There are a number of test data factories available from other developers within the Salesforce ecosystem that provide a series of ways of creating test data. Some utilize dynamic describe information on the object to retrieve a list of required fields and pre-populate the field with data, while others use default record templates. Some factories simply have methods defined by the developer for creating the data needed in the appropriate way. We could think of these three types as follows:

- Creating an object instance of this type with required fields populated through inspection
- Creating an object instance of this type using the defaults you can find in an ancillary class or data structure
- Creating an object instance *in this way*, where we provide a set of parameters to define the instance

It is for each team and organization to determine which of these different structures is the most appropriate for them. At one end of the spectrum, the first option requires the least thought by the developer as the code does all the heavy lifting to create the records. At the other end of the spectrum, you have greater control by defining exactly how you would like records to be created; however, you have more customized and bespoke code to manage over the application's life cycle.

So now, here, we are going to develop a test data factory that is of the second type: one that utilizes defaults set in an ancillary class or data structure. This will allow us to have more flexible code that is not only highly customized for this job but also has a greater degree of control than simply populating the default fields.

Salesforce Test Factory Open Source Library

We are going to build a simple test factory in this chapter to highlight some of the key features of a test factory and help build our understanding of how they work under the hood. For production environments, I recommend the use of a well-tested and well-used open source library such as the Salesforce Test Factory library created by Daniel Hoechst, which can be found at `https://github.com/dhoechst/Salesforce-Test-Factory`.

Let's define a simple test data factory class, as follows:

```
@isTest
public with sharing class TestDataFactory {

    public static SObject generateRecord(SObject obj) {
        return obj;
    }

}
```

This class has a single method, `generateRecord`, which takes in a `SObject` instance for us to populate with data and, for now, simply returns it.

For it to be able to populate this object, we are going to need a method of defining default values for the record. There are many options available for us to do this, but there are two that I want to focus on in particular: the use of an ancillary class to define the defaults, and loading the defaults from another data structure or file.

Let's first look at using an ancillary class to define these defaults. In this method, we need to define a `TestDataFactoryDefaults` class that will provide default field values for the different `SObject` types we create records for, as follows:

```
@isTest
public with sharing class TestDataFactoryDefaults {

}
```

Firstly, we should define some default data for our records. The simplest structure for us to store this in is `Map<Schema.SObjectField, Object>`, where the keys are the specific field to populate and the value is the value to populate the field with. We can define defaults for both the `Account` and `Contact` object types, as follows:

```
private static Map<Schema.SObjectField, Object> accountDefaults
= new Map<Schema.SObjectField, Object> {
    Account.Name => 'Test Account'
};

private static Map<Schema.SObjectField, Object> contactDefaults
= new Map<Schema.SObjectField, Object> {
    Contact.FirstName => 'John',
```

```
        Contact.LastName => 'Smith'
    };
```

We then need to associate these with the particular `SObjectType` that they apply to, again using a map collection, as follows:

```
private static Map<Schema.SObjectType, Map<Schema.SObjectField,
Object>> objectDefaultsMap = new Map<Schema.SObjectType,
Map<Schema.SObjectField, Object>>{
    Account.SObjectType => accountDefaults,
    Contact.SObjectType => contactDefaults
};
```

We have kept all of these variables `private` so far to maintain encapsulation, but we need a way of exposing them to our `TestDataFactory` class, which we can do with the following method:

```
public static Map<Schema.SObjectField, Object>
getDefaultValues(Schema.SObjectType sobjType) {
    return objectDefaultsMap.get(sobjType);
}
```

Now that we have this structure in place, we can update our `generateRecord` method and add some logic to populate the field values correctly so that our class looks like this:

```
@isTest
public with sharing class TestDataFactory {

    public static SObject generateRecord(SObject obj) {
        Map<Schema.SObjectField, Object> defaultValues =
TestDataFactoryDefaults.getDefaultValues(obj.getSObjectType());

        if(defaultValues != null) {
            populateFieldValues(obj, defaultValues);
        }

        return obj;
    }

    private static SObject populateFieldValues(SObject obj,
```

```
Map<Schema.SObjectField, Object> defaultValues) {
        for(Schema.SObjectField field : defaultValues.keySet())
    {
            obj.put(field, defaultValues.get(field));
        }

        return obj;
    }
}
```

In the preceding code, we have updated the `generateRecord` method to retrieve the default values map for `SObject` passed in, and return that instance with no changes if no such default value map can be found by our call to `TestDataFactoryDefaults.getDefaultValues`. If a map is found, we call `populateFieldValues`, which loops through the map and populates each field with the default value provided.

We should now test this code with a test class to verify it works as expected. The following test class does this for the different code paths (note that this will not show coverage for the `TestDataFactory` class as we have marked it as `@isTest`, excluding it from the code coverage calculations and making it easy for other developers to see that this class is only to be used for testing):

```
@isTest
private with sharing class TestDataFactory_Test {

    @isTest
    private static void testPopulateAccountWithDefaults() {
        Account acc = (Account)TestDataFactory.
        generateRecord(new Account());
        System.assertEquals('Test Account', acc.Name,
        'Incorrect default account name');
    }

    @isTest
    private static void testPopulateContactWithDefaults() {
        Contact con = (Contact)TestDataFactory.
        generateRecord(new Contact());
        System.assertEquals('John', con.FirstName, 'Incorrect
        default contact first name');
        System.assertEquals('Smith', con.LastName, 'Incorrect
```

```
default contact last name');
    }


    @isTest
    private static void testReturnEmptyObjectNoDefaults() {
        StaticResource res = (StaticResource)TestDataFactory.
        generateRecord(new StaticResource());
        System.assertEquals(null, res.Name, 'No values set for
        record as no default provided');
    }
}
```

If you are using this in a production organization, you should ensure that you have correctly set the parameters to any defaults provided in the organization and that a relevant object is used for the testReturnEmptyObjectNoDefaults method. I have used the StaticResource object here as it is rare that we will have instances of this created in code and needing to be defaulted in a test. You could replace StaticResource with any sObject that you will not be creating default values for here.

If you recall, when we defined this type of test data factory we mentioned that the defaults could be stored in an ancillary class (as we have seen) or in another data structure. We have the values stored in Apex for us to work with here; however, this has a couple of limitations, as follows:

- Any changes must be made by a developer.
- Changes require code deployments.

Both of these are acceptable limitations in most circumstances; however, we could store the data in another data format in a static resource and load the data in. This would allow the data to be updated more readily by administrators, and has some other benefits as well. Rather than develop a custom tool to do this, however, we should look at using the inbuilt tool Salesforce provides for allowing us to do this: the Test.loadData method.

Loading test data using Test.loadData

Depending on the type of work you are doing as a developer, your testing practices may vary greatly. For those who work on consultative projects, defining test data in the way we have just described will enable you to have a simple-to-use framework for adding new data as you work with a client and is a simple way for any other developer who works with that client to maintain the data. For **independent software vendor** (**ISV**) organizations and those who are part of a team working on a defined internal environment, a greater level of quality assurance may occur with dedicated testing teams, to validate the solution through the UI. This is not to say that this does not happen on consultative projects, but typically only organizations with an internal team dedicated to the solution will have the resources to perform such testing and management.

Using our test data factory structure from the preceding section presents us with a couple of potential issues. As highlighted, data cannot be easily updated by administrators and requires coding knowledge to manage and deploy. Secondly—and, I think, more importantly—the test data used by the developer may not be an entirely representative set of data compared to what the testing team or end users are utilizing. Often, developers may populate the bare minimum data to allow the process under test to be validated. There is nothing wrong with this per se, but it does leave a disconnect between the testing done manually and the testing done automatically.

Additionally, when an error is found by the testing team, it then requires greater effort on the part of the developer to replicate this error in code. Testers will typically work with a fixed set of test data for use in validating application paths. This is not least because when working in a new environment, they may load in a set of data for use that simulates a more realistic environment.

Whereas in our test data factory we had the default data stored in an ancillary class, an alternative option is to store it in a separate data format that can be updated and maintained by an administrator in the future. In testing setups where a dedicated test team reviews the application with a set of data, using this dataset can provide an additional level of confidence for everyone by simulating in code the tests that the testers are running. If an error or bug is found, the bug can quickly be replicated using the exact same data setup that the testing team used to find the error in the first place. As mentioned before, this makes it much easier to say with confidence that the bug has been replicated and then fixed.

Salesforce provides a mechanism for doing this, using the `Test.loadData` method. This method takes in two parameters: the type of data we wish to load, and the name of a static resource holding this data.

The data should be formatted as a **comma-separated values** (**CSV**) file, with the first line holding the field names for population. For example, we can create the following CSV fields for loading in a set of accounts:

```
Name,Phone,Website,Rating
Acme,111-111-1111,www.acme.corp,Warm
BIG inc,222-222-2222,www.big-inc.com,Hot
Castle Clothing,333-333-3333,www.castleclothing.com
```

Take this data and save it as a static resource called `AccountsData`. In our test class, we can now load in this data for use by running it as follows:

```
List<Account> accs = (List<Account>)Test.loadData(Account.
sObjectType, 'AccountsData');
```

This is an extremely useful way of loading in multiple pre-defined records for use in testing that can be updated at any point by simply updating the CSV file and re-uploading it as a new version of the static resource.

A nice but undocumented feature of this tool is that you can also create relationships between records as part of the loading process. We can include an `Id` column on our previous CSV file, populating it with a unique value, as follows:

```
Id,Name,Phone,Website,Rating
1,Acme,111-111-1111,www.acme.corp,Warm
2,BIG inc,222-222-2222,www.big-inc.com,Hot
3,Castle Clothing,333-333-3333,www.castleclothing.com
```

Next, define a new CSV file for loading in contact records, as follows:

```
AccountId,FirstName,LastName
1,John,Smith
2,Jane,Doe
3,Sarah,Connor
```

Save this file as a CSV static resource called `ContactsData`, for when we run the following code in a test:

```
List<Account> accs = (List<Account>)Test.loadData(Account.
sObjectType, 'AccountsData');
List<Contact> cons = (List<Contact>)Test.loadData(Contact.
sObjectType, 'ContactsData');
```

When we run our test, the contacts from the CSV file will be loaded into the system and relate to the relevant account using the fake ID we define. This is extremely useful in loading in sets of related data in a particular state to test.

When working on larger projects or testing the build of ISV applications, I find it useful to work with the testing team to define a set of test data that can be loaded in using the aforementioned format, to help validate processes more thoroughly and in an automated fashion. Unit testing separated down to the individual code method or function should still be undertaken, but as a system grows in complexity, the use of such a tool for loading data in for more coordinated integration testing can be invaluable.

Additionally, I find this tool best used with the `@TestSetup` annotation. The `@TestSetup` annotation defines a single method for a test class that is run once when the class is instantiated and creates test data for use by the methods within the class. Data is rolled back to this state after each test method is run and then expunged once the entire class has run.

I try to use the `@TestSetup` method for defining all test data within any test class; however, it is especially useful when calling `Test.loadData` to reduce resource usage in loading in the data (avoiding repeat runs of the save order of execution) by ensuring the data is only inserted once. A common reason for slow tests within Apex is a repeated **Data Manipulation Language (DML)** action to set up test data that invokes the save order of execution. Using the `@TestSetup` annotation can help reduce this, particularly when loading in larger volumes of data, as described here.

The use of static resources to improve our tests is not just limited to creating test data as we have seen here; we can also utilize static resources to help us when testing web service callouts, which is what we will be seeing next.

Testing RESTful web services with static resources

For obvious reasons, Salesforce does not make callouts to external web services when running Apex tests. There is no guarantee an endpoint is defined or available for testing, and the callout would hinder and slow down the running of any unit tests by an order of magnitude.

Because of this, we have to be able to provide mock responses to any web service callouts made within our tests and return the appropriate response for the test to utilize. For those unfamiliar with the terminology, mocking a service simply means providing an implementation to act in its place. In this case, we will be providing a placeholder for the responding endpoint for testing purposes.

Salesforce provides an interface called `HttpCalloutMock` that a developer can implement as part of their unit testing when handling **HyperText Transfer Protocol (HTTP)** callouts. Salesforce also provides a couple of standard implementations of this interface to help in testing, one of which is `StaticResourceCalloutMock`.

Consider the following code, which is making a callout to a web service:

```
public class AccountService {

    public static AccountWrapper getAccountJSON(String
    accountId) {

        HttpRequest req = new HttpRequest();
        req.setEndpoint('https://api.myexampleapp.com/
        accounts/' + accountId);
        req.setMethod('GET');

        Http http = new Http();

        HttpResponse res = http.send(req);
        if(res.getStatus() != 'OK') {
                //handle error
        }
        return JSON.deserialize(res.getBody(),
        AccountWrapper.class);
    }

    public class AccountWrapper {
        public String name;
    }
}
```

In this code block, we define a new request to an example endpoint that will retrieve the account with an identifier we provide in the method. The method sends the request and deserializes a successful response into an `AccountWrapper` instance for us to work with.

How would we test this code? We need to mock the web service response so that we can execute this code and deserialize the response.

To do this, we can create the following **JavaScript Object Notation (JSON)** file and save it as a static resource called `TestAccountCalloutResponse`:

```
{
    name: "Acme Anvils inc."
}
```

We then define a test for our `getAccountJSON` method, as follows:

```
@isTest
private class AccountService_Test {

    @isTest
    private static void testGetAccountJSON_ValidResponse() {

        StaticResourceCalloutMock mock = new
        StaticResourceCalloutMock();
        mock.
        setStaticResource('TestAccountCalloutResponse');
        mock.setStatusCode(200);
        mock.setHeader('Content-Type', 'application/json');

        Test.setMock(HttpCalloutMock.class, mock);

        Test.startTest();
        AccountService.AccountWrapper wrapper =
        AccountService.getAccountJSON('TestId');
        Test.stopTest();

        System.assertEquals('Acme Anvils inc.', wrapper.
        name, 'Incorrect name returned');
    }
}
```

This test method uses the static resource we have defined in a new `StaticResourceCalloutMock` instance. We tell the Apex testing framework to utilize this mock service by calling `Test.setMock(HttpCalloutMock.class, mock)`. When the code gets to the point where it would normally make the callout, it will then instead return the JSON code defined in our static resource as the body, with the status code and header we specified in the mock definition.

This makes it much quicker and easier to test web service callouts using either example responses provided by the **application programming interface (API)** vendor in their documentation or those obtained from manual testing. We can also extend this using the `MultiStaticResourceCalloutMock` class to allow the chaining of multiple responses. For example, it is common that you would require an authentication callout to get a token before making a resource callout. You can test this setup by using `MultiStaticResourceCalloutMock` to allow pre-defined responses to be returned. An example is shown here:

```
@isTest
private static void testAuthenticateThenCallEndpoint() {
    MultiStaticResourceCalloutMock multiMock = new
    MultiStaticResourceCalloutMock();
    multiMock.setStaticResource('https://api.myexampleapp.com/
authenticate', 'TestAuthenticateCalloutResponse');
    multiMock.setStaticResource('https://api.myexampleapp.com/
accounts/1234', 'TestAccountCalloutResponse');
    multiMock.setStatusCode(200);
    multiMock.setHeader('Content-Type', 'application/json');

    Test.setMock(HttpCalloutMock.class, mock);

    Test.startTest();
    AccountService.authenticate(); //Makes a callout to
    //authenticate
    AccountService.AccountWrapper wrapper = AccountService.
    getAccountJSON('TestId');
    Test.stopTest();

    System.assertEquals('Acme Anvils inc.', wrapper.name,
    'Incorrect name returned');
}
```

This code shows how `MultiStaticResourceCalloutMock` can be utilized to allow us to effectively test chained callouts in Apex easily and achieve the required testing confidence.

Testing best practices

I want to finish this chapter with some general testing best practices that developers should aim to follow when writing their test methods. We will cover scenario-specific best practices as we work through examples throughout the rest of the book, but these best practices will help your test code be more useful in validating the behavior of the code you have written and verifying that it will not exceed governor limits, whatever the scenario. The first best practice I want to discuss is the use of the `Test.startTest()` and `Test.stopTest()` methods.

Using Test.startTest and Test.stopTest to demarcate the code under test

In both of the preceding code snippets, we have used the `Test.startTest()` and `Test.stopTest()` methods before and after our callout code. Our callout code is the code we are testing and, as such, should be enclosed within these methods to have its own governor context and be demarcated. Calling `Test.startTest()` within a test method provides a new governor limit context for the test, allowing a developer to validate that their code will run as expected without exceeding any governor limits.

As your application grows and becomes more complex, you are likely to need a greater amount of test data in order to successfully run the code you wish to test. Each record you insert or update to create your test data will consume governor limits, as the related save order of execution for those DML actions occurs within a single Apex transaction. In some extreme cases, this can lead to a large volume of governor limits being consumed before the code under test is executed, and may then cause a `LimitException` to be thrown. We should therefore separate out the code under test and demarcate it into its own governor context using the `Test.startTest()` and `Test.stopTest()` method calls. Once `Test.stopTest()` is called, you will return to the original governor limit context.

Additionally, when working with asynchronous Apex, when the `Test.stopTest()` method is called, any asynchronous actions queued after `Test.startTest()` will be processed automatically. We will cover this in more detail in the chapters on our asynchronous Apex frameworks.

Using assertions to validate behavior

The other best practice I wish to highlight is the use of assertions to validate behavior. Salesforce provides the following three assertion method options in Apex:

- `System.assert(booleanCondition, optionalMessage)`
- `System.assertEquals(expectedValue, actualValue, optionalMessage)`
- `System.assertNotEquals(expectedValue, actualValue, optionalMessage)`

Put simply, a test method without an assertion is not a test at all—it verifies no behavior; it merely executes some code. We should ensure that we always provide at least one assertion within a test method to validate the outcome of the code we are testing. This will allow us to be confident that the code is functioning as intended and that we are obtaining the expected results.

Without such an assertion, a change may occur in the system that causes some behavior to break, but is not identified because the test is merely exercising and executing code rather than thoroughly testing that it is behaving as expected. By having an assertion within the test that validates the output, we can ensure that when changes are made they will not have an adverse effect on existing functionality.

Additionally, you should always use the `optionalMessage` parameter to provide a useful message as to why the test case has failed. If no value is provided, the developer or administrator running the tests will have to review the code itself to understand where and why the failure occurred. Providing a message saves them from having to do this and can help in debugging any failures.

Writing a test for any bug that occurs

Although it is the hope of any developer that they will write code that does not have any bugs, it is unrealistic to think that this will happen, and bugs or unexpected edge cases will be found throughout the life cycle of the system. I have mentioned already in this chapter, as well as in *Chapter 2, Debugging Apex*, that it is a good practice to write a test for any bug or defect that is found.

Doing so will allow you to verify that you can replicate the issue in a repeatable manner. If you cannot replicate the issue, you cannot understand it and therefore cannot fix it. Writing a test that replicates the bug provides you with a useful way of repeatably reproducing the issue and validating that it has been fixed.

Summary

In this chapter, we have dealt with the importance of testing our Apex code and how we can improve the quality and integrity of our tests. Testing is a key part of the software development life cycle, and writing clear and well-structured tests that validate assumptions and outcomes through assertions is extremely important in providing confidence in your system.

We also saw how we can improve the creation of test data for our tests in a number of ways. The largest performance problem for Apex tests is the repeated creation of data in different unit tests, as the system must run through the save order of execution multiple times, taking up time and governor resources. By separating our test data into a factory, we can ensure that data is created in a consistent manner and save ourselves additional rework should the code need updating to accommodate new required fields and processing. Calling our test data creation from a method annotated by `@TestSetup` ensures that the data is only created once and makes it easy for us to load data into our tests. Additionally, we can also utilize a tool such as the `Test.loadData` method to help us in loading a series of related records quickly and effectively to provide consistent test data, particularly in situations where we have more complex test steps requiring data setup or are working with a testing team using defined data.

We then looked at how we can utilize the `StaticResourceCalloutMock` and `MultiStaticResourceCalloutMock` classes to assist us in testing web services. We still have the option of writing our own implementations by implementing the `HttpCalloutMock` interface; however, from experience, I have learned that using the `StaticResourceCalloutMock` and `MultiStaticResourceCalloutMock` classes has been more than sufficient in allowing me to test my web service code and provides a neat way of managing the response data.

Finally, we finished the chapter by covering some general testing best practices that will make our tests more useful and less likely to hit governor limits as a solution grows and becomes more complex.

In the next chapter, we are going to finish the first section of this book by discussing secure programming within Apex. As with testing, security controls on code are often overlooked and can have notable consequences if not managed properly. In the next chapter, we will learn how we can work to avoid those issues.

6
Secure Apex Programming

In the previous chapters of this book, we have covered ways in which we can improve our Apex code to ensure that we minimize the number of basic errors we are receiving and also make it easier to handle and deal with them. In this chapter, we are going to finish this first section of the book by discussing how we can make Apex more secure, and ensure that users are not able to perform actions that we do not intend for them.

There are many reasons this is important, but key among them is ensuring that should a user become malicious or their account get compromised, then the damage they can do is limited. I worked with a client that had a faulty website integration design that allowed external users to view all contacts and accounts within the system. Their web developers had noticed this issue and recommended the client get it fixed by a Salesforce consultant (hence, my involvement).

At that time, the client was initially unsure of the severity and impact of this security hole, until they were shown how I could access all information for their contacts without too much trouble and then even edit some of the data. The organization represented an industry body, and so the potential reputational risk damage was huge. We worked with them to patch the hole rapidly and ensure their system was more secure.

To prevent such things from happening in our code, we will cover the following topics in the chapter:

- How permissions and sharing work on Salesforce

- Sharing and performance

- Enforcing sharing

- Sharing records using Apex

- Enforcing object and field permissions

- Understanding Apex class security

- Enforcing permissions and security within SOQL

- Avoiding SOQL injection vulnerabilities

Let's begin this chapter with an overview of how permissions and sharing work on the Salesforce platform to help us better understand the implications of the code we are writing.

How permissions and sharing work on Salesforce

The Salesforce platform has two main ways of controlling access to records—**permissions** and **sharing**. They are often confused for one another but have very different roles in managing access to data. Permissions in Salesforce focus on what you can do with a particular object in general; think of it as akin to a keycard that lets you access different levels of a building.

Sharing focuses on what records you can see for that object based on their ownership. This is like the different rooms our keycard can open on the floors we have access to. If our building was a corporate office block, then as a member of the IT team, we may have access to each floor (permission for each object) and the ability to look at everyone's desk. The CEO may have access to every floor but not into the server room in the basement for security and safety reasons.

With Salesforce's permissions and sharing tools, you can build up a very granular set of visibility permissions that control exactly who can access the different records within your org. The most basic control is *via permissions,* that is on a profile or permission set granting **Create, Read, Edit, and Delete (CRED)** access to an object, or in some instances, granting **view or modify-all permissions** to that object. When you attempt to retrieve a record in Salesforce, these permissions are checked before any further processing occurs.

Following this, sharing calculations are then run to verify whether you have access to the record or records that you are retrieving. In the following figure, we can see the various sharing options available to us, going from most restrictive and generic on the left with org-wide defaults, to broader and more open control mechanisms on the right:

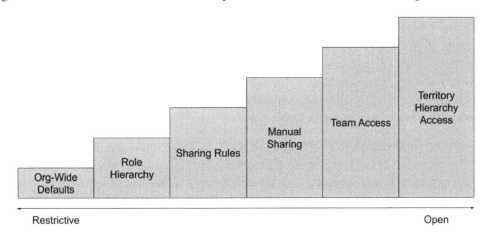

Figure 6.1 – Sharing options on the Salesforce platform

You can only increase visibility by moving further to the right on the chart; you can never restrict sharing through moving further right on the diagram. The most restrictive sharing settings are always those set by the org-wide defaults.

When working with data in code, we need to be mindful of these permissions to ensure that they are being enforced appropriately. Different contexts within our code will require us to either strictly enforce or purposefully ignore these permissions for different reasons.

Sharing and performance

One primary reason to ensure that your sharing and permissions are correctly configured is to improve your application's performance. As an application grows on the platform, the volume of data stored on it will also inevitably grow. The obvious side effect of this is that querying for records and loading lists of data can become much slower. Simply put, the more data you can see, the greater the volume of data to search through.

To help keep your application performant, you should reduce the amount of data every user can see to that which is strictly necessary. This will ensure that queries, list views, reports, and all manner of functionalities continue to run in an optimal way and don't slow down the user experience. We will be discussing performance in much greater detail in *Section 3* of this book, entitled *Apex Performance*. For now, we will return to understanding how we can work with the sharing framework within Apex.

Enforcing sharing

Once we have our sharing mechanisms set up within the system, we need to ensure that they are being enforced and followed throughout the application. There is no point restricting visibility of the data within the solution through the administrative tools and then ignore this using the automation setup.

By default, all Apex operations (and Process Builder and certain Flows) run in System Mode; that is, they execute as a generic system user that has access to all metadata and data within the org. This means that although we may have sharing rules and permissions configured to limit access, our code can still act without limitations. For record sharing, this has both positive and negative consequences:

- On the positive side, it means that our Apex code can retrieve data that the user cannot see to either provide more accurate values (for example, when running an aggregate query) or to retrieve data we wish to utilize in our solution, but not necessarily view.

  For example, we may have loans and payments against those loans stored within our system. Although we want members of our call center team to see the loans, we don't necessarily want them to see the detailed payment information, instead just seeing a read-only view of the last payment made. In this situation, they should not have any payment records shared with them, and our code could simply retrieve the last payment for display.

- On the negative side, if we do not enforce our sharing appropriately, this can lead to data being visible to users where it should not be. In the example of the customer I mentioned at the start of this chapter, their custom Apex API had been designed to not enforce sharing rules.

  By having this setup, they had made data available to external parties in the manner described earlier in our positive reasoning, but also shared additional data that led to the security flaw. In this case, the design should not have disregarded sharing, and we spent time reviewing and reimplementing the existing sharing model for increased security.

So how do we enforce sharing within our Apex configuration? As I am sure many readers will know, it is through the use of the `with sharing` keywords in our class definition. Imagine we had the following two classes—ClassA and ClassB:

```
public with sharing class ClassA {
    public static List<Account> getAccounts() {
        return [SELECT Name from Account];
    }
}

public without sharing class ClassB {
    public static List<Account> getAccounts() {
        return [SELECT Name from Account];
    }
}
```

Then we can say for certain that `ClassA.getAccounts().size() <= ClassB.getAccounts().size()` is always true, that is, the same query run in `ClassA` will always have less than or equal to the number of results returned by the same query in `ClassB`. Declaring either `with sharing` or `without sharing` explicitly, as we have done here, is a deliberate action for us to verify that we either do or do not want the sharing rules for the current user to be enforced. If we do not define a class as `with sharing` or `without sharing` explicitly, then the current sharing rules remain in force, as in the following example:

```
public with sharing class ClassA {
    public static List<Account> getAccounts() {
        return ClassC.getAccounts();
    }
}

public without sharing class ClassB {
    public static List<Account> getAccounts() {
        return ClassC.getAccounts();
    }
}

public class ClassC {
```

```
public static List<Account> getAccounts() {
    return [SELECT Name from Account];
}
}
```

This code has the same behavior as the previous block, with `ClassC.getAccounts` running using the sharing context from the class calling it.

What if `ClassC` was the entry point to our transaction? What sharing context is applied in this instance? In this case, `ClassC` would operate in `without sharing` mode by default. It is not necessarily clear however through the class definition whether that was intended by the developer or not, and can cause confusion and unintended consequences later in the application's life cycle.

Let's review an example. It is not uncommon in larger applications to have many utility classes defined that contain repeated code and are abstracted away to keep the application DRY, for example, a query may be abstracted away if it is used across multiple methods and classes. What sharing definition should be given for the utility class?

If we define it as `with sharing`, then the sharing rules will always be enforced. This may not be desirable in situations where we wish to utilize the fact that Apex can run in the system context to retrieve the data. Similarly, defining the class as `without sharing` means that we will potentially be returning additional data that should not be shared or displayed.

While the example here of a utility class may seem a little bit tenuous, for ISV partners and those publishing on the AppExchange, it is a common concern. I want my code to be able to be called and run by my customers in a way they see fit to enable them to extend the application, but also wish for the code to have a default mode of `with sharing` to ensure that I can meet the AppExchange security review guidelines.

To manage this, we can utilize the `inherited sharing` option as our default in situations where we want to default to a `with sharing` context, but enable the code to run in a `without sharing` context when called from a class defined as `without sharing`. In this way, whenever our code is used, it can be as any of the following:

- An Aura component controller
- A Visualforce controller
- An Apex REST service
- Any other entry point to an Apex transaction

Whenever we are defining our Apex classes, we should, therefore, apply the following rules to ensure our sharing is actually enforced as we anticipate it to be:

- Use `with sharing` when we know we want the sharing model to be enforced.

- Use `without sharing` when we know we want the sharing model to be ignored.

- Otherwise, use `inherited sharing` as a default.

Apex cannot only be used to enforce or ignore sharing rules, but we can also use Apex to create sharing rules when we have more complex sharing requirements than can be managed through the point-and-click sharing rules framework.

Sharing records using Apex

Salesforce has several ways of sharing records with users and groups of users such as **managed sharing, user-managed (or manual) sharing**, and **Apex managed sharing**:

- Managed sharing is the *point-and-click* sharing that most Salesforce developers and administrators are familiar with, and relies upon record ownership, the role hierarchy in the org, and any sharing rules.

- User-managed sharing or manual sharing is when a user chooses to share a record with a user or group of users using the **Share** button (currently only in Salesforce Classic).

- Apex managed sharing is the sharing of records with a user or group of users through the *use of Apex code* and is what we will be focusing on in this section.

All three of the methods described store records in the *share object* associated with the record within the Salesforce database. For every object, there is a corresponding share object. For standard objects, it is the object API name plus share, so `AccountShare`, `ContactShare`, `OpportunityShare`, and so on. For custom objects, `__c` in the object API name is replaced by `__Share`. Sharing via org-wide defaults, the role hierarchy, and permissions such as View All are not stored in these objects.

Apex managed sharing is commonly used when we have either a sharing requirement that is too complex for the point-and-click sharing rules or when we want to share a record that has no direct relationship. In these instances, we need to create sharing records using Apex to allow the record to be visible.

Let's consider the example where we are managing investments for individuals. Our users are investment managers who look after one or more investment funds (a custom object) and are connected via a fund team member (a custom object). A client (an Account object) can invest in one or more funds that are stored as an investment record (custom object). Both investments and fund team members are junction objects.

The investment manager should be able to see only the clients who have invested in their funds. For example, in the following diagram we have our investment managers, Alice and Bob, who look after two funds, **Acme Renewables Fund** and **Acme Tech Fund**. Finally, we have Carol and Dave, clients who have invested in either or both of these funds:

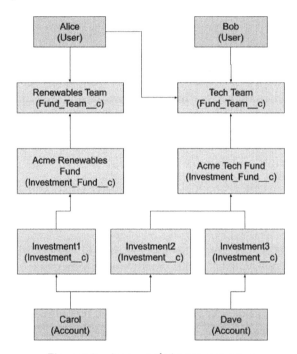

Figure 6.2 – An example investment setup

In this scenario, Alice should have visibility to both Carol and Dave's account records, while Bob should only be able to see Dave's account. Because of the object structure here, we need to manage this sharing using Apex managed sharing, creating the relevant share records when a new investment record is created. Some sample code for this might be on the creation of a new Investment__c record:

```
Set<Id> fundIds = new Set<Id>();

for(Investment__c investment : Trigger.new) {
    fundIds.add(invest.Fund__c); //The id of the fund being
```

```
        invested in
}


Map<Id, List<Id>> fundToTeamMemberIdMap = new Map<Id,
List<Id>>();


for(Fund_Team_Member__c member : [SELECT Investment_Manager__c,
Fund__c FROM Fund_Team__c WHERE Fund__c in :fundIds]) {
    if(!fundToTeamMemberIdMap.containsKey(member.Fund__c)) {
        fundToTeamMemberIdMap.put(member.Fund__c, new
        List<Id>());
    }
    fundToTeamMemberIdMap.get(member.Fund__c).add(member.
    Investment_Manager__c);
}


List<AccountShare> accShares = new List<AccountShare>();


for(Investment__c investment : Trigger.new) {
    for(Id userId : fundToTeamMemberIdMap.get(investment.
    Fund__c)) {
        AccountShare newShare = new AccountShare();
        newShare.ParentId = invetment.Investor__c; //The
        account making the investment
      newShare.UserOrGroupId = userId; //The investment
      manager
      newShare.AccessLevel = 'Read';
      newShare.RowCause = Schema.AccountShare.RowCause.
      Manual;
        accShares.add(newShare);
    }
}


insert accShares;
```

The key portion of this code is the creation of our `AccountShare` record at the end. The first portion of the code is to highlight that a query and some logic is required to allow us to retrieve the account information for sharing and so would be too complex for the standard sharing logic to handle.

For the `AccountShare` record, we require to set the following information:

- The ID of the record to be shared with the `ParentId` field.

- The user of group to be shared within the `UserOrGroupId` field.

- An access level, either `Edit` or `Read`, in the `AccessLevel` field.

- A reason for sharing in the `RowCause` field. The default value is `Manual`, as we have set here, however custom reasons can be set by adding them through the setup menu.

This works well and allows us to share the records appropriately, however, such record sharing must also be managed via Apex as well, and should an investment be removed, we would also need to ensure we had the correct trigger logic to remove sharing records where appropriate.

Now we have understood how we can both enforce sharing and then programmatically add further sharing rules to the system, we will look at how we can enforce object and field permissions through our code.

Enforcing object and field permissions

As previously mentioned, all Apex runs in System Mode and has access to all metadata and data within the org. This means that regardless of what permissions the user may have on an object or field, Apex can see all objects and fields. This again has some positive and negative consequences:

- On the positive side, we are now able to ensure that our code can act in ways that our user could not through a standard user interface. For example, we may have a field storing sensitive data that the user should not see or have access to for compliance reasons. Our code can still access this field on behalf of the user to enable it to be used within their workflow. As long as the code is correctly encapsulated and limited in how it is accessed, this is a great way of both enforcing permissions and allowing the desired business process to operate freely.

- On the negative side, this model means that if we are not careful, then we can accidentally expose records and permissions to users that should not have them. A good example here is allowing users to update fields on a custom page that they should not have access to. While many of the base components provided in Visualforce and Lightning do respect the set field-level security, custom user interface components do not and so can lead to the user's setting values on fields that they should not be able to see.

We have two ways of enforcing our object-level and field-level permissions in Apex code, the first of which is to utilize the describe methods within Apex to verify that the user had the correct permissions. The methods to verify the permissions for an sObject are as follows and are utilized on the Schema.DescribeSObjectResult instance for the given sObject:

- isAccessible
- isCreateable
- isUpdateable
- isDeletable

For example, we can verify permissions on a Contact object as follows:

```
if(Schema.sObjectType.Contact.isAccessible()) {
    // Read Contact records
}


if (Schema.sObjectType.Contact.isCreateable()) {
    // Create Contact records
}

if (Schema.sObjectType.Contact.isUpdateable()) {
    // Create Contact records
}

if (Schema.sObjectType.Contact.isDeletable()) {
    // Create Contact records
}
```

These methods can be helpful when building a custom user interface that displays or manipulates data from multiple different sObjects. Similarly, at the field level, on the Schema.DescribeFieldResult instance for a field, we have the following methods:

- isAccessible
- isCreateable
- isUpdateable

All of these are available to us to verify that we have the correct permissions to manipulate a field:

```
if(Schema.sObjectType.Contact.fields.Email.isAccessible()) {
    // Read Contact record Email
}


if (Schema.sObjectType.Contact.fields.Email.isCreateable()) {
    // Populate Contact record Email
}


if (Schema.sObjectType.Contact.fields.Email.isUpdateable()) {
    // Edit Contact record Email
}
```

These methods allow a very granular level of control over checking the permissions for a particular field and object and should be used when we wish to both ensure permissions are being enforced and that we are working with Apex in a context where this has not already been done. In my experience, these methods are of most use when working with custom Lightning web components or a custom user interface. In these scenarios, we want to ensure that we are enforcing the correct permissions as the system has not already done so with the standard base components.

Similarly, when working on providing an API to your application, it is a good practice to verify the permissions of the user calling into the API to ensure that they have the necessary access required. In some scenarios (server-to-server integrations, for example), there is less of a need for this as it is two systems synchronizing data between themselves.

However, when providing an API that is for individual users, you should validate the access to ensure that administrators can use the standard permissions system to effectively control these external users. Note that here, an API can also be an Apex API for other Apex classes; it does not need to be a RESTful or SOAP-based API.

We can also enforce field and object permissions using the `Security.stripInaccessible` method, which takes two parameters. The first is an access level that we wish to verify against, and the second is a `List<sObject>`. The method then removes any fields that the user does not have the stated access level for. It is also particularly useful for sanitizing records as a whole, such as when we are providing an API and receiving `sObject` data from external users.

For example, in the following code, we query some records from the database, then call the `Security.stripInaccessible` method on the records to remove those fields we have no access to:

```
List<Contact> contacts = [SELECT Id, FirstName, Email, Phone
FROM Contact];
SObjectAccessDecision accessDecision = Security.
stripInaccessible(AccessType.READABLE, contacts);

for(Contact con : (List<Contact>)accessDecision.getRecords()) {
    System.debug(con.isSet('Email')); //True if we have access
    to the Email field, false otherwise
    System.debug(con.isSet('Phone')); //True if we have access
    to the Phone field, false otherwise
}
```

In the preceding code, we are using the `isSet` method to check whether or not the field has a value to give us an indication of whether the user has access to the field. Note that this is not a foolproof mechanism as the `isSet` method will also return `false` if the field has not been set otherwise.

In the following code, we are using the `stripInaccessible` method to remove any fields that the user does not have update permissions on:

```
String jsonBody = '[{"FirstName":"Alice", "LastName":"Jones",
"Email": "ajones@test.com"}]';

List<Contact> contacts = JSON.deserializeStrict(jsonBody,
List<Contact>.class);

SObjectAccessDecision accessDecision = Security.
stripInaccessible(AccessType.UPDATABLE, contacts);

System.debug('The following fields were removed: ' +
```

```
accessDecision.getRemovedFields());

update accessDecision.getRecords();
```

In this code block, we are also outputting the list of fields that were removed (the return type is a map but we have a single object type). We can then comfortably call `update` on these stripped records.

I have found this method to be extremely useful when building out REST APIs to help me quickly enforce permissions. As a note, the `Id` field is always left in by the `stripInaccessible` method as a way of ensuring that no errors occur when updating records.

There is another way we can enforce these permissions within our SOQL queries, however, we will discuss that later in the chapter when discussing SOQL. The next area we will focus on, though, is Apex class security and how to manage this.

Understanding Apex class security

Access to an Apex class can be granted through either a Profile or a Permission Set. For internal users of the platform, it is unlikely that you will ever face major problems with Apex class access, as typically the user is not accessing the Apex class directly, rather accessing it via a user interface, Process Builder, or Flow, which separates them from direct Apex class access.

This is not the case when exposing classes for use as an API, that is, using the `webservice` keyword or classes annotated by `@RestResource`. In these situations, the user must be explicitly granted access through the use of a Profile or Permission Set. Note that only the top-level class, that is, the one directly invoked by the end user, must be granted access to it. Any other classes that this top-level class calls through its functions do not need access granted to them.

When defining APIs in Apex, care should be taken to construct the code in a way that firstly verifies the permissions for any data are correct (using techniques we saw in the previous section) and then access to only the minimum required set of Apex should be granted to maintain security.

Now we have looked at how we can restrict access to a class for external users, let's see how we can work with SOQL to also ensure that permissions are appropriately enforced.

Enforcing permissions and security within SOQL

When we discussed enforcing sharing rules earlier in this chapter, we noted how the use of the `with sharing` keywords on a class declaration would ensure that any query run within that class has the sharing rules for the user enforced upon the query. We also saw, in the *Enforcing object and field permissions* section, how we can work with results returned from a query and enforce permissions on these records using the `stripInaccessible` method.

In the Spring '20 release, Salesforce added the `WITH SECURITY_ENFORCED` clause to the SOQL language. Unlike the `stripInaccessible` method, if the user is lacking permissions for a field, an exception is thrown rather than the field simply being removed.

To apply this clause, we simply include `WITH SECURITY_ENFORCED` after any `WHERE` clause and before any `ORDER BY`, `LIMIT`, `OFFSET`, or aggregate function clauses. For example, consider the following:

```
List<Contact> = [SELECT FirstName, LastName, Email, Secret_
Field__c FROM Contact WITH SECURITY_ENFORCED];
```

In the preceding query, if the user has no access to `Secret_Field__c`, then an exception will be thrown, indicating insufficient permissions.

It is a reasonable question now to ask, *should I be including this clause on every query I write from now on?* In my opinion, no. This clause is perfect in situations where you want to take an *all-or-nothing* approach when it comes to enforcing permissions on the records. When using `stripInaccessible`, the original recordset can remain intact for comparison. Similarly, through using the `describe` methods we saw previously, we can provide a more nuanced experience, hiding and showing fields in the user interface or altering our code paths dependent upon permissions. With this clause, however, an exception is thrown and no data is returned.

Additionally, this clause is only available in API v48.0 and above. While any new code you write should utilize this new API version, the existing code would need to be migrated to this or a later version in order to operate appropriately. This can involve a greater set of changes in the codebase depending upon the availability of features between versions.

There is no strict reason to upgrade code between versions, although it is a good practice to try and move forward onto newer versions of the API for certain performance (and free) upgrades. To implement these upgrades just for the use of this clause alone would be a lot of additional effort. In general, it is a good practice to try and move to later API versions either when editing a piece of code and its related functionality, or on an annual basis as part of a cleanup.

Permissions are not the only way in which our SOQL code can compromise the security of our application. We can write dynamic SOQL queries that use a string that can be built up by other Apex logic and user input. If they are not correctly handled, these queries can lead to SOQL injection vulnerabilities, as we shall now discuss.

Avoiding SOQL injection vulnerabilities

It is a common use case to want to receive some user input and use this as part of a SOQL query filter. However, while this provides helpful user functionality, it can be misused by a malicious user to gain access to additional data that is not meant to be visible to them.

For example, we could be searching for a contact record with the last name in the form of an input string we have defined, as shown in the following code:

```
public String searchName {get; set;}
```

```
public PageReference search() {
    return Database.query('SELECT Id, FirstName, LastName,
Email FROM Contact WHERE LastName Like \'%' + searchName +
'%\'');
}
```

In this preceding code, we are defining a dynamic SOQL query where, when the user enters a search term, for example, Smith, the code will then search for contacts where the LastName field is like Smith, effectively running the following query:

```
SELECT Id, FirstName, LastName, Email FROM Contact WHERE
LastName Like '%Smith%'
```

What if the user entered a blank value? Our query then becomes the following:

```
SELECT Id, FirstName, LastName, Email FROM Contact WHERE
LastName Like '%%'
```

This query will return all the contacts within the system. We could add logic into our code to only run when the `searchName` is not blank. As I am sure we can see though, a malicious user could still enter a string that would return all the data from the `Contact` object. Should a user enter a value that is malicious in intent, such as `test%' OR LastName Like '%`, then our query string would become the following:

```
SELECT Id, FirstName, LastName, Email FROM Contact WHERE
LastName Like '%test%' OR LastName Like '%%'
```

This new query would return all contacts and again return more data than should be provided, particularly if this is being run in a class without sharing rules enforced.

So how do we defend against this? We have two options, the first and most simple of which is to ensure we are using Apex binding variables and static queries. We could rewrite our code as follows:

```
public String searchName {get; set;}
```

```
public PageReference search() {
    return [SELECT Id, FirstName, LastName, Email FROM Contact
    WHERE LastName Like :searchName];
}
```

By default, Apex binding variables are automatically escaped and so will ensure that the query would run as expected. There are instances however where we cannot revert to a static query and must use a dynamic query, for example, when building the query to include fields selected by a user or based upon the user's permissions. In these instances, we should ensure that we escape any input from the end user using our second option, the `escapeSingleQuotes` method:

```
public String searchName {get; set;}
```

```
public PageReference search() {
    return Database.query('SELECT Id, FirstName, LastName,
    Email FROM Contact WHERE LastName Like \'%' + String.
    escapeSingleQuotes(searchName) + '%\'');
}
```

With the same malicious input, our query string would now become this:

```
SELECT Id, FirstName, LastName, Email FROM Contact WHERE
LastName Like '%test%\' OR LastName Like \'%%'
```

This query will return no results for us (unless we have someone with a very peculiar LastName value) and we have avoided the injection attack. Furthermore, we could even add further string replacement in instances where it is needed to further increase security.

In my experience, it tends to be only ISV developers that regularly focus on handling such vulnerabilities as they are highlighted as part of the security review for listing on the AppExchange. The security scanner is available for any organization to run against their unpackaged code at `https://security.secure.force.com/security/tools/forcecom/scanner`. I recommend that if you are a consultant, you should run this scanner as a part of a regular release process to verify that you are following the security best practices and keeping your customers' data secure.

Summary

In this chapter, we have focused on the many ways in which we can ensure that we are maintaining the security of our application via our Apex code.

Trust has always been Salesforce's number-one value. As an organization, handling hundreds of billions of daily transactions with hundreds of thousands of customer storing their data, they have to make sure that you can be confident that they will not put your data at risk. As a part of that agreement, however, we as developers have to ensure that we are not accidentally exposing data or allowing users to access more data than they should be able to.

We started the chapter by looking at how sharing and permissions are managed on Salesforce before reviewing how we can enforce them within our Apex code, then looking at how we can create and manage custom sharing setups using Apex-managed sharing.

Following this, we moved to the other side of the Salesforce access control model, object, and field permissions. We saw how we can enforce these in Apex in multiple ways before discussing how to control access to Apex classes for external agents using APIs we have defined in Apex.

We then finished the chapter by discussing SOQL and how permissions can now be enforced using the WITH SECURITY_ENFORCED clause introduced in the Spring '20 release. We discussed the pros and cons of this approach before ending with a discussion of dynamic SOQL and SOQL injection vulnerabilities.

In my career, I have been lucky enough to work with a number of different organizations that were storing different types of sensitive data within Salesforce, including banks, pharmaceutical companies, health-care providers, insurers, oil and gas infrastructure providers, sporting event management organizations, and many more. The data that an organization holds is now one of the most important assets it has available to it, and as such we need to ensure we are not permitting internal or external users to see or act in a way that they should not be able to.

This chapter brings an end to this first section of the book, where our focus has been on avoiding errors and improving our Apex configuration to make it more robust and secure. In the next section, we are going to focus on working with asynchronous tools within Apex to help our application scale and grow, starting with the use of Future methods.

Section 2 – Asynchronous Apex and Apex REST

In this section, we will discuss the different asynchronous Apex options and how to use them to build applications that scale as our system is used more. As part of this, we will review common use cases, as well as the use of orchestration through platform events and allowing an external system to call into Apex.

This section covers the following chapters:

- *Chapter 7, Utilizing Future Methods*
- *Chapter 8, Working with Batch Apex*
- *Chapter 9, Working with Queueable Apex*
- *Chapter 10, Scheduling Apex Jobs*
- *Chapter 11, Using Platform Events*
- *Chapter 12, Apex REST and Custom Web Services*

7
Utilizing Future Methods

The first of the asynchronous Apex options we have are future methods. Future methods are a form of functions as a service that Salesforce provides. These methods enable you to execute some code in a *fire-and-forget* manner. In this paradigm, a function is called for execution (the firing) and placed on a queue to be processed when resources are available (forget). Salesforce will execute future method calls when resources are available on the Salesforce servers. In my experience, this tends to be near-instant unless you are performing a large volume of asynchronous processes.

In this chapter, we are going to discuss how to use future methods, some common use cases, and how to test them appropriately. As part of this discussion, we will also see where they fit into the different architectural options available to a developer working on the platform.

In this chapter, we will study the following topics:

- When to use a future method
- Defining future methods
- Calling future methods
- Testing future methods

Let's begin by discussing some common use cases for future methods.

Technical Requirements

The code for the chapter can be found here: `https://github.com/PacktPublishing/Mastering-Apex-Programming/tree/Chapter-7`

When to use a future method

There are two common use cases for future methods that most developers are familiar with—avoiding mixed DML errors and making background API requests. These are not the only use cases, but these are the two most common ones and so we will discuss them first.

Mixed DML

Certain sObjects cannot be used with other sObjects in DML operations without causing a mixed DML error. These are known as **setup objects** and are any object that affects a user's record access. The most common examples are when creating a `User` with a specified role, or updating a `User` and changing one of the following fields:

- `UserRoleId`
- `IsActive`
- `ForecastEnabled`
- `IsPortalEnabled`
- `Username`
- `ProfileId`

In these situations, it is a common practice to refactor the `User` (or another setup object) manipulation into a future method to be managed asynchronously. Most actions on these objects are not considered time-sensitive, for example, marking an inactive user as active is not a time-sensitive feature and does not need to be instantaneous.

A key point here is that when a mixed DML error occurs, you have very few choices in how to proceed to fix it. The DML operations within the functionality must be split in order to allow the code to execute with part of the process moving to an asynchronous callout (or in general, another execution transaction). Future methods are the simplest solution for this and the one recommended by Salesforce.

When making a callout to a third-party system you will likely encounter scenarios where the transaction with the external service does not need to happen immediately and in real time. Additionally, there may be instances where you are exchanging larger volumes of data (over 6MB) with a service. In both of these instances, a common practice is to extract the callout to run within a future method.

We have to do some additional work to enable the future method to make a callout, but only a small amount of extra work is required, as we will discuss when defining future methods in the rest of the chapter.

Other use cases for future methods

As noted at the start of this chapter, future methods are similar to functions as a service from other platforms. They do not truly match this paradigm as they are not an elastic scale in the same manner and have the Salesforce Governor limits applied to them, but it can be useful for us to think of them as a form of functions as a service, when determining whether a problem can be managed through future methods or not.

Firstly, future methods, as with all asynchronous Apex options we will cover, are limited in number per 24 hour period at either 250,000 or 200 multiplied by the number of user licenses in the org (whichever is the greater value) and so, when determining a use case for any of the asynchronous methods, we must consider whether we will surpass that limit or not with our intended use.

Once we are comfortable with the metrics here, we can ask the following key questions:

- Does this action need to happen in real time?
- What are the implications of a failure? Should a user be notified? Or an administrator?

Firstly, if the action needs to occur in real time, then future methods are not an appropriate use case for this functionality. Secondly, let's talk about failure and how to correctly handle it.

Future methods execute at some point in the future, separately from the transaction that called them. There is a chance that the future method may fail during its execution for some reason (for example, the external service may be down while making a callout). We therefore need to determine what the appropriate action following this will be. Let's get a better understanding through some examples.

Imagine we are implementing functionality for a call center that manages subscriptions for a streaming service. We have a new requirement to be able to cancel a customer's subscription over the phone so they are no longing receiving our service or a charge for it. As part of this process, we must make a callout to our billing system to cancel the subscription and any future payments, as well as check there are no outstanding payments. Could we do this in a future method?

In this scenario, we would want to avoid a future method as we want to allow the agent to confirm to the customer that the subscription has been removed and there are no outstanding payments at that point. Should there be an error or any payment amount remaining, this would need feeding back to the customer to be resolved before continuing. If we had a process to deactivate their community user record, this would be a good use case for a future method to help us avoid mixed DML errors, as well as being a process that can happen asynchronously.

Now we understand some of the use cases for future methods, let's look at how we define them for use.

Defining future methods

A future method must be defined as a `static` method with a `void` return type, as shown in the following code snippet. We annotate the method with the `@future` annotation to inform the compiler that this method should be called and placed onto the asynchronous processing queue:

```
@future
public static void myFutureMethod() {
    //method for execution
}
```

The method must be `static` so that it can be called and executed without the need for any state to be stored for it to execute.

We can also specify `callout = true` in the `@future` annotation to declare that the method can make callouts. By default, a standalone `@future` annotation is the same as `@future(callout = false)`, barring our future method from making callouts to external systems. A method defined to make callouts would then be declared as follows:

```
@future(callout = true)
public static void myFutureCalloutMethod() {
    //make an API request
}
```

Our future method may have parameters in its definition, however, they can only be primitive data types, arrays of primitive data types, or collections of primitive data types. The most common parameter used is a set of record `Ids` for some processing to occur, as we can see here:

```
@future
public static void myFutureMethod(Set<Id> idsToProcess) {
    //Retrieve the records for those Ids and process them
}
```

When utilizing future methods, therefore, you will almost always need to perform one or more queries to retrieve the data needed to perform the desired action. For example, if we wanted to make a callout to a third-party service providing some contact information, we would take in the set of contact IDs to send over and query these within our method, as shown in the following code block:

```
@future(callout = true)
public static void sendUpdatedContactInfo(Set<Id> contactIds) {
    List<Map<String, String>> calloutBodyMap = new
    List<Map<String, String>>();

    for(Contact con : [SELECT FirstName, LastName, Email,
    ExternalId__c FROM Contact WHERE Id in :contactIds]) {
        Map<String, String> contactInfo = new Map<String,
        String>();
        contactInfo.put('first_name', con.FirstName);
        contactInfo.put('last_name', con.LastName);
        contactInfo.put('email', con.Email);
        contactInfo.put('id', con.ExternalId__c);
        calloutBodyMap.add(contactInfo);
    }

    HttpRequest req = new HttpRequest();
    req.setBody(JSON.serialize(calloutBodyMap));
    req.setMethod('PUT');
    req.setEndpoint('https://some.external.service.com/
    contacts');
    Http http = new Http();
    HttpResponse resp =      http.send(req);
```

```
    if(resp.getStatusCode() != 200) {
        throw new CalloutException('Incorrect status
        returned : ' + resp.getStatusCode());
    }
}
```

This code example shows how we can use a query in our future methods to retrieve the data we need and then process it appropriately to communicate with a faux web service. It should also be noted that we have bulkified this method by default here. Whenever creating future methods, a best practice is to try and bulkify the method to ensure that it can be used within any of the potential contexts that a developer may wish to operate in, for example, a trigger. This code snippet would be the type of structure you would recommend if you had to synchronize data updates from Salesforce to an external system. This code could be called from a trigger and operate in a bulkified manner, helping to reduce the overall number of callouts required.

Passing state and coordinating data

What about instances where we need to pass in complex data types, or where utilizing primitives only may not suffice? While these use cases are rare, they do exist and in some circumstances you may find yourself going from a context where a lot of data is available around what functionality needs to be performed, to a future context where this state would need to be rebuilt. We will see in later chapters other asynchronous Apex options that can also do this work; however, the discussion here is also important in seeing how we can more readily capture information around errors from future methods as well.

We can also see in our previous code snippet that we have to consider carefully how we might deal with failures from our future method, as we cannot return any data. Should the callout in the preceding code fail, for example, we may want to retry the callout again (for example, the external web service may have been unavailable) and have some information available to us as to the nature of the failure.

One method of allowing us to both pass state and return responses is through a message queue or job object. This is a concept we will revisit a number of times over the coming chapters as it pertains to many different situations where we want a semi-permanent data store for information we are using in asynchronous processes.

The idea behind this object is that we have a custom object in which we can store data that persists on the database and can be used to coordinate logic across these transaction boundaries. A basic setup for such an object, Future_Job__c, is shown in the following screenshot. We have two long text area fields to store data for processing in a JSON format and any error information:

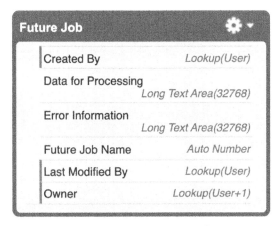

Figure 7.1 – Future Job object definition

Instead of requiring our future method to have parameters for lots of different pieces of data, we can now create a custom data type and store it within JSON in our **Data for Processing** field, `Data_for_Processing__c`, then simply deserialize this data within our future method.

We can deserialize to either a primitive data type or record, or a custom Apex type where appropriate. For example, imagine we had the custom Apex type `ContactWrapper` as shown in the following snippet:

```
public class ContactWrapper {
    private String firstName;
    private String lastName;
    private String email;

    public Contact generateContact() {
        //populate User record using data above
    }
}
```

We could then serialize an instance of this object into JSON and place it within our `Data_for_Processing__c` field. If we insert our `Future_Job__c` record into the database and pass its `Id` into our future method, we can deserialize this data in our future method and create users, shown as follows:

```
public class CreateUser_Future {
    @future
    public static void createUser(Id futureJobId) {
```

```
        Future_Job__c job = [SELECT Data_for_Processing__c,
Error_Information__c FROM Future_Job__c WHERE Id =
:futureJobId];
        ContactWrapper wrapper = (ContactWrapper)(JSON.
deserializeStrict(job.Data_for_Processing__c, ContactWrapper));
        try {
            insert wrapper.generateContact();
            delete job;
        } catch(Exception ex) {
            job.Error_Information__c = JSON.
            serializePretty(ex);
            update job;
        }
    }
}
```

This code could be utilized to create a contact from some data in a different execution thread, without the need to retrieve all of the data to generate the contact. Note that should the process fail, we capture the exception and output its information on the Future_Job__c record for us to review. In the example of a service being unavailable, we could simply empty the error field and provide the user a button to call the future method with this record again. We are also deleting the record once processing has succeeded, as there is no longer any need for the data to be stored.

This does have some drawbacks; we are now implicitly tying together processes on different threads to reuse code between them, in this case, the ContactWrapper class. In this situation, the wrapper gives us a single location to make any updates to how we wish to generate our contact and so enables us to keep our code DRY by avoiding multiple locations to make updates. When using this method to communicate and persist data across transaction boundaries, you should be aware of the trade-offs you are making and where possible provide useful commentary on code for its usage. I include this here as an example to show how this is possible, although in practice some of the other asynchronous Apex options we will review in the following chapters are more applicable.

Note that our previous logging setup from *Chapter 4*, *Exceptions and Exception Handling*, could also be used here to help record the errors. Often in situations like this, it is easier to record the error on the coordinating record (such as with the Future_Job__c) as the data and context are held directly on the record itself, making it easier to debug.

In the example we have just seen, we are creating a `Contact` record (possibly from a `User` for HR management, for example), however, it should be noted that if we were operating on a record such as `User` in this future method, we should not utilize the same `Future_Job__c` record and structure. This is because the `Future_Job__c` object cannot have DML performed on it in the same context as our `User` object, which was one of the original use cases in the first place. We will see an instance of this in the *Monitoring execution of future method invocations* section.

We have now covered how we can define future methods and coordinate the passing of data to the method, so we should now review how we can call our future methods to execute.

Calling future methods

As noted in the previous section, our future method is simply a `static` method, meaning we can call the method in the same way we would call any `static` method. For example, imagine our method was defined as follows:

```
public class FutureClass {
    @future
    public static void myFutureMethod() {
        //Method code
    }
}
```

Then, to invoke this method we would simply execute the following line of code within our code to call the function:

```
FutureClass.myFutureMethod();
```

We can call future methods from almost any Apex code we are executing with only a small number of exceptions. You cannot chain future methods together, so the following code would compile but would throw an exception when `futureB()` was invoked:

```
@future
public static void futureA() {
    //Code for futureA method
}

@future
public static void futureB() {
```

```
    //Execute some other code
    futureA(); //this would compile, but fail at runtime,
    //future methods cannot invoke other future methods
}
```

If we call our future method from a trigger context, we cannot invoke that trigger context from another future method. So, imagine we had the following trigger code:

```
trigger ContactTrigger on Contact(after update) {
    FutureExample.myFirstFutureMethod();
}
```

Then, we could not invoke the `after update` context on the `Contact` record from another future method, such as the following:

```
@future
public static void mySecondFutureMethod() {
    //Method code to execute
    update someContacts;
}
```

We would receive the following error at runtime:

```
System.AsyncException: Future method cannot be called from a
future or batch method: FutureExample.myFirstFutureMethod()
```

When defining and calling future methods, we should therefore be careful about ensuring that our code path will not contain chaining inadvertently, as this can cause unexpected errors.

Monitoring execution of future method invocations

Once you have invoked a future method, it is placed on the Apex job queue to be executed when resources are next available. As we will see in later chapters, many different types of asynchronous Apex operations are placed on that queue, and each job is given a unique identifier for you to track its progress. Some of these asynchronous Apex types return this identifier when invoked; however, future methods do not.

We can still monitor the status of a future job in the **Apex Jobs** page in the **Setup** menu under **Environments | Jobs**, as shown in the following screenshot:

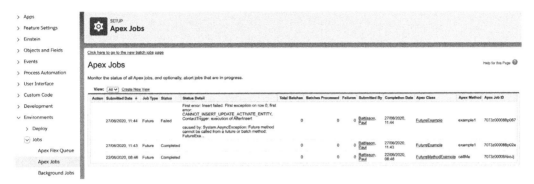

Figure 7.2 – Apex Job queue

We can also query for the status of a future job through SOQL, using a query such as the following:

```
SELECT Id, Status, ApexClassID, MethodName FROM AsyncApexJob
WHERE JobType = 'Future' ORDER BY CreatedDate DESC
```

This query will list out for review all Apex jobs that are a future invocation, returning information relating to which method was invoked and its status.

We have now seen how we can define and invoke a future method, so the final step is for us to test the future method prior to deploying it to production. Let's now discuss how we can do this and effectively test future methods.

Testing future methods

By its nature, asynchronous Apex methods does not execute on the same thread and in the same execution context as other Apex methods, so when testing we must force the Salesforce test runner to execute any asynchronous Apex methods synchronously to allow us to assert on the operation of the code.

The way by which we will do this for all our asynchronous code is through the use of the `Test.startTest()` and `Test.stopTest()` methods. These methods define an execution context with its own set of Governor Limits and resources available to it. Any asynchronous code that is invoked after `Test.startTest()` is called will be executed synchronously by the test runner when `Test.stopTest()` is called. This allows us to verify that our code operates as expected.

Let's say we have the following future method and Apex class to test, which deactivates a user given their record Id:

```
public with sharing class DeactivateUser_Future {

    @future
    public static void deactivateUser(Id userId) {
        User u = [SELECT Id, IsActive FROM User WHERE Id =
        :userId];
        u.isActive = false;
        update u;
    }

}
```

To test this class, then, we need to test both positive and negative use cases. Firstly, let's define a test class and add our scaffold positive test case:

```
@isTest
private with sharing class DeactivateUser_Future_Test {
    @isTest
    private static void testDeactivateUser() {

    }
}
```

In order to deactivate a user, we will need to create one that we can safely deactivate in the test. Let's add some code to the testDeactivateUser method to do this:

```
@isTest
    private static void testDeactivateUser() {
        Profile communityProfile = [SELECT Id, Name FROM
        Profile WHERE Name = 'Standard User' LIMIT 1];

        User testUser = new User();
        testUser.FirstName = 'Test';
        testUser.LastName = 'User';
        testUser.Email = 'test@paul.test.com1';
        testUser.Username = 'test@paul.test.com1';
```

```
            testUser.Alias = 'TestUser';
            testUser.ProfileId = communityProfile.Id;
            testUser.LocaleSidKey = 'en_GB';
            testUser.TimeZoneSidKey = 'Europe/London';
            testUser.LanguageLocaleKey = 'en_US';
            testUser.EmailEncodingKey = 'UTF-8';
            testUser.IsActive = true;

            insert testUser;
    }
}
```

This code creates a new user for us. We can then call `Test.startTest()`, invoke our future method, and call `Test.stopTest()` to get it to execute synchronously in the test runner:

```
Test.startTest();

DeactivateUser_Future.deactivateUser(testUser.Id);

Test.stopTest();
```

We can then assert that the user is no longer active, as follows:

```
List<User> users = [SELECT Id, IsActive FROM User WHERE Email =
'test@paul.test.com1'];
System.assertEquals(1, users.size(), 'Incorrect number of users
returned');
System.assert(!users[0].IsActive, 'User should be inactive');
```

This test will enable us to verify that the code works as expected. For the negative use case, we simply need to provide a `userId` for a non-existent record and then assert that an exception is thrown:

```
@isTest
private static void testError() {

    try {
        Test.startTest();
        DeactivateUser_Future.
```

```
deactivateUser('0053z00000BXnI5AAL');
    Test.stopTest();
        System.assert(false, 'Error should be thrown');
    } catch(Exception ex) {
        System.assert(true, 'Exception was thrown');
    }

}
```

As we discussed in the preceding code, we cannot use our logging framework here to persist an error for us to work with, nor could we use a structure such as the Future_Job__c object, because of the fact that we would then receive a mixed DML error from updating a user record and then acting on a Log__c or Future_Job__c record.

Summary

As we have seen in this chapter, future methods are a versatile and easy-to-work-with asynchronous processing option within Apex. They allow us to define discrete bundles of code that can be used for making long-running callouts or to avoid mixed DML errors when working with setup objects.

We have also seen some different methods of interacting with future methods to persist state and errors between transaction contexts, and finally saw how our future methods can be tested.

The reason we focus on future methods first in this section is that they are the simplest to invoke (just a static method call) and therefore are easier to test. They also have limited out-of-the-box support for state transmission, which has to be mangled through the use of an object that persists across the transaction context.

In the next chapter, we are going to look into batch Apex, where state persistence and use cases differ from what we have seen.

8
Working with Batch Apex

In *Chapter 7, Utilizing Future Methods*, we reviewed how we can utilize future methods to process data in different transactions to avoid issues such as mixed DML errors and make long-running callouts. Future methods are still constrained by Governor Limits, which, while slightly more generous than the standard framework, still do not allow large-scale processing of data.

In this chapter, we are going to discuss Batch Apex, a tool within the Apex language designed specifically to allow processing of large volumes of data asynchronously.

In this chapter, we are going to understand the following topics:

- When to use Batch Apex
- Defining Batch Apex
- Invoking Batch Apex
- Monitoring Batch Apex
- Exception handling and platform events

Technical Requirements

The code for the chapter can be found here: `https://github.com/PacktPublishing/Mastering-Apex-Programming/tree/Chapter-8`

When to use Batch Apex

Batch Apex has a number of key use cases, which we will discuss here. But before discussing them, it is worth spending some time understanding how Batch Apex processes data.

As we will see in the following diagram, Batch Apex is great for working with large volumes of data. When utilizing Batch Apex, we define a set of data to be iterated over, either through a query or a custom iterable. Salesforce then chunks this data into batches and processes the batches one by one. So, if we had 200,000 records to process and wanted to process them in batches of 1,000, Salesforce would chunk the job into batches of 1,000 and process them one by one.

Refer to the following diagram:

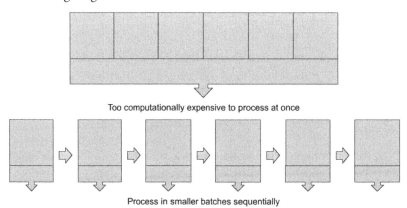

Too computationally expensive to process at once

Process in smaller batches sequentially

Figure 8.1 – Batch processing

This makes Batch Apex fantastic at some tasks and less useful at others. Let's now look through some use cases where having these processes executed in a sequential series of batches makes the most sense.

Large data volumes

Imagine we have a scenario where we are in an existing org with 1,250,000 contact records. We are going to add a new field that needs populating on each contact to provide a new unique key that is a combination of data from this contact and a field on the related account. How could we do this?

A potential answer is using the data loader, by exporting all the contacts into a spreadsheet tool such as Excel, performing the updates on the spreadsheet, and then uploading the new data. At the time of writing, Excel does not support over approximately 1 million rows of data, and so we would need to split this into two uploads. Additionally, those who have worked with large Excel files over 10,000 rows of data will attest to the fact that your computer may not always run as fast when doing this.

Another option is to use Batch Apex to update these records. A Batch Apex job can retrieve and process up to 50 million rows of data when using a query locator and will process them in the background without human intervention needed; only the code is required to define the update. If you are dealing with performing an update on a large volume of data, I recommend you check to see whether a Batch Apex process might be a better option than a data load.

Complex logical manipulation processes

A particular example of when Batch Apex is more appropriate for working with large data volumes is when the logic involved is more complex than can be achieved in a data load.

Reviewing our previous example of updating a large volume of contact records, if we are simply populating an individual field such as a total, the logic to perform this is simple and does not require anything more than a formula within Excel, or even a formula field itself.

However, for an update, if we need to retrieve data from other records based upon a query or using logical choices (`if`...`else` or `switch` statements), then Batch Apex should be our tool of choice.

High-volume web service callouts

Sometimes there will be a need to perform a large volume of callouts to an external system that we do not want to block the main execution context. This could be either a one-off job, such as an initial sync between two systems, or a regular transmission of data in a nightly process. In any instance where we want to send a large amount of data between systems using web services, we should consider Batch Apex. Callouts can be made from a Batch Apex class and allow us to bulkify the way in which we send data across, to improve overall performance. For example, we may be sending data to an external service whenever a record within Salesforce is saved. If this external service cannot utilize a solution such as **Change Data Capture**, then we can use Batch Apex to send these changes in state in a bulkified manner. We will see an example of this now in processing an asynchronous queue.

Asynchronous queue processing

When dealing with certain use cases, we will want to produce our own asynchronous queue of work to be processed. One organization I worked with required changes in contact information to be synchronized to a website backend for display on the website. Tools such as Heroku Connect were unavailable as the site was running on a .NET-based backend, and Change Data Capture would have provided too much data. The solution here was to create a custom message queue (like the `Future_Job__c` we discussed in *Chapter 7*, *Utilizing Future Methods*) that would store the details of the change we needed to communicate to the external system. A Batch Apex class would then run and process all these records, sending the updates to the website for display. This ties in with the high-volume web service callouts use case above.

When the need arises to create your own queue of work to be processed asynchronously, utilize Batch Apex to process the queue records in a scalable and performant manner. The processing of the queue is done on a scheduled basis—another good use case for Batch Apex, which we will now discuss.

Scheduling updates to lots of records

Scheduled Batch Apex classes are a powerful tool that allow you to perform updates to many records on a scheduled basis to meet a multitude of business requirements. One example is for marking records to be archived to an external system (and then archiving them), a scheduled process can be run nightly to review changed data within the past 24 hours.

Another organization I worked with needed to get the latest score for a set of records from an external system every evening. We utilized a scheduled Batch Apex class to make the necessary callouts and process the data. The power of a scheduled Batch Apex job is that the job will scale to meet data volumes of up to 50 million records. If you find a situation where you are updating over 50 million records every night, then you should review your architecture.

We will dive deeper into Scheduled Apex jobs in *Chapter 10*, *Scheduling Apex Jobs*, but the use of Scheduled and Batch Apex together is a powerful combination and is separate from just a scheduled Batch Apex execution, which is done through the user interface rather than via code.

I also utilize a scheduled Batch Apex job to make many one-off updates to data post deployment where required, using the `System.scheduleBatch` method. This method schedules a one-time run of a Batch Apex class at a defined point in the future (or as close as resource availability allows). Often, when working on complex large environments, a new field will be introduced that needs retrospectively populating on all existing records as discussed previously. You can schedule this update to occur when the usage of the system is low (for example, outside working hours) to minimize any disruption to end users.

Managed sharing recalculations

In *Chapter 6*, *Secure Apex Programming*, we discussed the use of Apex **Managed sharing** to help control access to records within the system. Over time, particularly in large Salesforce deployments, this can lead to a large volume of sharing records that need managing and maintaining. If a recalculation of a large enough portion of these is required, then Batch Apex is an optimal tool to help us recalculate these records in bulk. We can also use some features such as one-off scheduling to help ensure this is happening outside working hours when the sharing can be best recalculated with minimum impact on a user.

A note on testability

Before we move on to how we define a Batch Apex class, I want to highlight that one of the key features of Batch Apex that makes it so useful for the preceding use cases is its testability. Because we are writing Apex code, we have to meet our testing requirements to deploy the code to our production environment for it to run. Unlike updates via Data Loader, which we can only verify through a visual check and experience, we can (and in fact have to) write Apex tests for our code that allow us to verify in a repeatable and consistent manner that the code works as we expect. This gives an additional level of comfort that when we make an update that may impact millions of records, it operates as we expect and can even verify that automation such as triggers, workflow, Process Builder, and flows are not impacting our intended outcomes.

Now we have understood the potential use cases for Batch Apex, we will look at how we define a Batch Apex class and the different permutations we can define.

Defining a Batch Apex class

When we refer to a Batch Apex class, we actually mean a class implementing the `Database.Batchable` interface and its related interfaces. As we will see when we discuss invoking Batch Apex in the next main section of the chapter, this provides us with some benefits in making our code dynamic in certain situations. In this section, we will review defining a Batch Apex class using the base interface and the additional related interfaces we can also apply.

The base interface

The simplest Batch Apex class definition is one in which we define a class that implements the `Database.Batchable` interface, as shown in the following code snippet:

```
public class ExampleBatch implements Database.
Batchable<sObject> {

    public Database.QueryLocator start(Database.
    BatchableContext bc) {
        //Retrieve our data for processing
    }

    public void execute(Database.BatchableContext bc,
    List<sObject> records){
        //Process our records
    }

    public void finish(Database.BatchableContext bc){
        //Run any post-processing operations
    }
}
```

The preceding code is the most common form of declaration in my experience and allows us to define a query for a set of data that we will iterate over in our batches. The `Database.Batchable` interface has three methods that must be implemented—`start`, `execute`, and `finish`.

The `start` method defines the objects or records for us to process within the batches. We can return either a `Database.QueryLocator` instance or an `Iterable<sObject>` instance for processing, which is handed to the `execute` method.

The `execute` method contains the logic we wish to perform on each batch, typically including any DML. Each invocation of this method is handed a batch of records and so you should ensure that you have correctly bulkified your code to run in the intended manner with what can be up to 2,000 records. When invoking a batch job, you can provide a scope parameter to define the number of records to process per job. For classes returning a `Database.QueryLocator` object, the scope parameter defaults to 200 and can be set to a maximum of 2,000 (setting it higher will still only return 2,000). For implementations using iterator classes, there is no upper scope limit.

Once all the batches have been processed, the `finish` method is called and post-processing actions can be taken. Typically, these take the form of sending an email or cleaning up any unrequired data. We will also see later in this chapter, in the *Chaining batches* section, how we can use this method to help us work with Batch Apex in different ways to improve flexibility.

Each batch execution is independent of other batches and so cannot share data between contexts. To do this, we have to add state that can be shared. Let's look at how we can extend the base Batch Apex declaration to include state that allows us to keep a common set of data in memory across the different batches.

Stateful batch implementations

As mentioned in the preceding paragraph, there are a number of different interfaces that a batch class can implement alongside the `Database.Batchable` interface. One of these additional interfaces is `Database.Stateful`, which allows us to maintain state between the different batches of records, so we can share information. A typical use case is for aggregate or summary information, or for maintaining a count.

As an example, I once worked with an organization where we needed to generate a unique sequential username for 40,000 new community members in the form of XXXXXX@company.id, where XXXXXX is a number such as `045271`. To do this, we need to maintain the current number we are using so that we can increment and populate the username appropriately, as well as storing the value at the end of processing for future use. This was a prime use case for a stateful Batch Apex class.

To define a Batch Apex class that maintains state, we implement the additional `Database.Stateful` interface in our class definition, as follows:

```
public class ExampleStatefulBatch implements Database.
Batchable<sObject>, Database.Stateful {

    private Integer statefulCount;
```

```
public Database.QueryLocator start(Database.
BatchableContext bc) {
    //Retrieve our data for processing
}

public void execute(Database.BatchableContext bc,
List<sObject> records){
    //Process our records
}

public void finish(Database.BatchableContext bc){
    //Run any post-processing operations
}
}
```

In the preceding code snippet, the `statefulCount` member variable is shared across the batches and the value can be used to count records as the batch job progresses.

It should be noted that only member variables persist their state across batches; static variables are scoped to the transaction (that is, batch) and reset after each batch has completed. We can see this in the following code snippet:

```
public class ExampleStatefulBatch implements Database.
Batchable<sObject>, Database.Stateful {

    private Integer statefulCount = 0;
    private static Integer staticCount = 0;

    public Database.QueryLocator start(Database.
    BatchableContext bc) {
        //Retrieve our data for processing
    }

    public void execute(Database.BatchableContext bc,
    List<sObject> records){
        for(Account acc : (List<Account>)records) {
                statefulCount++;
                staticCount++;
        }
```

```
    }

    public void finish(Database.BatchableContext bc){
        System.debug(statefulCount);
        System.debug(staticCount);
    }
}
```

When our `finish` method executes the value of our `statefulCount`, it will return whatever the overall count was, whereas our `staticCount` will output the number of items processed in that batch as the value of the `staticCount` variable will be reset on each batch.

We have now seen how we can maintain state across the different batches, but how about making callouts? We noted at the start of this chapter that another use case for Batch Apex was to make high-volume callouts to a web service or to process a custom queue. Let's now look at how we can enable our class to make callouts.

Callout-enabled batch classes

To enable a Batch Apex class to make web service callouts, we need to have it implement the `Database.AllowCallouts` interface. This interface, like the `Database.Stateful` interface, does not have any additional methods that we need to implement as part of the interface implementation, but instead makes the ability to make callouts possible on the class. An example class would then be the following:

```
public class ExampleCalloutBatch implements Database.
Batchable<sObject>, Database.AllowCallouts {

    public Database.QueryLocator start(Database.
    BatchableContext bc) {
        //Retrieve our data for processing
    }

    public void execute(Database.BatchableContext bc,
    List<sObject> records){
        //Process our records and make some callouts
    }

    public void finish(Database.BatchableContext bc){
```

```
            //Run any post-processing operations
    }
}
```

Each of our `start`, `finish`, and `execute` methods can implement up to 100 callouts each; however, from experience, it is a best practice to try and limit the callouts to the `execute` method.

Note that because we have a limit of 100 callouts per batch (that is, per invocation of the `execute` method), when defining a batch class that makes callouts, we will want to be aware of the scope size for the batch. As noted in the *The base interface* section, the default scope size (when using `QueryLocator`) is 200 records and a maximum of 2,000 records. If we were making a callout per record to an external service, we would surpass this limit in either situation and would therefore need to limit the scope to a maximum of 100 records. In practice, you will want to do some testing to find the best-balanced position to operate in using bulkified callouts that call endpoints with multiple records at once while keeping the request size small enough to maintain performance.

The scope limit we mention here is for when we are working with `QueryLocator` and not `Iterable`. So far, all the examples we have seen show the use of `QueryLocator`, but what are the differences between the two options and when would it be best to use one over the other? Let's see, in the next section.

Iterable versus QueryLocator in Batch Apex

When defining the scope for our Batch Apex class, we can use either an `Iterable`, that is, a class that implements the `Iterable` interface, or `QueryLocator`. So far, all the examples we have seen have shown the use of a `QueryLocator` instead of an `Iterable`. Is there a reason for this?

In my experience, the most common scope for a Batch Apex class is the result set from a SOQL query. In order to maximize the available volumes within the batch job, you should return a `QueryLocator` object for the SOQL query, which will enable you to retrieve up to 50 million records, whereas any standard query is limited to 50,000 at the time of writing. `Iterable` implementations of a Batch Apex class will still have this 50,000-record limit in place for any querying that is done as part of generating the `Iterable`.

In most situations, therefore, you will encounter Batch Apex classes using a `QueryLocator` to define scope; however, a custom iterator can be useful in defining and providing scope where more complex ordering may be needed, or when working with external objects.

For example, if we wanted to process all the accounts within an account hierarchy, that is, from the very top-level account down through all of its subsidiaries, we would require multiple queries to retrieve all the necessary data, which cannot be done in a `QueryLocator`. It is a safe assumption that we have no accounts with a hierarchy of over 100 levels (the maximum number of SOQL queries we can make) and that we have less than 50,000 accounts in the hierarchy to do this in an `Iterable` solution.

> **Important note**
>
> Note that if we had a hierarchy over 100 levels deep and with more than 50,000 records, then we would likely experience a large data skew within the org. We should spend time rearchitecting how we store these records. Having a data structure like this would likely indicate that the org is storing data at a level that is too granular and should be reworked or split into multiple accounts.
>
> To add some perspective, according to the Statista website, the world's largest food chain, Subway, had 41,600 stores worldwide as of 2019. Using this as a baseline, it is extremely unlikely we would have over 50,000 records in a hierarchy without having a serious flaw in our data model. Performing a thought experiment like this can be a useful way of determining the likelihood of breaking such a limit.

A possible variation of such a custom iterator is shown in the following code:

```
public with sharing class CustomAccountIterable implements
Iterable<Account> {
    private CustomAccountIterator iterator;

    public CustomAccountIterable(Id accountId) {
        iterator = new CustomAccountIterator(accountId);
    }

    public Iterator<Account> iterator() {
        return iterator;
    }
}
```

Firstly, we implement the `Iterable<sObject>` interface providing the API name of the `sObject` we wish to create the iterator for. The `Iterable` interface has a single method to implement, `iterator()`, which must return an implementation of the `Iterator<sObject>` interface. Here, we also have a constructor that takes in the `Id` of the account at the top of the hierarchy we are creating the `Iterable` for.

The bulk of our customized logic is within our implementation of the `Iterator<sObject>` interface in the following code. This class creates a flattened hierarchy through the use of a repeated query and a `while` loop to retrieve all the necessary records. The interface requires us to provide the `hasNext()` and `next()` methods, which inform `Iterable` whether more records are available to iterate through, and if so, provides the next item:

```apex
public with sharing class CustomAccountIterator implements
Iterator<Account> {

    private List<Account> accounts;
    private Integer iterator = 0;


    public CustomAccountIterator(Id globalParentId) {
        Boolean hasChildAccounts = true;
        Set<Id> parentIds = new Set<Id> { globalParentId };
        accounts = [SELECT Id, Name FROM Account WHERE Id =
        :globalParentId];

        while(hasChildAccounts) {
            Map<Id,Account> childAccounts =
            getChildAccounts(parentIds);
            if(childAccounts.size() > 0) {
                parentIds.clear();
                parentIds.addAll(childAccounts.keySet());
                accounts.addAll(childAccounts.values());
            } else {
                hasChildAccounts = false;
            }
        }
    }

    public Boolean hasNext() {
```

```
            return iterator < accounts.size();
    }


    public Account next() {
        if(iterator < accounts.size()) {
            iterator++;
            return accounts[iterator-1];
        }
        return null;
    }


    private Map<Id, Account> getChildAccounts(Set<Id>
    parentAccountIds) {
        return new Map<Id, Account>([SELECT Id, Name FROM
        Account WHERE ParentId in :parentAccountIds]);
    }
}
```

As was mentioned, it is more commonplace to use QueryLocator instances in Batch Apex due to the greater volumes of data they provide, however, custom iterators and implementations of the Iterable interface provide a useful way of delivering data for processing when more complex logic is involved in the retrieval. It should also be noted that the standard Apex list collection also implements the Iterable interface to provide a simple way of creating Iterable instances for processing. You should also avoid bringing back child records within a QueryLocator where possible to help maximize and improve performance.

Now that we have understood how to define our Batch Apex classes to enable us to process the data, let's look at how we can invoke and execute our Batch Apex to process the desired data.

Invoking Batch Apex

There are a number of different ways in which we can invoke a Batch Apex class to run, which will be useful in different circumstances and use cases. In this section, we will review the different ways in which you can invoke Batch Apex and when each of them might be applicable. We will also discuss some ways in which you can utilize a number of Salesforce features together to allow you to invoke Batch Apex in a more dynamic and configuration controlled fashion. Let's begin with the first one.

Using Database.executeBatch

The first way to invoke Batch Apex is through the use of the standard `Database.executeBatch()` method. This method takes in an instance of a class implementing the `Database.Batchable` interface and a second optional parameter to define the size of the scope of each batch. As mentioned in the *The base interface* section, for implementations using `QueryLocator` instances, this defaults to 200 records and has a maximum value of 2,000 records, while for implementations using an `Iterable` instance there is no upper limit.

To invoke our `ExampleBatch` class from before, we would therefore execute it as follows:

```
Database.executeBatch(new ExampleBatch()); //Invoke batch
process with batch size/scope set to 200 records
Database.executeBatch(new ExampleBatch(), 1500); //Invoke batch
process with batch size/scope set to 1500 records
```

Both calls would get the batch process to run only once, processing all the data returned by the `QueryLocator` or `Iterable` and then ending. This form of invocation is extremely useful when running a one-off job to update data that we do not want to run repeatedly, such as the earlier example of generating usernames.

For managing one-off batch jobs in production environments, I typically create a `OneOffBatch` class that I will update with the code that is needed to perform the required job and redeploy as necessary. This means I do not pollute my code base with many classes that are only going to be used once but that I must maintain.

What if we wanted to run a one-off batch job in 2 hours' time? For example, if I were processing and updating all the sharing rules within my organization, I would want to do this when no users were in the system, say from 8 p.m. onwards. How would I invoke this job without me having to be at my machine? Let's see how.

Scheduling batch classes

In this instance, you could use the `System.scheduleBatch()` method to schedule the batch class to run after a specific number of minutes have passed, for example:

```
System.scheduleBatch(new ExampleBatch(), 'example batch job',
60, 1200);
```

This method call will schedule the `ExampleBatch` job to run in `60` minutes time with a batch size of `1200` records. We also provide a name for the job here for us to use when monitoring jobs. Note that the scope parameter is optional and that we can use the default scope by running the following:

```
System.scheduleBatch(new ExampleBatch(), 'example batch job',
60);
```

Although the job is scheduled for the specified time (in the preceding example, that is 1 hour from when the code is executed), the actual execution time may vary depending on resource availability but will not be before the scheduled time. This is helpful to ensure that we can wait to execute our code until after a certain time, for example, at 3 p.m. we might schedule our job to run in 4 hours' time, that is, on or after 7 p.m., to ensure no users are in the system.

When a call is made to `System.scheduleBatch`, a scheduled job `Id` is returned, which is an `Id` for the `CronTrigger` `sObject`. We can use this `Id` to query the `CronTrigger` object and retrieve any status information that might be required, as follows:

```
String jobId = System.scheduleBatch(new ExampleBatch(),
'example batch job', 60);
CronTrigger ct = [SELECT Id, State, NextFireTime FROM
CronTrigger WHERE Id = :jobId];
System.debug('Job in status of: ' + ct.State);
System.debug('Next execution at: ' + ct.NextFireTime);
```

Note that this is different from the monitoring of regular batch jobs, which we'll cover in more detail in the *Monitoring Batch Apex* section of this chapter.

This form of scheduling is very useful for one-off scheduling, but what about repeated scheduling, for example, running a process every night at midnight?

Working with a scheduled class and custom metadata

We can combine both the scheduled Apex and Batch Apex frameworks to allow us to have Batch Apex classes that run on a regular, scheduled basis. We will cover the `Schedulable` interface in more detail in *Chapter 10, Scheduling Apex Jobs*; however, I want to present here a pattern that I have worked with multiple times that allows you to schedule and control the execution of multiple Batch Apex jobs through the use of custom metadata.

> **Note**
>
> It is assumed that you are familiar with custom metadata types and records, however, if you are not, then I recommend pausing to briefly review the *Get Started with Custom Metadata Types* Trailhead module.

I have encountered a number of situations over the years while working with Salesforce where there has been a need to run a series of Batch Apex jobs on a regular interval, be they for callout processing or for data cleanup (many companies have data retention rules that can be automated). In these instances, it is helpful to have a way in which we can quickly add, manage, and update the Batch Apex classes we wish to run on this schedule.

Firstly, we need to define a custom metadata type called **Batch Job** and two fields, **Active** and **Scope**, as shown in the following screenshot. We will use this custom metadata type to hold the details of Batch Apex classes that we wish to run, as well as any scope we wish to apply to them:

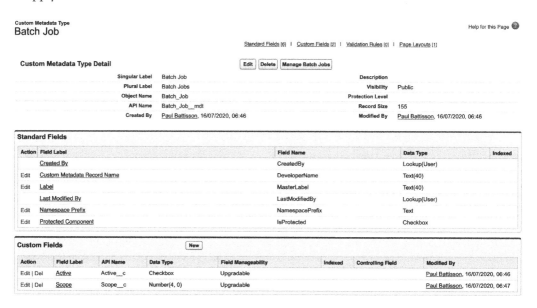

Figure 8.2 – Custom metadata definition

We can then create records to hold the details of classes we wish to execute; for example, the following screenshot shows the definition for our `ExampleBatch` class with a scope size of `2000`:

Batch Job

Figure 8.3 – ExampleBatch definition in custom metadata

We will dive into the specifics of working with scheduled Apex later, but for now, we should note that a scheduled Apex class has a single `execute` method that contains the code to execute on the desired schedule. In order to use our batch custom metadata, we would then populate that method with code such as the following:

```
List<Batch_Job__mdt> jobs = [SELECT DeveloperName, Scope__c
FROM Batch_Job__mdt WHERE Active__c = true];


for(Batch_Job__mdt job : jobs) {
    Type jobType = Type.forName(job.DeveloperName);
    Database.executeBatch((Database.Batchable<sObject>)
    jobType.newInstance(), job.Scope__c);
}
```

The preceding code allows us to define through configuration the Batch Apex classes we want to run on a specified schedule and turn the execution on or off using the `Active__c` flag. This can be extremely useful and powerful in allowing you to manage these items as needed as well as making the deployment of a new batch job simpler—you simply deploy the Batch Apex class and the custom metadata record, ensure the record is marked with `Active__c = true` and the job will run. This removes inherent dependencies within the code, making it more scalable and fault-tolerant to any changes.

Note that submitting these multiple jobs does not necessarily have them fire straight away. Jobs that are submitted are added to the Apex Flex Queue, which can hold a maximum of 100 Batch Apex jobs in the **Holding** status. The queue will then work through and allocate resources as they become available until the maximum of five concurrent jobs are in a queued or running status. This is something you should be aware of when using this structure to ensure you have code that runs as anticipated. I would, however, suggest that should you have more than five scheduled batch jobs running regularly as you may want to review your processes and architecture.

What about processes that depend on each other? What if I wanted to run another batch job once my first had finished, for example, after processing all the account records, I wished to process my contact records? We can do this by chaining together batches.

Chaining batches

In 2014, I delivered a talk called *Building Machine Learning Systems in Apex* with my then colleague Jen Wyher. The system we built was the first instance I am aware of where machine learning or artificial intelligence systems were working on Salesforce, but in building the system we encountered a number of unique challenges (some of which I will discuss in *Section 3, Apex Performance*) including the need to process a large volume of data dynamically. We needed a system that would process a set of data, determine whether its knowledge of the data had improved and, if so, make another attempt to improve; otherwise, end and revert to the best guess.

To do this, we utilized Batch Apex and the ability to chain Batch Apex processes. In the `finish` method of a Batch Apex class, you can make another call to `Database.executeBatch` to allow you to start another batch process on a series of records. This can enable you to chain together extremely long-running processes or multiple related jobs to coordinate them appropriately.

Executing multiple batches in parallel

What if, instead of chaining, you wanted to improve batch processing performance by executing multiple batches in parallel? As we have just seen, Batch Apex can chain processes as needed, but they still run in a serial fashion. For some situations you will want to process the batches in parallel if possible, to improve performance and ensure that work is performed in a timely manner. In order to process items in parallel, you have a couple of options.

Firstly, you can use a stateful batch implementation to build up a set of records to process in each of the batches and then fire these batches off in the `finish` method; for example, if we wanted to process all the accounts in our org we could use a parallel structure as follows:

```
public class ExampleStatefulParallelBatch implements Database.
Batchable<sObject>, Database.Stateful {

    private Set<Id> idSet1 = new Set<Id>();
    private Set<Id> idSet2 = new Set<Id>();
    private Set<Id> idSet3 = new Set<Id>();
    private Set<Id> idSet4 = new Set<Id>();
```

```
    private Set<Id> idSet5 = new Set<Id>();
    private Integer count = 0;

    public Database.QueryLocator start(Database.
    BatchableContext bc) {
        //Retrieve all our data for processing using
            return Database.getQueryLocator('SELECT Id FROM
            Account');
    }

    public void execute(Database.BatchableContext bc,
    List<sObject> records){
        for(Account acc : (List<Account>)records) {
                switch on Math.mod(count, 5) {
                        when 0 {
                                idSet1.add(acc.Id);
                        }
                        when 1 {
                                idSet1.add(acc.Id);
                        }
                        when 2 {
                                idSet1.add(acc.Id);
                        }
                        when 3 {
                                idSet1.add(acc.Id);
                        }
                        when else {
                                idSet5.add(acc.Id);
                        }
                }
                count++;
        }
    }

    public void finish(Database.BatchableContext bc){
        ExampleInitialisedBatch batch1 - new
        ExampleInitialisedBatch(idSet1);
```

```
        Database.executeBatch(batch1);
        ExampleInitialisedBatch batch2 = new
        ExampleInitialisedBatch(idSet2);
        Database.executeBatch(batch2);
        ExampleInitialisedBatch batch3 = new
        ExampleInitialisedBatch(idSet3);
        Database.executeBatch(batch3);
        ExampleInitialisedBatch batch4 = new
        ExampleInitialisedBatch(idSet4);
        Database.executeBatch(batch4);
        ExampleInitialisedBatch batch5 = new
        ExampleInitialisedBatch(idSet5);
        Database.executeBatch(batch5);
    }
}
```

This code separates all of our accounts into five sets to then distribute across batches. We have to be careful here to avoid the heap size Apex governor limit of 12 MB or this will cause an error. It is therefore wise when running a job like this to consider how you test and verify that you will not exceed governor limits by verifying against large data volumes in a full copy sandbox.

We pass the IDs into the `ExampleInitialisedBatch` instances via the constructor and store them in a `private final` variable for use in our query to define the scope, as is shown in the following example code:

```
public class ExampleInitialisedBatch implements Database.
Batchable<sObject> {

    private final Set<Id> processIds;

    public ExampleinitialisedBatch(Set<Id> recordIds) {
        processIds = recordIds;
    }

    public Database.QueryLocator start(Database.
    BatchableContext bc) {
        //Retrieve our data for processing
        return Database.getQueryLocator('SELECT Id, Name FROM
        Account WHERE Id in :processIds');
```

```
    }

    public void execute(Database.BatchableContext bc,
List<sObject> records){
        // Process records
    }

    public void finish(Database.BatchableContext bc){
        //Any required clean up code or trigger a new batch
    }
}
```

An alternative method to this for parallelizing work is to perform some analytics on the dataset separately to allow you to define chunks of data to work with that you can then specify dynamically. For example, if we wanted to update all of our accounts, we may run some basic analytics in SOQL to determine that a good way of splitting the data into roughly equal groups is by the year in which they were created. We could then pass this into the constructor of our batch class as we did with `ExampleInitialisedBatch` to define our scope. Some example code would then be the following:

```
public class ExampleInitialisedBatch implements Database.
Batchable<sObject> {

    private final Integer year;

    public ExampleinitialisedBatch(Integer filterYear) {
        year = filterYear;
    }

    public Database.QueryLocator start(Database.
BatchableContext bc) {
        //Retrieve our data for processing
        return Database.getQueryLocator('SELECT Id, Name FROM
Account WHERE CALENDAR_YEAR(CreatedDate) = ' + year);
    }

    public void execute(Database.BatchableContext bc,
List<sObject> records){
        // Process records
```

```
        }

    public void finish(Database.BatchableContext bc){
        //Any required clean up code or trigger a new batch
    }
}
```

This provides us with another way of generating batches that can be triggered in parallel by using platform features in tandem.

We have now seen a number of ways in which we can invoke Batch Apex in both a serial and parallelized fashion, but how can we monitor batches once they have been submitted?

Monitoring Batch Apex

Once we have submitted a Batch Apex job for processing, we will want to be able to monitor its execution to see how it is performing. Whenever we make a call to `Database.executeBatch`, we are returning an `Id` for the `AsyncApexJob` `sObject`, which we can use to retrieve the status of the batch job through a query, as shown in the following snippet, that can be executed in the `Execute Anonymous` window:

```
Id batchJobId = Database.executeBatch(new ExampleBatch());

AsyncApexJob apexJob = [SELECT Id, Status, JobItemsProcessed,
TotalJobItems, NumberOfErrors
                FROM AsyncApexJob WHERE ID = :batchJobId];

System.debug('Job has status of ' + apexJob.Status + ' and
has processed ' +  apexJob.JobItemsProcessed + '/' + apexJob.
TotalJobItems + ' with ' + apexJob.NumberOfErrors + '
errors.');
```

We can also monitor the batch jobs we have submitted in the **Apex Jobs** view in **SETUP**, as shown in the following screenshot:

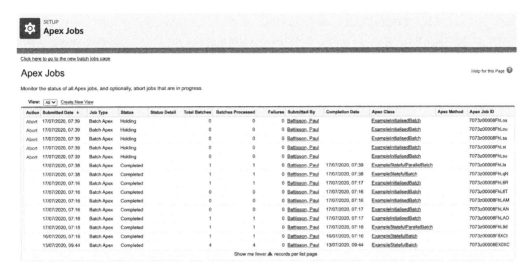

Figure 8.4 – Viewing Apex Jobs in an org through the SETUP menu

When a batch job is submitted, it may be immediately processed by the system, in which case it will show in the **Apex Jobs** list shown in the previous screenshot. You can have a maximum of five queued or active batch jobs, after which jobs will be added to the **Apex Flex Queue** where up to 100 jobs can be queued in a holding status.

In the following screenshot, you can see the **Apex Flex Queue** holding a set of additional jobs that have been submitted. You can view this queue thorough the **SETUP** menu:

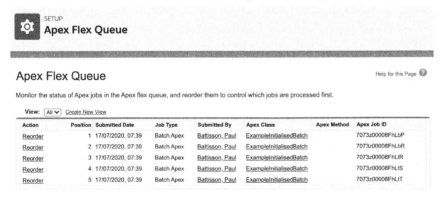

Figure 8.5 – Apex Flex Queue view

Jobs within the **Apex Flex Queue** can be reordered should priorities for the jobs change after submission. We can do this using the **Reorder** link seen in the preceding screenshot, or through the use of an Apex method such as the following:

```
Boolean movedSucessfully = System.FlexQueue.
moveJobToFront(jobToMoveId);
```

The `System.FlexQueue` class has a number of methods that allow you to move a job before or after another specified job as well as to the start or end of the queue. Should you find that you need to manage your job queue programmatically, these methods will enable you to do so easily from the Execute Anonymous window.

We saw in the preceding sections how we can see the number of errors that have occurred using the `AsyncApexJob` object, but how can we notify administrators of these errors in a more effective manner that allows them to check the data and stop the error from occurring again? This is what our next section is about.

Exception handling and platform events

There are two predominant ways of handling errors and exceptions within a Batch Apex job. The first, which was previously the standard mechanism, was to create a logging framework like what we discussed in *Chapter 4, Exceptions and Exception Handling*, and store the exception information as a record within the system through a `catch` statement and/or the `finish` method.

In API v44, Salesforce introduced the `BatchApexErrorEvent` platform event, which will automatically post errors to this channel for you to subscribe to. This can enable a custom error logging framework to subscribe to these notifications either through code or a declarative tool such as Process Builder or Flow.

In order to send these events, your Batch Apex class needs to implement the `Database.RaisesPlatformEvents` interface. Any errors or exceptions that are not handled will then be streamed to this channel. The following code snippet shows an Apex trigger that captures these events and simply debugs the information:

```
trigger BatchApexErrorEventTrigger on BatchApexErrorEvent
(after insert) {
    List<Account> records = new List<Account>();
    for(BatchApexErrorEvent evt : Trigger.new){
    System.debug('Failure on job with id: ' + evt.
    AsyncApexJobId);
        List<String> recordIds = evt.JobScope.split(',');
        System.debug('The error impacted ' + recordIds.
        size() + ' records');
    }
}
```

You will typically want to use the record IDs returned by the scope to mark the records in a fashion that makes them easy to reprocess again later. Note as well that because this is a platform event, it can be consumed by an external streaming channel as part of any DevOps and monitoring process that the organization may have. Obviously, we wish to avoid any errors occurring and the best way to do this is through thorough testing.

Testing Batch Apex

We have now seen in this chapter the different use cases and ways of invoking Batch Apex jobs. The final thing we need to do is be able to test our batch code appropriately to ensure that the code runs as expected. This is a critical step as Batch Apex processes run across a large volume of data and can therefore have repercussions if incorrect updates or changes are made. For example, if a batch job is used to recreate the sharing settings for an organization and makes the incorrect adjustments, this can have severe consequences and potential legal implications around data sharing.

Batch Apex is like other forms of asynchronous Apex where we test it using the `Test.startTest()` and `Test.stopTest()` methods to trigger the asynchronous operation to fire; for example:

```
Test.startTest();
Database.executeBatch(new ExampleBatch());
Test.stopTest();
//Verify behaviour of batch class was as expected
```

While this is simple to implement and follows the same pattern as other asynchronous methods, there are a number of items we must test within a batch class to ensure that we do not have unhandled exceptions and unintended consequences. The following are all items you should test for:

- Consider what batch size you will be running and testing with a data volume that matches. If you choose to set the batch size to 2,000, then you should verify that the code will run at that scale.

- Apex unit tests will only ever execute a single batch even if enough data is provided to run multiple batches. Be mindful of this when generating test data.

- Create a varied set of test data that can match the different states of your data that will impact the batch job. For example, if you are taking different actions within the batch dependent on a field value, create a suite of test data that verifies the different values that are possible to exercise all the code paths.

- Ensure you assert on outcome values. All tests should include assertions, as discussed in *Chapter 5*, *Testing Apex Code*; however, it is particularly important here to verify that the code has no unintended consequences.

- Test the operation in a full copy sandbox to verify data manually if you have access to such an environment.

If you take these items into consideration, you will have more confidence in the code you are running and be less likely to have large data changes that are unintended.

Summary

In this chapter, we have seen how we can effectively utilize Batch Apex as a tool to enable us to make changes against large volumes of data or process work as and when resources are available.

We started the chapter by reviewing what Batch Apex is and the different common use cases for Batch Apex. Some of these use cases can also be achieved with other tools and so it is important that when you are reviewing Batch Apex as a potential tool, you compare it appropriately with other options. It is not a silver bullet to simply help you work with an increased set of governor limits.

Following this, we looked at the different ways in which we can define a Batch Apex class to meet these use cases and the difference between using a `QueryLocator` and an `Iterable` to define the scope of the job. As noted, it is most common to use a `QueryLocator` object as it allows the greatest amount of scale for data volumes.

We then looked at how we can invoke Batch Apex processes in both a one-off, scheduled, and repeated manner, including using a simple framework involving custom metadata to help us control the execution of the various scheduled jobs that we may have. We also reviewed how to monitor jobs we have started and handle errors from those jobs using the `BatchApexErrorEvent` platform event.

We finished the chapter by looking at how we can test Batch Apex effectively and the key things we should be testing for. You should now feel more confident about defining and using Batch Apex in a number of different scenarios. One of the scenarios we discussed was the chaining together of batch classes.

In the next chapter, we will review queueable Apex, which is another way of chaining together large asynchronous processes.

9
Working with Queueable Apex

So far in this section on asynchronous processing in Apex, we have dealt with both future methods and Batch Apex, two different ways of processing data asynchronously with different use cases and benefits. In this chapter, we are going to discuss another asynchronous processing option that is somewhat of a hybrid of both—Queueable Apex.

We will discuss what Queueable Apex is and how it compares to both Batch Apex and future methods. This will help us to then define and understand use cases for Queueable Apex before we see how we define a Queueable Apex implementation. After defining a Queueable Apex implementation, we will see how to invoke a queueable job and how to chain jobs. We'll then finish the chapter by reviewing how we test our Queueable Apex classes.

In this chapter, we'll cover the following topics:

- What Queueable Apex is
- When to use Queueable Apex
- Defining Queueable Apex implementations
- Invoking Queueable Apex
- Testing Queueable Apex

What is Queueable Apex?

Queueable Apex was first introduced in the Winter '15 Salesforce release, that was some time around the end of 2014. It was delivered as a response to the growing use of both Batch Apex and future methods and developers finding use cases where neither was an ideal solution. This led to the development of Queueable Apex. Queueable Apex allows a developer to submit a job for processing and then at the end of that job, start another job, chaining multiple jobs together, something like this:

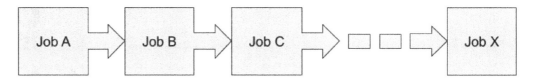

Figure 9.1 – Jobs are chained together with each job

From *Figure 9.1*, we see that each chained job is invoking another job, in the process, if needed until the full process is complete. Perhaps the best way to understand Queueable Apex is to understand the original reason it was designed. In his detailed blog post (`https://developer.salesforce.com/blogs/engineering/2014/10/new-apex-queueable-interface.html`), Josh Kaplan from the Salesforce product management team shared that one of the primary reasons that the Queueable Apex toolkit was developed was due to a large number of empty Batch Apex jobs being submitted.

Given our understanding of both future methods and Batch Apex, let's try and figure out why this occurred.

Within our asynchronous Apex options, we have an increased set of governor limits, but still do not have an unlimited set of resources. Let's consider a scenario where we have received an order from a user by closing an opportunity. Once that opportunity is marked as `Closed Won`, we have a series of steps that occur in the background but do not need to be synchronous:

1. We must first make a call to the inventory management system and verify we have the required stock for the order.

2. If we do not have enough stock, then we must place an order in the inventory system for the stock and record that against our opportunity.

3. If we do have the right amount of stock, we make a second callout to the inventory management system to take that stock and remove it from the inventory and prepare it for our order.

4. We then make a callout to our fulfillment system, generating a print label and postage information for the order.

5. On successfully retrieving the postage, we then send a callout to our warehouse and packing system to send the package with the given inventory, order information, and postage. This example process is shown in the following flow diagram:

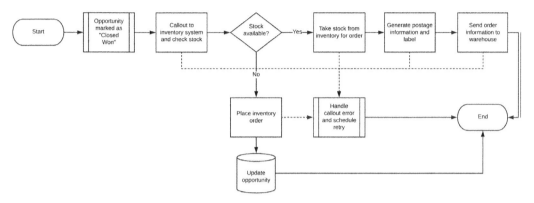

Figure 9.2 – An example process with multiple callouts, failure options, and branching logic

This process involves a number of callouts, database operations, and other logic processing that means that we may not be able to complete the entire process in a single transaction, or that if there is a failure from a callout, we will want to be able to re-attempt the process. This gives us the following pair of requirements:

1. Can we make callouts?

2. Can we reschedule/repeat the process if we have a failure (for instance, calling the same method again)?

Are we able to meet these requirements using our existing asynchronous options?

Let's firstly consider future methods. We can make callouts from future methods (this is one of the use cases for them) and so we can meet the first requirement. A future method cannot call another asynchronous method though, and so we cannot meet the second requirement using a future method.

Now let's think about Batch Apex. Batch Apex is able to make callouts, and Batch Apex can be chained to allow you to call items multiple times. So, it seems that Batch Apex would be a good option here, however, a feature of Batch Apex is that we always run at least two messages through the Apex queue.

The first is to run the `start` method, and the second is to run the `execute` method. In a situation where we have no batches to process, this is expensive and slow. In building out a solution for this problem, we would likely be creating some form of job record to process, or for marking our opportunity in some way, to define its status within this process. This would then get picked up by our Batch Apex `start` method for processing, but if no records were to be processed (perhaps picked up by another, earlier batch run), then we would have an expensive call to make.

This is where a Queueable Apex job comes in, and as noted, was one of the reasons that Queueable Apex was developed, to avoid these scenarios with empty batches. Queueable Apex allows you to chain methods together in an inexpensive way while providing you the governor limits and resource benefits of being in an asynchronous context. Let's have a look at how Queueable Apex compares to both future methods and Batch Apex more explicitly.

Queueable versus future

Future methods, as discussed in *Chapter 7, Utilizing Future Methods*, are designed for one-off long-running processes. We can pass in simple primitive data types to a future method, which will then retrieve the data needed to run the remaining code in the process. When retrieving records from the database to use directly, this is a simple task, however, if the data needs processing into a different format to work with, we may end up repeating the effort we have already undertaken in determining how the record should be processed.

Additionally, as noted in the previous section, we cannot call a future method from within a future method. This means, for situations where we are making a callout that we may wish to retry, we cannot have a simple way of automatically retrying the callout, and instead have to log the exception in some format again, for processing.

Finally, when you invoke a future method, no job ID is returned, making it difficult to monitor the status of the job and ensure that it has processed correctly or see if an error has occurred.

Queueable Apex resolves all of these issues. Firstly, Queueable Apex, like Batch Apex, provides an interface that allows you to set non-primitive member variables that can be accessed when the job executes. Upon enqueuing the job, you receive a job ID in the same way you do for a Batch Apex invocation. This allows you to monitor the job through your Apex code, making it easier to report any statuses to end users. Finally, Queueable Apex jobs can enqueue other Queueable Apex jobs, allowing you to chain jobs together.

Does this mean we should only use Queueable Apex and not future methods? Absolutely not. Future methods are a far better solution when making one-off callouts or requests to external systems, or when trying to circumvent issues such as the mixed DML error we discussed at the start of *Chapter 7, Utilizing Future Methods*.

As an example, I was integrating with a solution that provided analytics on email and chat data from within Service Cloud. Whenever an email was sent to a customer or a chat with a customer was finished, the transcript of the email/chat and other information needed to be sent to the third-party system to analyze how well the agent was performing. This functionality was achieved using future methods as we did not need to retry on failure (there was no need for all messages to be processed) and would be sending data from the relevant sObject and so we only required the ID for the record to load the records for sending into memory.

Queueable versus Batch

As discussed in the *What Is Queueable Apex?* section, whenever you invoke a Batch Apex job, at least two messages will run through the Apex queue, the first to process the `start` method within the Batch Apex class and the second to process the `execute` method. This is expensive from the perspective of the platform as it may be running these two messages when there is only a single record to process, which could instead be handled by a future method or Queueable Apex job.

I like to think of Queueable Apex as a Batch Apex job that I can chain more easily and that I have to define the inputs for explicitly. In a Batch Apex implementation, we have the `start` method to define scope for the batches we are processing. In Queueable Apex, we have to manually set the scope through the Queueable instance instantiation and can then work with the data as we wish.

As a note, when re-queuing jobs using Queueable Apex, a delay will be added before the job is enqueued again, starting at 1 second and rising to 1 minute. To promote the use of Queueable Apex over Batch Apex for these use cases, the same done in Batch Apex has a maximum enqueuing gap of 4 minutes, meaning that if you are creating a near-infinite loop of jobs, the job will be 4 times slower in a Batch Apex implementation than using Queueable Apex.

Now that we have understood what the driver behind the creation of the Queueable Apex framework was at a high level and how it compares to both future methods and Batch Apex, we will next review some common use cases for Queueable Apex.

When to use Queueable Apex

There are three primary use cases for Queueable Apex, which we will discuss in this section, however, you may notice that some of them overlap with use cases we previously discussed for future methods and Batch Apex. This is because there is typically no one right answer for how you should look to architect and develop a solution—although there are often many wrong ways of doing things. When working on some of these overlapping use cases, the key question to consider is whether you wish to chain the asynchronous process you are building. If the answer is yes, then you are almost always going to get the best results using a Queueable Apex implementation. Let's now look at some common use cases in the following sections.

Extensive or complex processes

The first key use case is for extensive or complex database processes. What do I mean by this? As we know, Salesforce has a series of governor limits that are in place to ensure that resources are not monopolized by a single user or process. For most transactions, this is not a problem and the governor limits merely act as guide rails to keep you on the right track. However, in certain instances, you will need to perform a task that will consume a larger volume of resources than is available. This is one such use case for splitting the job into a multi-stage process using Queueable Apex.

Let's look at an example. We are managing tech conferences and typically organizing events where around 5,000 people attend. We have created a tool in Apex to manage the building of agendas for attendees and wish to pre-populate the agenda with certain items for attendees:

- All attendees should have the opening and closing keynotes added to their agenda.

- If the attendee has a premium pass (around 500 of the attendees), the CEO briefing session should be added to their agenda.

- If the attendee has indicated they are a developer, the developer keynote should be added to their agenda.

Agenda items are stored as a junction record between attendee and session. This simple-sounding example highlights a prime extensive process that would be best solved using a Queueable Apex job.

Firstly, note that we cannot do this in a single transaction (synchronous or asynchronous) as this would break the governor limit for the maximum number of 10,000 records processed by DML statements. We should therefore split this into four Queueable Apex jobs that chain together:

1. Create the opening keynote entries.
2. Create the closing keynote entries.
3. Create the premium pass entries.
4. Create the developer entries.

By separating out the process like this, we can ensure that all of our updates are done in an asynchronous manner, that we stay inside our governor limits, and that we have separated out our code into a cleaner structure, whereby each job here has its own function.

Callouts

Another common use case is when dealing with callouts. There are, broadly speaking, two situations you will find you have when managing callouts: you will either need the callouts to all succeed and be received by the external system, or you will have a situation where failed messages do not need retrying. It is also common to require a series of callouts to a web service to perform an action, particularly when working with RESTful services. If we consider the example of placing an order that was highlighted at the beginning of the chapter, we have a combination of both callouts that should be retried on certain failure conditions and that are reliant on information from previous callouts.

Again, this is a good use case for Queueable Apex. Should a callout fail within a Queueable Apex job, you can re-enqueue the job and attempt to retry the callout. This is particularly important for callouts that while asynchronous are still somewhat time-sensitive—the job can be re-enqueued and should undergo processing within a minute.

Chained processes

We have already discussed how chaining is a key feature of Queueable Apex, and in the two use cases in the preceding sections, we have highlighted how useful it is to be able to chain Queueable Apex jobs together. In this use case for chained processes, I am referring in particular to those processes where the order of execution is important.

For example, say we had a requirement to process and update a large volume of accounts, then the related contacts, and then any open opportunities within those accounts. An example may be that we have updated our account model for organizations denoted as high-value, key target, and so on, and wish to update relevant data to reflect this. We would want to update the account information first, then use this information when updating the contacts and opportunities. In this type of ordered process, a Queueable Apex implementation allows us to maintain the order of processing we desire and split the work appropriately.

Now that we have discussed some of the main Queueable Apex use cases, we will look at how we can define a Queueable Apex class.

Defining Queueable Apex implementations

Queueable Apex, like Batch Apex, is defined through the implementation of an Apex interface, in this case, the `Queueable` interface.

To define a Queueable Apex job, we simply implement this interface, which has a single method, `execute(QueueableContext context)`. A very basic implementation would then be the following:

```
public class ExampleQueueable implements Queueable {
    public void execute(QueueableContext context) {
        //Do something
    }
}
```

As we discussed, unlike our Batch Apex implementations, we must define the scope for the Queueable Apex job to process. We can do this in two ways. We can do it through the use of a query within our `execute` method:

```
public class ExampleQueueable implements Queueable {
    public void execute(QueueableContext context) {
        List<Account> accs = [SELECT Id, Name FROM Account
        WHERE NumberOfEmployees > 1000];
        //Process accs
    }
}
```

Or the second way—through the use of member variables:

```
public class ExampleQueueable implements Queueable {

    public List<Account> accs;

    public ExampleQueueable(List<Account> scope) {
        accs = scope;
    }

    public void execute(QueueableContext context) {
        //Process accs
    }
}
```

This is similar to how we would define a future method, a single method (in this case, always called `execute`) that is invoked asynchronously, however, instead of the method being separated from any state, we can now define the state through the use of member variables that allow us a far greater degree of control. Note that the ExampleQueueable class is like any other Apex class and so can have complex Apex types as member variables should the developer wish to pass some custom data state to the queueable job. Refer to the following code block:

```
public class ExampleQueueable implements Queueable {

    public List<MyCustomApexType> dataToProcess;

    public ExampleQueueable(List<MyCustomApexType> scope) {
        dataToProcess = scope;
    }

    public void execute(QueueableContext context) {
        //Process accs
    }
}
```

This is similar to the `ExampleInitialisedBatch` case we saw in *Chapter 8, Working with Batch Apex.*

Allowing callouts

Also similar to our Batch Apex constructs, we enable the class to make callouts to external services by implementing the `Database.AllowsCallouts` interface. Refer to the following code:

```
public class ExampleCalloutQueueable implements Queueable,
Database.AllowsCallouts {
    public void execute(QueueableContext context) {
        //Generate and send a HTTP request
    }
}
```

Our `execute` method is limited to 100 callouts per invocation, however, I have found it easier to chain together different Queueable jobs when making a high volume of callouts in this manner. Most notably, it can become very difficult to manage and handle the responses from such a large number of callouts in a way that is easy to read.

Apex does not have the concept of promises or `async/await` functions and so merely blocks the transaction until the callout is complete. As we require a callout to succeed before another can be made, it is a common practice to group callouts in such long-running processes into smaller bundles to execute and chain together.

We have now seen how we can implement the `Queueable` interface to provide a Queueable Apex class, but how do we enqueue our job? Let's see in the next section.

Invoking Queueable Apex

Queueable Apex jobs are invoked using the `System.enqueueJob` method as shown in the following code snippet:

```
Id apexJobId = System.enqueueJob(new ExampleQueueable());
```

As is shown, the `System.enqueueJob` method returns an `Id` for an `AsyncApexJob` sObject instance that we can use to monitor the status of the Queueable Apex job in the same way we monitor the job in a Batch Apex context. It should be noted, however, that as Queueable Apex does not process batches of records, `JobItemsProcessed` and `TotalJobItems` will always return 0.

From a synchronous Apex process, we can enqueue 50 jobs but can only enqueue a single job when enqueuing from a Batch Apex or Queueable Apex class (more on this in the next section). There are some shared ways of circumventing this that can be found on the internet, such as scheduling another Apex job that will enqueue the job should you be at the limit of the available jobs in the queue. I would not recommend this for a number of reasons. Firstly, you should see this as a code smell for your architecture. If you have more than 50 jobs enqueued at once, then you should consider whether you need to segment your system further and consider a more distributed event-driven architecture with platform events (see *Chapter 11, Using Platform Events*) or whether your processes are taking too long to complete. Secondly, as your system usage grows, you are likely to continue to encounter this problem, except now the scheduled job will be failing instead and there will be a less direct debugging connection. Let's see more about this in the next section.

Enqueuing child/chained jobs

As mentioned many times throughout this chapter, one of the key features of the Queueable Apex framework is the ability to chain jobs together. A Queueable Apex job can enqueue another job using the same `System.enqueueJob` method as in the preceding section:

```
public class ExampleQueueable1 implements Queueable {
    public void execute(QueueableContext context) {
        //Perform processing
        System.enqueueJob(new ExampleQueueable2());
    }
}
```

As highlighted in the preceding code, you are limited to a single call to `System.enqueueJob` from within a `Queueable` Apex method.

When writing code that chains multiple jobs together, you should include a check for whether the code is currently running in a test context using the `Test.isRunningTest` method. If you attempt to chain a queueable job inside a test context, an exception will be thrown. To avoid this, you should structure your chaining call as follows:

```
public class ExampleQueueable1 implements Queueable {
    public void execute(QueueableContext context) {
        //Perform processing
        if(!Test.isRunningTest()) {
```

```
                    System.enqueueJob(new ExampleQueueable2());
            }
        }
    }
```

Finally, let's look at how we can test Queueable Apex more generally.

Testing Queueable Apex

To test Queueable Apex, we follow the same pattern we have used for all our asynchronous code. We place the `System.enqueueJob` call between a `Test.startTest` method call and a `Test.stopTest` method call to run the asynchronous process synchronously:

```
@isTest
private class ExampleQueueable_Test {

    @isTest
    private static void testExecute() {
        Test.startTest();
        System.enqueueJob(new ExampleQueueable());
        Test.stopTest();
        //Assert on expected changes
    }
}
```

Note that if you were to run the following code:

```
@isTest
private class ExampleQueueable_Test {

    @isTest
    private static void testExecute() {
        Test.startTest();
        Id apexJobId = System.enqueueJob(new
        ExampleQueueable());
        Test.stopTest();
        System.assertNotEquals(null, apexJobId);
    }
}
```

The test would fail as the `System.enqueueJob` method does not return an `Id` from within a test context, instead always returning `null`.

Summary

In this chapter, we have looked at how we can use Queueable Apex as a way of allowing us to perform long-running or chained processes efficiently. As we have seen, Queueable Apex is a hybrid of future methods and Batch Apex, allowing developers to build out solutions that can execute efficiently and chain processes together where required.

We started the chapter by seeing how Queueable Apex compares to both future methods and Batch Apex, including discussing the historical context behind the tool being introduced. We then looked at specific use cases that are well suited to Queueable Apex, namely those where we may want to chain multiple items together. We also discussed how we can think about separating out our existing processes into a format that will work well in a queueable context and avoid governor limits.

We then saw how we define and invoke Queueable Apex classes and how to chain jobs together. Finally, we discussed some of the nuances of testing Queueable Apex to ensure that we do not receive errors when chaining jobs or attempt to refer to the `AsyncApexJob` ID, which is not returned in a test context.

In the next chapter, we will discuss how to use Scheduled Apex. We have already highlighted some of the use cases of Scheduled Apex in *Chapter 8, Working with Batch Apex*, and now we will build upon some of this earlier discussion to review how we can most effectively schedule Apex jobs.

10
Scheduling
Apex Jobs

In this chapter, we are going to discuss how we can schedule Apex jobs to run at some predetermined point in the future or on a regular basis. All the asynchronous processing options we have seen so far – future methods, Batch Apex, and Queueable Apex – run when resources are available after being invoked in as near to real time as possible (except for scheduled Batch Apex, which we will discuss in more detail later). We invoke our future, batch, or queueable method, and whenever resources are available, Salesforce will process the request and execute our code.

Scheduled Apex jobs, on the other hand (including scheduled batch jobs), execute on or after a desired time is set is by the developer. This could be a single time as a one-off execution (for example, updating a series of records when a new field is added), or on a more regular scheduled basis, based on your use case – for example, nightly integration sync.

In this chapter, we are going to review some of these use cases and the different ways in which we can schedule an Apex job to run, as well as how to monitor it once it has been scheduled.

Technical Requirements

The code for the chapter can be found here: `https://github.com/PacktPublishing/Mastering-Apex-Programming/tree/Chapter-10`

The following topics are covered in this chapter:

- When to use Scheduled Apex jobs
- Defining a Schedulable Apex class
- Invoking Scheduled Apex
- Testing scheduled jobs and Apex scheduling

Let's start by reviewing the two main use cases for Scheduled Apex.

When to use Scheduled Apex jobs

Quite simply, and somewhat obviously, as the name implies, you should use Scheduled Apex whenever you wish to schedule an Apex job you have defined to run at some point in the future, without a need for you as a developer or system administrator to begin the execution or invoke the job at that time. Broadly, speaking there are two types of jobs you will want to schedule: one-off executions and repeating jobs. We will now review both of those use cases.

One-off executions

A one-off execution is any Apex job that you wish to fire once, and only once, throughout the life cycle of the application. Typically, you will want to run this job at a time of day when it is not ideal for you to be available, such as after working hours when you can update data with no end users on the system.

An example of this type of job is populating a new field on an object en masse when it cannot be done via a data loader. If we have a complex process to populate a large volume of records, then we will likely perform this through a Batch Apex job. We will typically want to run this update outside of standard working hours, such as in the evening or on the weekend, when we will minimize the chance of impacting users. However, this is not an ideal time for a developer or system administrator to be logging in to perform the work. A better option, therefore, is to schedule this job to run at a preset time to avoid the need for any manual intervention and allow the operation to run when resources become available.

Repeating jobs

Unlike a one-off job, such as an update, you may have repeating jobs that you wish to process on a regularly scheduled basis. A good example is a nightly synchronization with an external system. In this scenario, we will want any changes made throughout the day to synchronize with the external system out of hours, say at midnight, to keep the two systems aligned. This is particularly common when working with legacy enterprise systems.

We can also schedule jobs more regularly than this – for example, running every 5 minutes – however, we will need to be mindful of the fact that when we schedule work in Apex, the job will execute as soon as resources are available to process the job after the scheduled time. This means that while we may have the job scheduled to run at 3 P.M. (for example), it may not actually run until 3:03 P.M. due to resource unavailability. If the process then does not complete until 3:06 P.M. (a batch job with callouts, for example), then our second job may have fired at 3:05 P.M.. This can cause clashes due to record locking, or further delay in the running of later jobs as resources are unavailable. From experience, I would suggest, therefore, that you aim to have any scheduled jobs running at most every 10 or 15 minutes to minimize this risk.

Let's now look at how we define an Apex class that we can schedule.

Defining a schedulable Apex class

We define an Apex class that can be scheduled by implementing the `Schedulable` interface. Similar to our `Queueable` interface, it provides a single method, `execute`, which we must implement. We can see this in the following code:

```
public class SchedulableExample implements Schedulable {
    public void execute(SchedulableContext SC) {
        //Do something
    }
}
```

From the preceding code, we see that within the `execute` method, it is best practice to make a call to another class containing the logic we wish to run, rather than explicitly declaring the logic within the `execute` method itself. This primarily helps to ensure that you reuse code as much as possible and manage your separation of concerns, but this also makes the processing code easier to test by allowing you to test separately from the scheduled execution setup.

It is also important to recognize that our `SchedulableExample` class can contain member variables and other functions, just as our Batch Apex and Queueable Apex implementations could. Should we wish to propagate some state through to the `execute` method, we could do so using a member variable, for example:

```
public class SchedulableExample implements Schedulable {

    private Id accountId;

    public SchedulableExample(Id accId) {
        accountId = accId;
    }

    public void execute(SchedulableContext SC) {
      AccountUtility.doSomethingToThisAccount(accountId);
    }
}
```

From the preceding code, we can see that defining an Apex class for scheduling is a simple process, but once we have defined a class, how do we schedule it for use?

Scheduling an Apex class

We can schedule an Apex class using either the point-and-click **Apex Scheduler**, or programmatically using the `System.schedule` method. Both options have pros and cons, which we will discuss as we see how to schedule an Apex class in this section.

Using the Apex Scheduler

The simplest way to schedule an Apex job is to use the built-in point-and-click **Apex Scheduler**. To access the scheduler, go to the **Apex Classes** page within the **SETUP** menu and press the **Schedule Apex** button, as highlighted in the following screenshot:

Figure 10.1 – The Schedule Apex button

Upon clicking this button, you will be presented with the **Apex Scheduler** page, which will allow you to schedule an Apex class, as seen in the following screenshot. You need to provide the following values for your scheduled job:

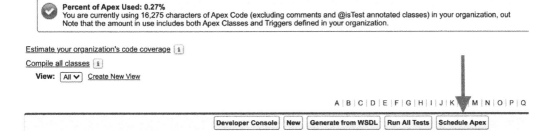

Figure 10.2 – Scheduling an Apex job

As can be seen from the preceding screenshot, we have the following fields:

- **Job Name**: A name for the job that you can use when monitoring.

- **Apex Class**: This must be an Apex class implementing the `Schedulable` interface.

- **Frequency**: Select how often you wish the job to run. Note that a weekly job with each day selected is a daily job.

- **Start**: Choose a date on which this job should begin executing.

- **End**: Choose a final execution date for this job. I have selected the same date, so this job will execute only once.

- **Preferred Start Time**: When you would like the job to execute. Note that this is in the running user's locale.

Upon clicking **Save**, the job will be scheduled.

In this example, I scheduled the following `SchedulableExample` class:

```
public class SchedulableExample implements Schedulable {
    public void execute(SchedulableContext SC) {
        System.debug('I was executed at ' + Datetime.now());
    }
}
```

In the `execute` method, we are outputting the actual time that the method was executed. This code was scheduled to run at 9 A.M. in a Developer Edition with no other work ongoing, so it executed at the time we expected, as shown in *Figure 10.3*:

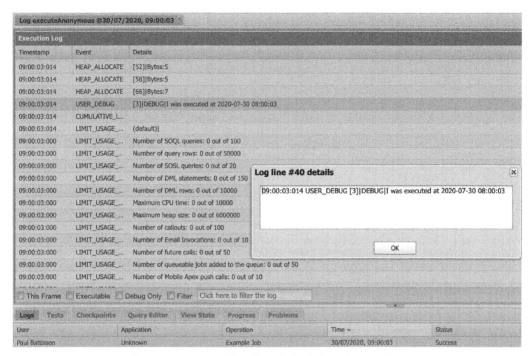

Figure 10.3 – The debug log of scheduled job execution

Note that the time displayed in the log is in UTC time and my locale is British Summer Time, at the time of writing, and so it is 1 hour ahead of UTC.

This is the simplest way of scheduling an Apex class to run but limits you to a single daily execution that must be on the hour; you cannot select, for example, 09:30 as the start time. While the Apex Scheduler is therefore extremely useful in certain situations, if we require more control over the start time or wish to schedule items programmatically, we need to use the `System.schedule` method. So, let's see that next.

Using the System.schedule method

The `System.schedule` method allows you to define a more precise string to define the date and time at which you want a job to run, using a CRON expression. The `System.schedule` method takes in the following three parameters:

- A name for the job run

- A CRON expression to represent the date and time the job should run

- The name of the Apex class to run, which must implement the `Schedulable` interface

The CRON expression here follows the standard CRON conventions used in UNIX-based systems. The expression is a string in the following format:

```
Seconds Minutes Hours Day_of_Month Month Day_of_Week Year_
Optional
```

The parameters here all have strict values that can and cannot be set, as shown in this table:

Parameter	Available Values	Available Special Characters
Seconds	0–59	None
Minutes	0–59	None
Hours	0–23	None
Day_of_Month	1–31	, - * ? / L W
Month	1–12 or the following:	, - * /
	JAN	
	FEB	
	MAR	
	APR	
	MAY	
	JUN	
	JUL	
	AUG	
	SEP	
	OCT	
	NOV	
	DEC	
Day_of_Week	1–7 or the following:	, - * ? / L #
	SUN	
	MON	
	TUE	
	WED	
	THU	
	FRI	
	SAT	
Year_Optional	1970–2099 if provided or null	, - * /

Table 10.1

The special characters noted in the preceding table have the following meaning:

Character	Meaning
,	Used as a delimiter for a list of values – for example, JUN, JUL, AUG when specifying multiple months.
-	Used to specify a range of values – for example, MON-WED when specifying multiple days.
*	Specifies all values – for example, if Day_of_Month is given as *, then it will run every day of the month.
?	Denotes no specific value and is used by Day_of_Week or Day_of_Month when a value is specified in the other parameter.
/	Used to specify increments, with the number before / denoting the interval start and the number following is the interval amount. In the Day_of_Month parameter, 3/4 denotes the first instance as the third of the month, with every fourth day following.
L	Specifies the last value in a range – for example, January 31 or February 29 on a leap year when used in the Day_of_Month parameter. This character can be used alone in the Day_of_Week parameter to denote SAT or 7, or be used in conjunction with a day value to choose the last instance of that day in the month – for example, 6L is the last Friday of the month.
W	This is used to specify the nearest weekday for a given day in the Day_of_Month parameter – for example, 4W will run on the nearest weekday to the fourth of the month.
#	Denotes the nth day of the month in the Day_of_Week parameter. The number before # is the day of the week and the value after is the day of the month. 3#2 is the second Tuesday of the month.

Table 10.2

We can then use these values to create more specific and complex scheduling strings, such as the following:

- The 0 0 20 * * ? expression will run the class daily at 8 P.M., a standard daily job.

- The 0 30 22 ? * LW expression will run the class on the last weekday of every month at 10:30 P.M., a job such as an end-of-month invoicing run.

If we wished to schedule our `SchedulableExample` class to run every working weekday (Monday–Friday) at 6 A.M. in 2021, the code snippet would be as follows:

```
String cronExp = '0 0 6 ? * MON-FRI 2021';
System.schedule('Daily 6A.M. Job 2021', cronExp, new
SchedulableExample());
```

This is an extremely granular level of control for scheduling our jobs and allows us, as developers, a more succinct programmatic way of controlling program behavior. As the CRON expression is a simple string, it is not uncommon to wrap the call to `System.schedule` within a `public` method that accepts the CRON expression as a parameter to enable the developer to schedule the job using Execute Anonymous.

System.schedule versus System.scheduleBatch for Batch Apex classes

In *Chapter 8, Working with Batch Apex*, we saw the `System.scheduleBatch` method as a way of scheduling a Batch Apex class to run at some point in the future. I briefly want to touch on the usage of `System.scheduleBatch` versus the use of `System.schedule`.

`System.scheduleBatch` will only schedule a Batch Apex class for a single execution at the desired time; it will not allow the job to be scheduled for repeated execution. It is also available for any Batch Apex class and does not require you to implement the `Schedulable` interface. Should you need to run a Batch Apex job once, then the `System.scheduleBatch` method should be the preferred method.

We also saw, in the *Working with a scheduled class and custom metadata* section in *Chapter 8, Working with Batch Apex*, that we can use a scheduled job and custom metadata to enable us to execute multiple Batch Apex jobs on a scheduled basis. The code we had to retrieve our custom metadata and execute our batches was as follows:

```
List<Batch_Job__mdt> jobs = [SELECT DeveloperName, Scope__c
FROM Batch_Job__mdt WHERE Active__c = true];

for(Batch_Job__mdt job : jobs) {
    Type jobType = Type.forName(job.DeveloperName);
    Database.executeBatch((Database.Batchable<sObject>)
    jobType.newInstance(), job.Scope__c);
}
```

If we wished to have this series of batch jobs that were run every night, then we would include this code in the execute method of our class implementing the Schedulable interface, as follows:

```
public class NightlyBatches implements Schedulable {
    public void execute(SchedulableContext SC) {
        List<Batch_Job__mdt> jobs = [SELECT DeveloperName,
        Scope__c FROM Batch_Job__mdt WHERE Active__c = true];

        for(Batch_Job__mdt job : jobs) {
            Type jobType = Type.forName(job.
            DeveloperName);
            Database.executeBatch((Database.
            Batchable<sObject>)jobType.newInstance(),
            job.Scope__c);
        }
    }
}
```

We could then schedule our NightlyBatches class to run at 11 P.M. every night:

```
String cronExp = '0 0 23 * * ?';
System.schedule('Nightly batch jobs', cronExp, new
NightlyBatches());
```

This is a common pattern for executing multiple nightly batch jobs for archiving and data deletion scenarios. We have shown a nightly schedule here, but you could easily extend this class to take in parameters via the constructor to filter the Batch_Job__mdt records returned, allowing you to have a more universal scheduling class. It is not uncommon to see organizations have multiple scheduling classes that could be abstracted to become more dynamic and allow the running of batches to be determined at runtime.

From within a Scheduled Apex class, you can call to execute a Batch Apex class, a Queueable Apex class, and a future method. You can also schedule another Scheduled Apex class from within a scheduled job. However, this is not advised and it is known as suicidal scheduling, which we will now discuss.

Suicidal scheduling

Historically, there was a situation where developers would call the `System.schedule` method from within a scheduled job, and then abort the scheduled job they were in. This is known as *suicidal scheduling*. A common use case for this was to enable a developer to run a scheduled job at a high frequency, such as every minute.

Salesforce as a solution has a shared set of resources among all users of the platform. These resources are shared and controlled through the use of governor limits to ensure that every customer on the platform gets their fair usage of the resources as part of the multi-tenant framework. Suicidal scheduling is one attempt to try and circumvent this set of limits to allow a single tenant to run jobs at a high frequency. It should be noted that in general, Salesforce is a transactional database platform and is not suited to such a high-volume approach where you want to run such scheduled jobs. It is an extremely powerful and performant platform but is not suitable for running such loads. If you find yourself needing to run a scheduled job at such a frequency, then you should consider adding an external processing solution to your architecture, such as Heroku, to perform this processing for you. An example use case is checking a third-party API for changes. You can either update the logic to run more infrequently, as we will discuss ahead, or migrate this portion of processing to an external platform such as Heroku to query for the changes and push them into Salesforce.

Salesforce has imposed a limit of a minimum 5-minute window before any call to `System.schedule` inside a scheduled job for it to execute. Should you wish to run a scheduled job every 5 minutes, the best practice is to make a series of 30 independent calls to `System.schedule` to create 30 independent jobs scheduled to run every 5 minutes. In my experience, a frequency of every 5 minutes is more than reasonable for 99% of use cases and will allow you to stay within the execution limits.

Once we have scheduled a job, be it using the **Apex Scheduler** or the `System.schedule` method one or more times, how do we then monitor the jobs?

Monitoring a scheduled job

There are a number of ways in which we can monitor a job once it has been scheduled that provide different capabilities. The simplest, and in my opinion the most useful, of these is the **Scheduled Jobs** page within the **SETUP** menu:

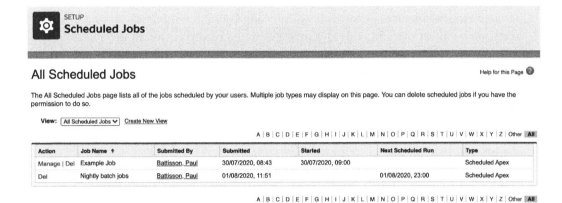

Figure 10.4 – The Scheduled Jobs page

From the page, we can see all the jobs that have been scheduled, their status, and when they are next scheduled to run. We can also remove scheduled jobs by clicking the **Del** link on the far left of the list view. For jobs that have executed and are no longer running, such as our example job in the top row, we can also use the **Manage** link to reschedule the job. This page provides the simplest view of all our scheduled jobs and provides an easy way to manage them.

Scheduled jobs are a form of asynchronous Apex that also show in the **Apex Jobs** page in the **SETUP** menu, as shown in the following screenshot. While available for monitoring here, the information provided is limited, and this view does not allow us to take any action:

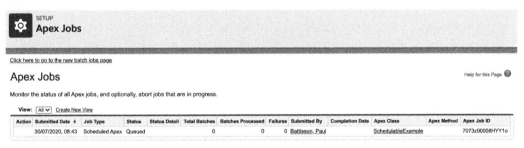

Figure 10.5 – The Apex Jobs page with a scheduled job

What the view does include, however, is an Apex job ID value, which is returned by our `System.schedule` method. This ID correlates to the record ID for an instance of the `CronTrigger` sObject. If we query the `CronTrigger` sObject using this ID, we can retrieve information about the scheduled job and its status, as shown in the following query:

```
CronTrigger ct = [SELECT TimesTriggered, NextFireTime, State,
CronJobDetail.Id, CronJobDetail.Name FROM CronTrigger WHERE Id
= :jobID];
```

In this query, we are also getting information from the associated `CronJobDetail` record, which holds information about the scheduled job and its type. The use of the job ID and queries allows more customized reporting to be produced should it be needed. If you need, the scheduled job can also obtain its own job ID within the `execute` method using the `SchedulableContext` instance passed into the `execute` method. Assuming you have followed the same naming convention for `SC` as the `SchedulableContext` instance parameter, you can retrieve the ID using the following:

```
SC.getTriggerId()
```

The `CronDetail` sObject also includes a `JobType` field that details the type of job that is scheduled. The full list of values can be found in the Salesforce documentation, but the value 7 corresponds to a Scheduled Apex job. We could, therefore, retrieve a count of all the currently scheduled jobs that are of the Scheduled Apex type by running the following query:

```
SELECT COUNT() FROM CronTrigger WHERE CronJobDetail.JobType =
'7'
```

This is a useful query to have as it can allow us to ensure that we stay within the governor limits for the number of scheduled jobs we can have within an org. Let's now review some of the limits around Scheduled Apex.

Scheduled job limits

There are two primary limits that we must be aware of when working with Scheduled Apex. The first is the overall org limit for the number of asynchronous Apex jobs in a 24-hour period (set at the maximum of 250,000 or 200 x the number of user licenses). As discussed, this limit is shared among all the asynchronous Apex functions within the org, and so we need to ensure that we keep this in mind when architecting and designing our solution.

The other primary limit for Scheduled Apex is the limit to the maximum number of Scheduled Apex jobs of 100. The query utilizing the `CronJobDetail.JobType` parameter we ended the last section with provides a simple way of allowing us to easily verify that we are not going to surpass that limit when scheduling a new job. The most common instances where this occurs are when a developer has decided to schedule an Apex job from a trigger context without considering situations involving bulk API updates, data loading, or mass record changes. Particular attention should be paid to ensuring that when adding code to schedule an Apex job, it will not be accidentally invoked a large number of times in a bulk situation.

It should be noted that while web service callouts are not possible within a Scheduled Apex job – that is, in a synchronous manner – the scheduled class can still make callouts asynchronously through the use of future methods annotated as `@future(callout = true)` or by invoking a Batch or Queueable Apex job.

Finally, during a scheduled maintenance window for Salesforce, scheduled jobs that would run during the window will run after the maintenance has occurred and will be rolled back and restarted after the window, if they were executing when maintenance occurred. There may be an increased delay before a job starts after a maintenance window as resource usage spikes.

Now that we understand how to monitor jobs we have scheduled, let's finish this chapter by discussing how to correctly test Scheduled Apex classes.

Testing scheduled jobs and Apex scheduling

Scheduled Apex, as discussed, is a form of asynchronous Apex and, therefore, we should utilize the `Test.startTest()` and `Test.stopTest` methods to ensure that the asynchronous code executes within our test method. Suppose we had the following class for testing:

```
public class SchedulableExample implements Schedulable {
    public void execute(SchedulableContext SC) {
        Account a = new Account();
        a.Name = String.valueOf(DateTime.now());
        insert a;
    }
}
```

This code is not overly useful, but will allow us to illustrate the testing of Scheduled Apex. If we are scheduling this job using the Apex Scheduler or the `System.schedule` method via Execute Anonymous, we can write our test to simply schedule the class at any point and verify the results of the action once the `Test.stopTest` method has occurred. Some example code to do this is as follows:

```
@isTest
private class SchedulableExample_Test {

    @isTest
    private static void testScheduleAndCreateNewAccount() {

        Test.startTest();
        String cronExp = '0 0 23 * * ?';
        System.schedule('Example Scheduled Job', cronExp,
        new SchedulableExample());
        Test.stopTest();

        List<AggregateResult> results = [SELECT Count(Id) FROM
        Account];

        System.assertEquals(1, results[0].get('expr0'),
        'Account not created as expected');
    }
}
```

This code verifies that the `Account` record instance was created (as we are in a test context not using `seeAllData = true`, we know the only `Account` we can retrieve is our created record) and that our class executed as anticipated.

If we were executing `System.schedule` within another method and scheduling the code as part of another process, then we may wish to query the `CronTrigger` object to verify that it has been scheduled and that the expected execution time matches the schedule we have set.

Note that we have to be considerate here that tests can be run at any point, so we will not necessarily have an easy way of knowing what the date portion of the NextFireTime field will be. We can see an example of using these parameters in the following snippet:

```
@isTest
private class SchedulableExample_Test {

    @isTest
    private static void testScheduleAndCreateNewAccount() {

        Test.startTest();
        String cronExp = '0 0 23 * * ?';
        String jobId = System.schedule('Example Scheduled
        Job', cronExp, new SchedulableExample());

        CronTrigger ct = [SELECT Id, TimesTriggered,
        NextFireTime FROM CronTrigger WHERE id = :jobId];

        System.assertEquals(0, ct.TimesTriggered);

        Time expected = Time.newInstance(23, 0, 0, 0);
        System.assertEquals(expected, ct.NextFireTime.time());

        Test.stopTest();

        List<AggregateResult> results = [SELECT Count(Id) FROM
        Account];

        System.assertEquals(1, results[0].get('expr0'),
        'Account not created as expected');
    }
}
```

In this updated snippet, we are verifying before calling `Test.stopTest()` that the time portion of our `NextFireTime` field is correct (this allows us to be agnostic of the timing of the test run from a date perspective. If we were verifying the date portion and ran this test at 23:01, we would need to accommodate for that in the code). We also check that the scheduled class has not been executed using the `TimesTriggered` field to confirm that we have scheduled the class as expected and that it has not fired immediately.

Summary

In this chapter, we looked in detail at how to use Scheduled Apex to define Apex classes that can be set to execute at some point in the future. We began the chapter by discussing the use cases for Scheduled Apex, namely one-off executions and repeating jobs. After discussing the definition of these use cases and how we might utilize Scheduled Apex, we looked at how we define an Apex class for scheduling by implementing the `Schedulable` interface.

The majority of the chapter was spent discussing the different ways we can schedule an Apex class, using either the Apex Scheduler or the `System.schedule` method, and the difference between this and `System.scheduleBatch`. After discussing the issues and limitations in place to prevent so-called *suicidal scheduling*, we looked at monitoring scheduled jobs and the limits in place around scheduling Apex classes.

We finished the chapter by reviewing how we can test Scheduled Apex code and the different ways of verifying behavior. This chapter finishes our discussion of the standard asynchronous Apex options within Salesforce. In the next chapter, we are going to discuss platform events, a relatively newer Salesforce feature that enables us to architect our application in an event-driven manner with certain functioning occurring asynchronously.

11
Using Platform Events

So far in our discussion of asynchronous processing, we have focused solely on the ways in which we can run Apex code asynchronously to handle appropriate tasks. While this is one asynchronous programming model available on the Salesforce platform, the primary focus of using the asynchronous methods we have discussed thus far is to allow you to work with an increased set of governor resources to perform some complex functionality, or to run a job at a pre-determined point in the future.

In this chapter, we are going to discuss a different model using platform events. Platform events are a relatively new addition to the Salesforce platform and enable developers and architects to design solutions differently, in a way that allows us to decouple and scale applications more readily.

In this chapter, we will discuss the following:

- What event-driven architecture is and how the event bus works
- When to use platform events
- How to define and publish a platform event using a variety of different mechanisms
- How to handle and subscribe to platform events on the Salesforce platform
- The relationship between platform events and the Change Data Capture functionality
- How to test platform events

Technical Requirements

The code for the chapter can be found here: `https://github.com/PacktPublishing/Mastering-Apex-Programming/tree/Chapter-11`

An overview of event-driven architecture and the event bus

At the time of writing, I have been working with the Salesforce platform for a little over 11 years. In that time, what started as a platform based primarily around sales and service-related applications has grown into a broad platform, delivering all manner of applications. In my work with Salesforce, I have delivered applications outside the traditional sales, service, and marketing business areas to banks, insurers, pharmaceutical companies, research organizations, retailers, fashion brands, and charities, to name just a handful.

As the scope and type of application on the platform has grown, architects have had to think of different ways to organize and manage applications to enable organizations to continue to deliver rapidly and operate at scale. Salesforce introduced platform events to assist architects and developers in meeting these needs using event-driven architectures.

Exploring event-driven architecture

We can think of an application as a series of modules, each focused on a single area of functionality, such as sales, billing, service, order management, and so on. A customer will typically move through many of these different modules within their life cycle, which we need to account for. For example, they may begin in the sales system as a prospect, before a deal with them is closed, upon which they enter both the billing and order management systems. Later, they may need assistance from the service department with their order during its processing, or after the order has been delivered.

While these separate modules are related, we can think of the interactions between them as being based upon a series of events. For example, the deal being closed is an event that the sales module can notify other modules about. Similarly, the order being dispatched is an event that the order management system can notify the other modules about.

By thinking of our application as a series of modules that are aware of specific events that they can act upon, we can think of a series of events being published by a variety of modules and then subscribed to, and consumed by other modules:

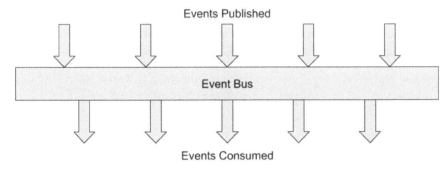

Figure 11.1 – Event publishers and subscribers

Figure 11.1 gives us this simple visualization. One or more different events or event types is published, with one or more subscribers consuming the events. There is no requirement for a one-to-one mapping between publishers and subscribers; an event can be published and consumed by 0 or more different subscribers. The place where these events are placed is called the **event bus**, which we will discuss now.

The event bus

When dealing with events as a means of application control, architects and developers can choose to use either an event bus or a message queue for managing the flow of events or messages throughout the system. While these terms are now used in a largely interchangeable way by many vendors, there is a difference in the way in which the underlying solutions work that is of particular importance for us.

In a message queue, messages are sent between systems in first-in-first-out order with a single subscriber pulling messages off a queue for processing. Each subscriber (or set of subscribers in a more horizontally scaled system) will have a separate queue or channel for messages to be sent to, from which it will pull messages for processing.

By comparison, with an event bus, events are published to a channel on the bus and every subscriber of the channel is notified. This allows for a single event or message to be pushed to multiple subscribers for processing. This difference is beneficial for us as it allows us as developers to decouple our application modules more loosely and add new subscribers as we need.

Salesforce platform events use an event bus, which allows us to have multiple subscribers to a single event channel for processing. The simplest analogy to think of when picturing how platform events operate is a social network such as Twitter. On Twitter, I can publish events (tweets) to my channel (timeline with my Twitter handle). Others can then choose to subscribe to my events (follow my handle) and consume these events as they are published (by reading my tweets). Some consumers will take actions based upon the event details (a like or retweet), or may publish their own event in response (a reply). There is no limit to how many subscribers there are for a single Twitter user, and similarly, platform events can have many subscribers. If you can understand how Twitter works, then you can easily understand how platform events and the event bus operate.

With this basic understanding of event-driven architecture and what an event bus is, we will now review some of the primary use cases for platform events.

When to use platform events

In general, platform events can be used anywhere in the system where we wish to communicate asynchronously with another part of the system. I use the term asynchronously here as processors of platform events (as we will see) run in their own transaction and therefore may have a slight delay in processing. What follows are therefore the broad use cases most suitable for using platform events.

Asynchronous processes

A primary use case is that of running asynchronous processing of records that does not require an increased set of resources or heightened governor limits but may still not be possible in the current transaction. An example here would be if we were creating or updating a contact record and wanted to create a user for a community from this contact. This would lead to a mixed DML error in a single transaction, which can be triggered through a platform event once the contact has been updated.

Again, it is worth noting here that working with platform events will not provide you with a new transaction with increased governor limits, but will provide you with a second transaction. Asynchronous processing in this context is therefore more focused on splitting applications (refer to the *Decoupling applications* section ahead) instead of providing a method of performing long-running processes. For callouts and similar asynchronous functionality, platform events provide a useful mechanism, as we will discuss now.

External connections

A common scenario for developers is the need to connect to an external system and provide that system with updates from Salesforce. Although Salesforce does have a product for this in **Change Data Capture**, not all external systems can handle the connection required to process the updates, or there may be a need to send over data to the external system in a more processed or exact format. We may also want to trigger specific actions on an external system based upon events occurring within our Salesforce application, for example sending a notification to a user when a specific event occurs.

When working with platform events and external systems, we have two options for connecting: either the external system can consume the event directly or we can handle the event within Salesforce and make a callout to the external system via an API. Both options have their benefits and disadvantages, but the primary factor when deciding is whether the external system can be updated to consume events through a CometD polling channel. If so, then handling the event on the external application is typically the cleaner implementation and allows the applications to be decoupled in the best way. We will discuss handling platform events both on Salesforce and via a CometD connection from an external system later in this chapter.

I have noted in both of these first use cases that decoupling an application is a factor driving how to connect to an external application both using platform events and when running asynchronous processes. What do I mean by decoupling an application in this context and why is it a good use case, or driver of use cases, for platform events? Let's see.

Decoupling applications

At the beginning of this chapter, we started thinking of an application as a series of modules that work together to form the full application. Each of these modules, in an ideal structure, has its own locus of control and handles a discrete set of functionality. These modules can be entire systems or simply groups of functionality in an application. Ideally, we want to be able to keep these modules well delineated and separated to make it easier to switch or update modules in the future as part of our work to have both a scalable and flexible architecture.

To do this most effectively, we want to find a way for the separate modules to communicate without explicitly knowing about each other. For example, earlier we discussed the concept of a closed won opportunity creating an order in an order management system. The communication between these systems should be such that neither system is tied closely to the other. This is where we can utilize platform events for communication to great effect. When a particular state is reached or an action occurs, we can publish a platform event that can be consumed by any subscribing system to action. The publishing system does not need to be informed of which modules are consuming the events, nor does the consumer need to know which module is publishing.

Applications involving Salesforce have grown far more complex and involve a higher number of people and processes than ever before, and so decoupling an application as discussed can be a useful way to help ensure that a system can scale and grow appropriately, both in terms of processing performance and the ability of the organization to make changes to the application.

Now that we understand why we would utilize platform events, let's look at how we define a platform event for use.

Defining and publishing a platform event

A platform event is defined through the **Setup** menu under **Integrations | Platform Events**. Press the **New Platform Event** button to define a new platform event. From the perspective of metadata, platform events are similar to custom objects, except that they are suffixed by __e instead of __c. In the following screenshot, you can see the definition for a new platform event I will use within this chapter, `Demonstration`:

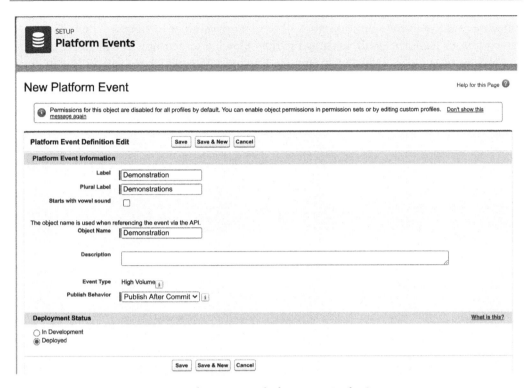

Figure 11.2 – Defining a new platform event in the Setup menu

Most of this screen looks identical to the screen to define a new custom object; however, we have one difference in the **Publish Behavior** picklist. The options available here are **Publish Immediately** or **Publish After Commit**. If the default **Publish After Commit** option is selected as shown, platform events published within a transaction will not be published until the end of the transaction, after any work has been committed and the transaction has succeeded. If an error occurs that causes the transaction to fail after the publish call is made, the event will not be published.

The alternative option is **Publish Immediately**. Choosing this will ensure that the platform event is published as soon as the publish call is made regardless of what else happens in the transaction. This can have potential side effects. For example, we may have an event published where we include the ID for a record to retrieve that has not been committed to the database yet. We therefore need to be cognizant of any assumptions we have in the order of how items are being processed and fired.

Once we save this event definition, we will see a screen similar to an object definition screen for our platform event, as shown in the following screenshot. The platform event contains some standard fields, including the **ReplayId** field, which we will discuss in detail later when looking at best practices for monitoring platform events:

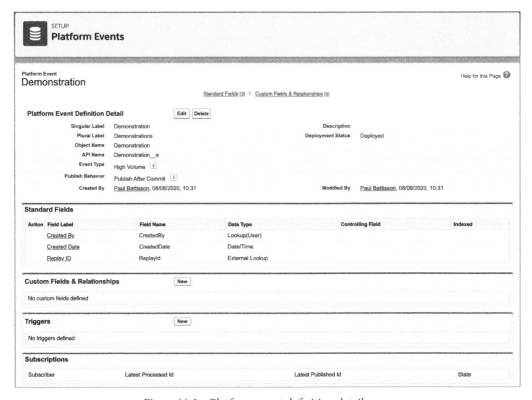

Figure 11.3 – Platform event definition detail page

We can also add custom fields to our platform events to allow us to send data throughout the system. Not all of the standard field types are supported for platform events, with only support for basic primitives.

In the following screenshot, we can see the definition for a custom field, `Message__c`, which will be used in the example code in the chapter to transfer a message:

Custom Fields & Relationships   New

Action	Field Label	API Name	Data Type	Indexed	Controlling Field
Edit | Del	Message	Message__c	Text(100)		

Figure 11.4 – Custom Message__c field definition

Now that we have a simple platform event defined, let's look at the different ways in which we can publish events to the event bus.

So, one of the best features of platform events is the fact that they can be published from a variety of sources within Salesforce, covering both programmatic and point-and-click tooling. This will allow us as developers to create scalable and decoupled applications that can be easily worked with by administrators. In this section, we will look at how we can publish platform events to the event bus using these different tools. While this book is focused on Apex, I think it is still important to cover these other options here to ensure that you can use the best tool available for the given use case.

Using Apex

When working with platform events in Apex, we must first define an instance of the event in memory, like we would do with a custom object, and then publish the event to the event bus. Just as with custom and standard objects, Salesforce automatically creates an Apex class for any platform event defined, which we can use to work with platform events in Apex.

In the following code snippet, we define a `public static` method, which allows us to pass a `message` string into the method and publish a `Demonstration__e` event to the event bus containing that message:

```
public with sharing class DemonstrationEventPublisher {

    public static void publishEventWithMessage(String message)
    {
        Demonstration__e demo = new Demonstration__e();
        demo.Message__c = message;
        Database.SaveResult result = Eventbus.publish(demo);
        System.debug('The publish event was a success: ' +
        result.isSuccess());
    }
}
```

If you save the preceding code and then call the `publishEventWithMessage` method through the **Execute Anonymous** window, you can publish an event to the event bus with the message we define, as follows:

```
DemonstrationEventPublisher.publishEventWithMessage('Hello');
```

If you view the debug log for this, you will see that the message was successfully published, as shown in the following screenshot:

Figure 11.5 – Successful publishing of our first event

We use the EventBus.publish() method to publish either a single platform event as shown, or multiple platform events by passing in a list. We could add a publishEventsWithMessages method that handles a list of messages as shown in the following code snippet, publishing all the events at once:

```
public static void publishEventsWithMessages (List<String>
messages) {
    List<Demonstration__e> demos = new List<Demonstration__
    e>();
    for(String message : messages) {
        Demonstration__e demo = new Demonstration__e();
        demo.Message__c = message;
        demos.add(demo);
    }
    Database.SaveResult result = Eventbus.publish(demos);
    System.debug('The publish event was a success: ' + result.
    isSuccess());
}
```

As we can see, it is simple to publish one or more events to the event bus in Apex using the provided Apex classes. Let's now look at how we can also send the same events using Process Builder.

Using Process Builder to publish events

We use the **Create a Record** action within Process Builder to fire platform events. In the following screenshot, you can see the base definition for a new process that will handle all actions for when a contact is inserted into the system:

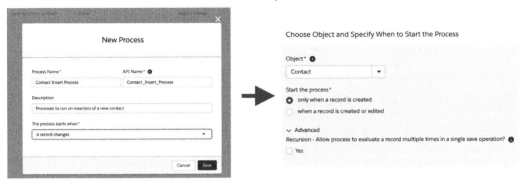

Figure 11.6 – Contact insert process definition

We then define a criterion called **Send Hello Message** that will fire whenever a new contact is inserted, that is, there are no set criteria, as shown in the following screenshot:

Define Criteria for this Action Group

Criteria Name * ⓘ

Send Hello Message

Criteria for Executing Actions *

○ Conditions are met

○ Formula evaluates to true

◉ No criteria–just execute the actions!

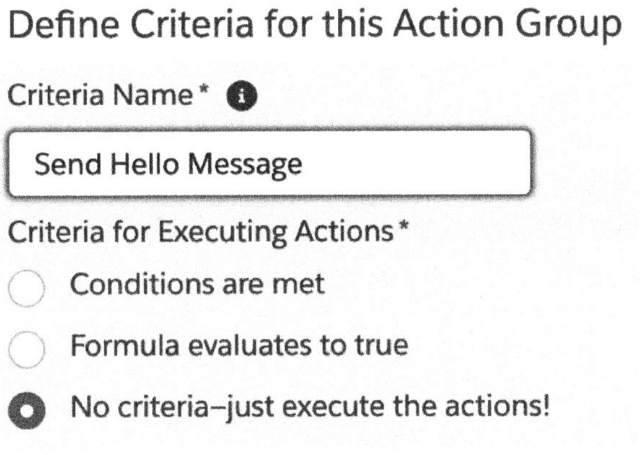

Figure 11.7 – Criteria set to fire whenever new record inserted

Finally, we define an action to **Create a Record** that will create a new record of type `Demonstration__e` and populate the message field with a formula that will read **Hello** plus the first name of the newly created contact. You can see this in the following screenshot:

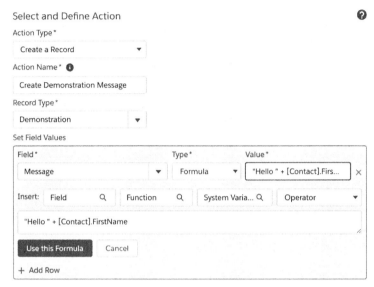

Figure 11.8 – Creating a Demonstration__e record and populating the Message__c field using a formula

The full process we have defined is shown in the following figure for completeness:

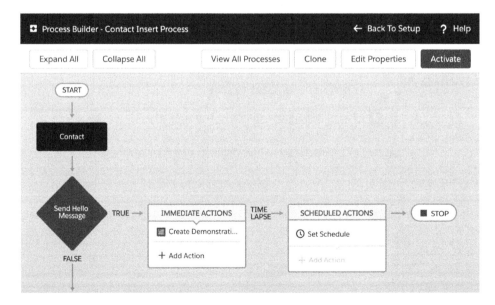

Figure 11.9 – Full process definition

If this process is activated, whenever a new contact record is inserted, a `Demonstration__e` event will be sent along with the populated message that had been handled.

The use of platform events within Process Builder allows administrators and developers to collaborate more closely in working with a decoupled and event-driven architecture. Looking back at our earlier example of sending an event when an opportunity is marked as closed won, the admin and the developer can agree together the structure of the platform event record and then independently work on the logic to publish and handle the event.

Another declarative way of publishing events is through the use of Flow, which we will discuss now.

Publishing platform events through Flow

Flow is a powerful declarative tool within Salesforce to allow administrators and developers to rapidly build background processes and simple user interfaces. Similar to how we publish events in Process Builder using the **Create a Record** action, platform events are published within flows using the **Create Records** element. When working with this element, we must be careful to correctly publish events with consideration of the way in which Flow handles the **Create Records** element and transactions.

A flow can be made up of one or more transactions. If the flow is an auto-launched flow, it will either be its own transaction or part of a wider transaction, depending on how it is invoked. For example, if the flow was invoked as part of a save process via Apex code, its transaction will form part of the overall save order of execution for that transaction and await the whole transaction ending. If the flow is a screen-based flow, then the transaction will end whenever a **Screen** or **Local Action** element is executed. Additionally, if in either flow type a `Pause` element is used, the transaction will end.

This is important to consider: we need to be aware of the implications of firing platform events from a flow and when they will be sent. For example, if we send a platform event from step 1 in a screen-based flow that had 3 steps, the event may be handled before the second step has occurred, and any data we are relying upon may not have been saved yet. When publishing platform events from within Flow, it is common to wait until the end of the Flow to publish to avoid any such issues, unless you require the event to fire earlier.

As mentioned, to publish a platform event using a flow, you use the **Create Records** element. In the following screenshot, we have defined a screen flow for us to use to publish our platform event called **Send Demonstration Message**:

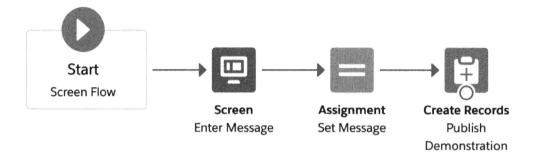

Figure 11.10 – Send demonstration message's full screen flow

Let's see how this works:

1. The first step in the flow is adding a screen element to capture the message we wish to send, as detailed in the following screenshot:

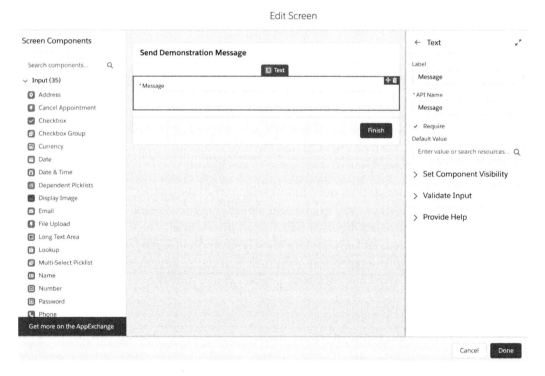

Figure 11.11 – Screen element to capture the message for the platform event

2. We then work with a record variable, which will be the platform event instance we wish to publish containing the message the user has just input:

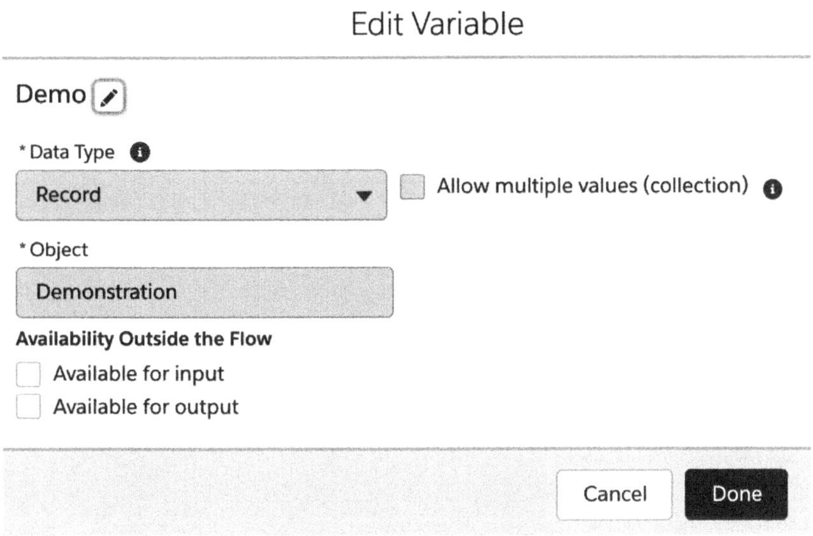

Edit Variable

Demo ✏️

* Data Type ℹ️

| Record ▼ |

☐ Allow multiple values (collection) ℹ️

* Object

| Demonstration |

Availability Outside the Flow

☐ Available for input
☐ Available for output

Cancel   **Done**

Figure 11.12 – Record variable to hold our platform event

3. We then assign the user input message to the `Messsage__c` field on the record variable, as shown in the following screenshot:

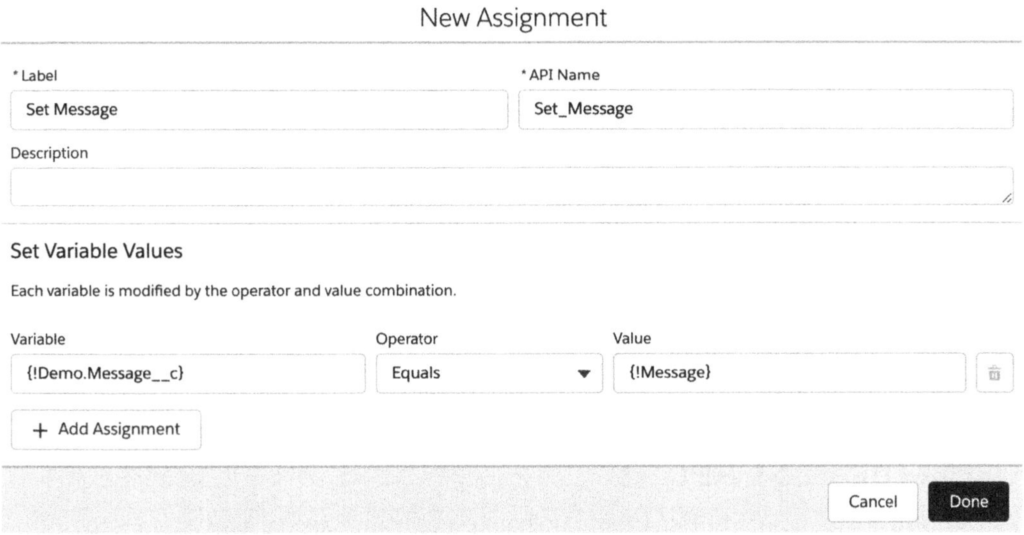

New Assignment

* Label	* API Name
Set Message	Set_Message

Description

Set Variable Values

Each variable is modified by the operator and value combination.

Variable	Operator	Value	
{!Demo.Message__c}	Equals ▼	{!Message}	🗑️

+ Add Assignment

Cancel   **Done**

Figure 11.13 – Setting the Message__c field on our record variable to match the message input by the user

4. The final step in our flow is to use a **Create Records** element to publish the platform event:

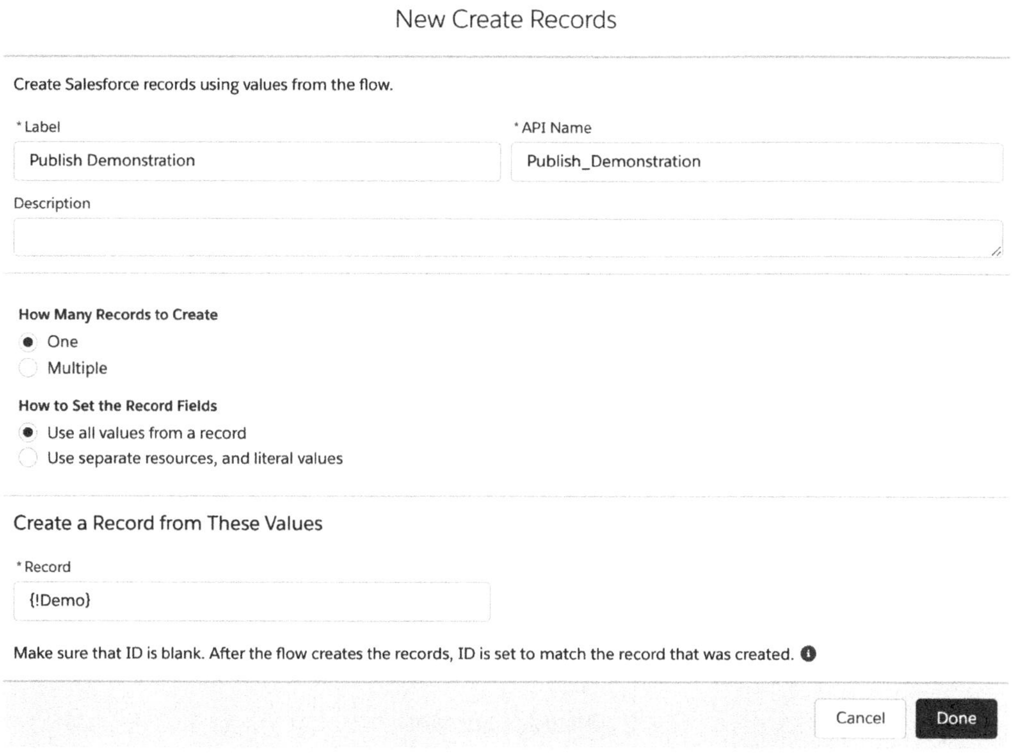

New Create Records

Create Salesforce records using values from the flow.

* Label

Publish Demonstration

* API Name

Publish_Demonstration

Description

How Many Records to Create
● One
○ Multiple

How to Set the Record Fields
● Use all values from a record
○ Use separate resources, and literal values

Create a Record from These Values

* Record

{!Demo}

Make sure that ID is blank. After the flow creates the records, ID is set to match the record that was created. ●

Cancel   Done

Figure 11.14 – Using the Create Records element to publish a platform event

If you run the flow, you can enter a message and it will be sent as the value on our `Demonstration__e` platform event.

When publishing a platform event in both Process Builder and Flow, we are using the standard create record functionality to create a record that can be either a standard or custom object. This helps provide some insight into how well integrated Salesforce have made platform events with the rest of the underlying platform, considering it a first-class metadata component alongside objects. It also gives us a hint as to how we might publish an event through the REST API, as we will now discuss.

Using the REST API

As with Process Builder and Flow, to publish an event from an external system into Salesforce, you simply need to use the REST API and `POST` with the sObject's endpoint, as you would do if you were creating a standard or custom object record via the API.

For each platform event we define, Salesforce provides an endpoint for creating, retrieving, updating, and deleting records of that type following this naming convention:

```
/services/data/v49.0/sobjects/Platform_Event_Name__e
```

To publish a platform event of a particular type, we make a POST request to this endpoint, passing in any field value as a request body. To publish an instance of our Demonstration__e event, we would send a POST request to the endpoint:

```
/services/data/v49.0/sobjects/Demonstration__e
```

And then we'd pass a request body to set the value of the Message__c field:

```
{
    "Message__c" : "This is sent via the REST API"
}
```

If you have created the Demonstration__e event in a development environment, you can test this through the Workbench REST Explorer tool at https://workbench. developerforce.com/restExplorer.php. The following screenshot shows what the screen will look like when you make such a request:

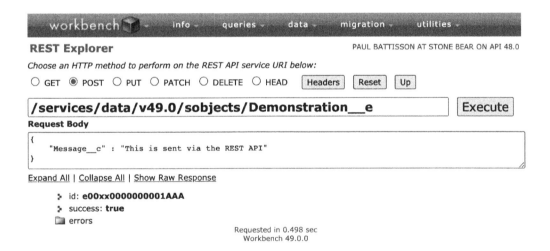

Figure 11.15 – Publishing a platform event via the REST API

Note that a set of items are returned in the `errors` property, although if you inspect them, they will inform you that the error has a status code of `OPERATION_ENQUEUED`. This error is therefore not a real error and somewhat misleading, hence why when publishing an event and wishing to check the success of the publish action, you should use the `success` parameter in either the REST API response body or the `isSuccess()` method on the `SaveResult` instance, as shown when we published our event using Apex.

Now that we have seen the various methods of publishing platform events, we will look at the different ways we can subscribe to and handle platform events.

Subscribing to and handling platform events

One of the key features of platform events is that we can subscribe to and then act upon an event from a variety of different solutions. In this section, we are going to talk through the available solutions on the Salesforce platform itself before looking at handling events off-platform in the next section.

Handling platform events using Apex triggers

For Apex developers, the simplest way to subscribe to a platform event channel in Apex is to use a trigger on the platform event. Triggers defined for a platform event can only operate in the `after insert` context, as no other context exists for an event. In the following code snippet, you can see a simple trigger for our `Demonstration__e` platform event:

```
trigger DemonstrationTrigger on Demonstration__e (after insert)
{
    for(Demonstration__e demo : (List<Demonstration__e>)
    Trigger.new) {
        System.debug(demo.Message__c);
    }
}
```

As we can see in the preceding code, the trigger can access any events within the context using the `Trigger.new` context variable. Unlike the case with standard triggers, which have a batch size of 200, for platform events, a trigger may receive a batch of up to 2,000 events. This makes it far easier to exceed governor limits within the transaction, and we must ensure that we architect and develop our code correctly to handle this.

One way in which we can do that is by setting a checkpoint for the event stream to resume and artificially batching our events into smaller chunks. Each event is given a `ReplayId` instance, which can be used to resume processing from a particular point in the event stream.

Let's update our existing trigger code to handle only 300 events at a time to match the standard object limits. This is a somewhat arbitrary limit for now; in practice, I would advise you to review what your code is doing and then act accordingly. For example, if your code requires a greater volume of query rows, you should monitor the usage of query rows to restart once a threshold is reached. Note that if the trigger ends through an unhandled exception, such as a limit exception, the trigger will be fired again using the last set `ReplayId`; however, it is a better practice to ensure that exceptions are handled gracefully and we control the execution flow appropriately.

Firstly, lets update our trigger to include a counter and increment it during our `trigger` loop:

```
trigger DemonstrationTrigger on Demonstration__e (after insert)
{
    Integer iterations = 0;
    for(Demonstration__e demo : (List<Demonstration__e>)
    Trigger.new) {
        System.debug(demo.Message__c);
            iterations++;
    }
}
```

We want to exit the `for` loop and therefore the trigger when the `iterations` variable reaches `299`:

```
trigger DemonstrationTrigger on Demonstration__e (after insert)
{
    Integer iterations = 0;
    for(Demonstration__e demo : (List<Demonstration__e>)
    Trigger.new) {
        System.debug(demo.Message__c);
```

```
            iterations++;
            if(iterations == 299) {
                break;
            }
        }
    }
}
```

Finally, we need to add in the setting of the `ReplayId` before we perform our check to allow Salesforce to resume the event stream from the correct position. We do this using the `setResumeCheckpoint()` method on the current event bus trigger context, which can be retrieved and used as shown in the following code:

```
trigger DemonstrationTrigger on Demonstration__e (after insert)
{
    Integer iterations = 0;
    for(Demonstration__e demo : (List<Demonstration__e>)
    Trigger.new) {
        System.debug(demo.Message__c);
        EventBus.TriggerContext.currentContext().
        setResumeCheckpoint(demo.ReplayId);
        iterations++;
        if(iterations == 299) {
            break;
        }
    }
}
```

It should be noted that there is no guarantee that if you publish 2,000 messages they will all be passed into a single trigger context. The use of the `ReplayId` instance to restart processing that we are showing here is a defensive coding practice to handle errors should they occur.

An alternative option for us is to throw an instance of `EventBus.RetryableException`. If an error occurs during the processing of our code, throwing an instance of `EventBus.RetryableException` will lead to an attempt to re-run the trigger after a small delay, up to a maximum of 10 times, with the delay increasing each retry time. Following the 10th attempt, the event is moved into the error status. It should be noted that unlike with the previous `setResumeCheckpoint()` call, all work is rolled back and the trigger will start processing the items in the failing batch afresh, plus any new items.

We shall now look at how we can subscribe to platform events declaratively in Process Builder and Flow.

Subscribing to platform events in Process Builder

Process Builder processes can use a platform event firing as the operation that causes them to start by choosing the **A platform event message is received** option, as shown in the following screenshot:

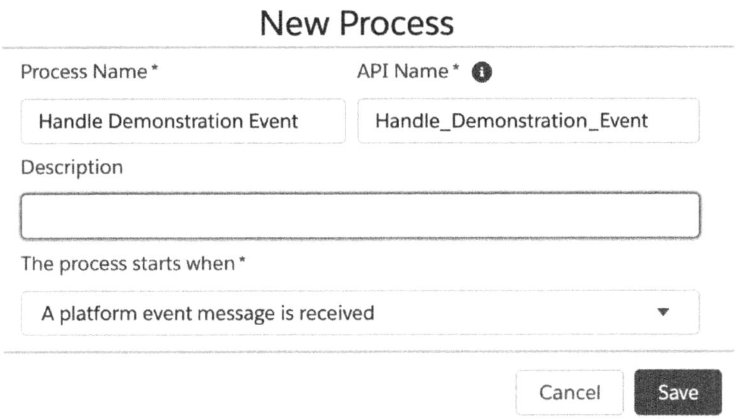

New Process

Process Name *

Handle Demonstration Event

API Name * 🛈

Handle_Demonstration_Event

Description

The process starts when *

A platform event message is received ▼

Cancel   Save

Figure 11.16 – Starting a Process Builder process from a platform event

With this option selected, you must then choose how to retrieve a relevant record from the database for the process to operate on by matching the field on the target object to a value on the platform event, as shown in the following figure:

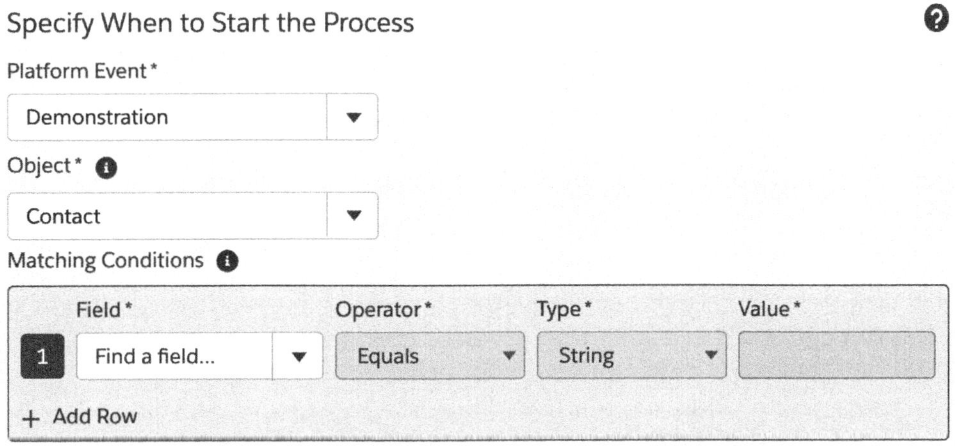

Specify When to Start the Process   ❓

Platform Event *

Demonstration ▼

Object * 🛈

Contact ▼

Matching Conditions 🛈

	Field *	Operator *	Type *	Value *
1	Find a field... ▼	Equals ▼	String ▼	

+ Add Row

Figure 11.17 – Specifying how to retrieve a record instance using a platform event

As we can see from this, without adding a new field to hold a unique record identifier, we could not utilize our `Demonstration__e` platform event in this process to retrieve a matching record. We could, for example, publish a platform event when an opportunity reaches is marked as closed won and have Process Builder retrieve the opportunity for some additional processing, such as creating an additional record related to the opportunity. We could not, however, have a platform event that is not connected to a record cause an action within Process Builder.

To perform this form of action, we would need to use Flow. When choosing the type of flow we wish to create, we can select **Platform Event-Triggered Flow** as shown in the following screenshot:

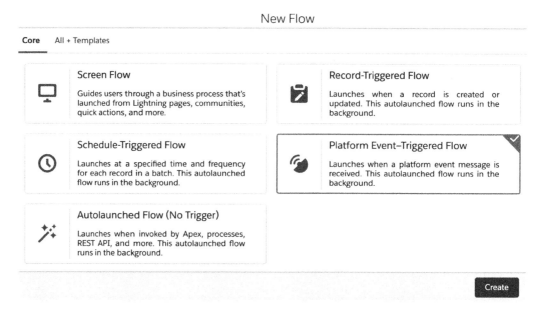

Figure 11.18 – Defining a platform event-triggered flow

And then we can select our `Demonstration__e` event as shown here:

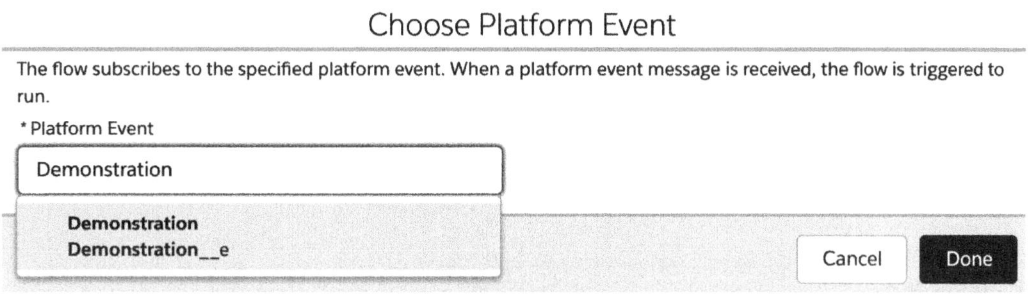

Choose Platform Event

The flow subscribes to the specified platform event. When a platform event message is received, the flow is triggered to run.

* Platform Event

Demonstration

Demonstration
Demonstration__e

Cancel   Done

Figure 11.19 – Choosing our Demonstration__e platform event

From this point onward, we can then perform any actions we want using the data on the platform event as desired. Unlike Process Builder, there is no requirement to retrieve a record or act in a particular way. As an example here, I have created a new record variable called `MessageTask` that will allow us to insert a new `Task` record when an event is received, which sets the `Subject` field of `Task` to the value of the `Message__c` field on the event. You can see the record variable definition in the following screenshot:

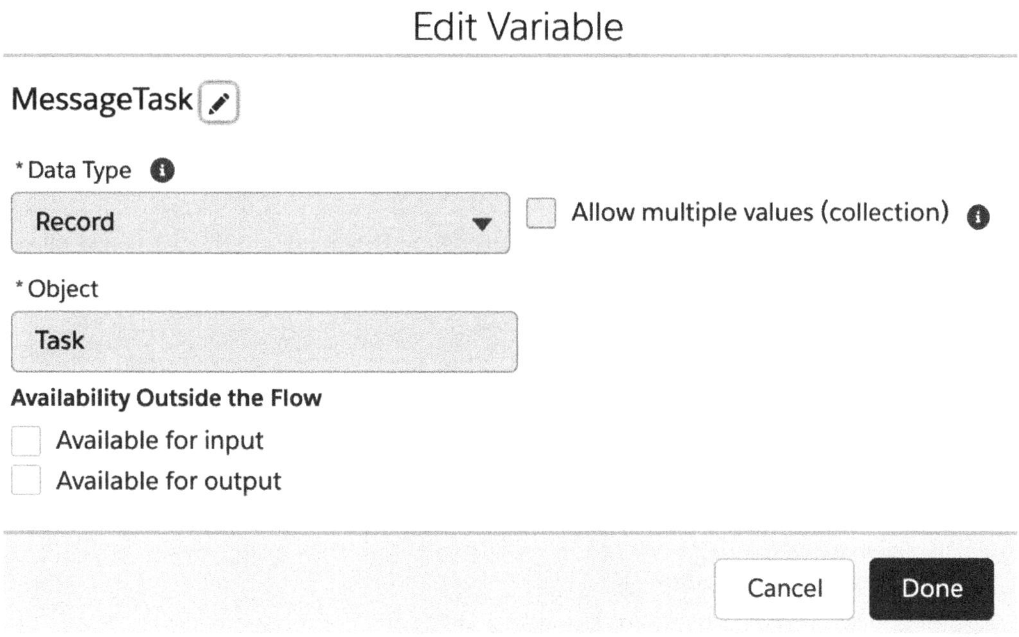

Edit Variable

MessageTask

* Data Type

Record   ▼   ☐ Allow multiple values (collection)

* Object

Task

Availability Outside the Flow

☐ Available for input
☐ Available for output

Cancel   Done

Figure 11.20 – Creating a variable for our Task record

This is followed by an assignment operation to set the `Subject` field using the value of the `Message__c` field on the platform event:

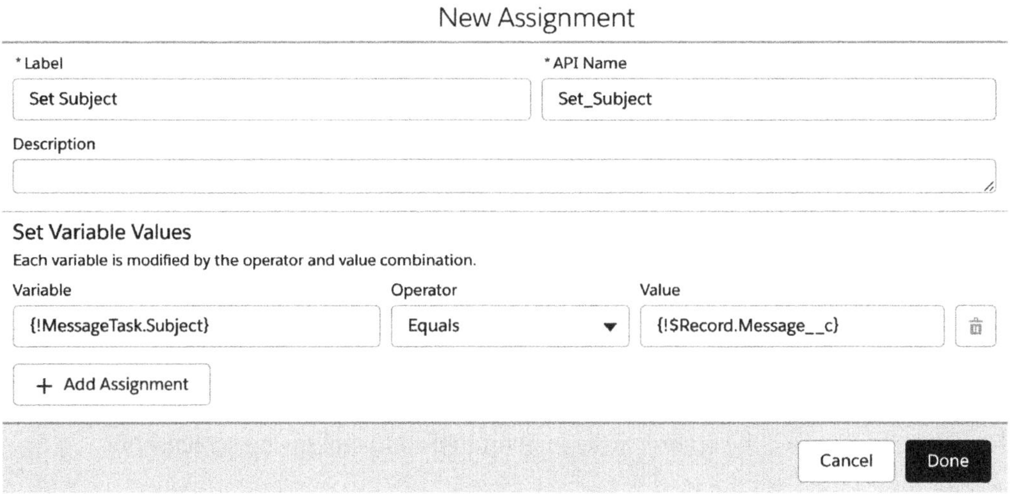

New Assignment

* Label	* API Name
Set Subject	Set_Subject

Description

Set Variable Values

Each variable is modified by the operator and value combination.

Variable	Operator	Value	
{!MessageTask.Subject}	Equals ▼	{!$Record.Message__c}	🗑

+ Add Assignment

Cancel   Done

Figure 11.21 – Setting the Subject field of the Task to be the contents of the Message__c field from the platform event

Finally, we use a **Create Records** element to insert the new **Task** record:

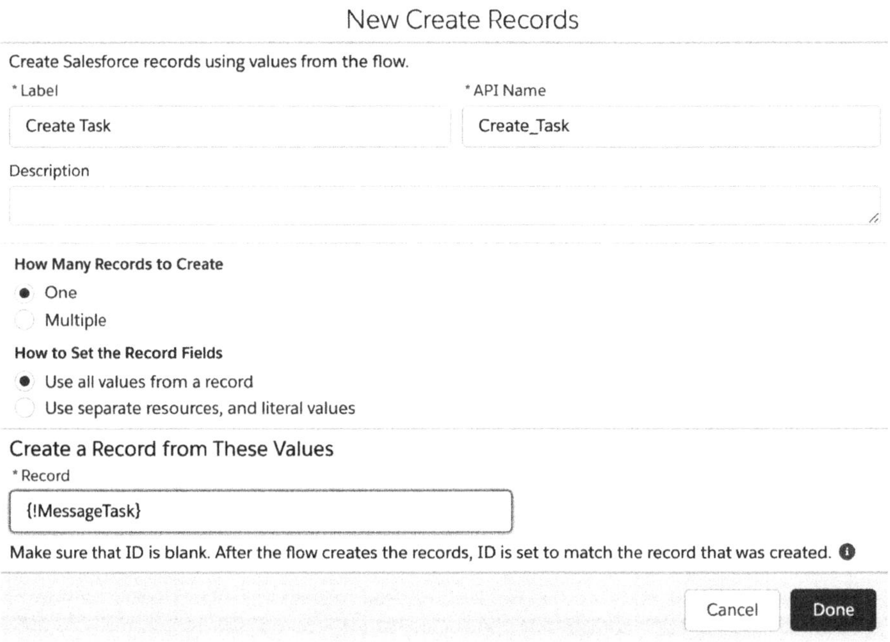

New Create Records

Create Salesforce records using values from the flow.

* Label	* API Name
Create Task	Create_Task

Description

How Many Records to Create

● One
○ Multiple

How to Set the Record Fields

● Use all values from a record
○ Use separate resources, and literal values

Create a Record from These Values

* Record

{!MessageTask}

Make sure that ID is blank. After the flow creates the records, ID is set to match the record that was created. ❶

Cancel   Done

Figure 11.22 – The Create Records element to insert the Task

If you save and activate the flow, you can then test the handling of a platform event to ensure that a `Task` record is created by publishing a platform event using the `DemonstrationEventPublisher` class we defined earlier through **Execute Anonymous**. I executed the following code snippet:

```
DemonstrationEventPublisher.publishEventWithMessage('Hello');
```

This is the **Task** record for me:

Figure 11.23 – An example task created

This structure is a powerful way of coordinating logic between administrators and developers to allow systems to communicate. It also provides a simple way for an external service to integrate with Salesforce using only point-and-click development skills on the Salesforce side by having an external service publish platform events that a flow can subscribe to. While this book is focused on the Apex language, I think it is important for developers to consider all the tooling available to them and how they can best support and work with administrators in different situations.

Finally, if a flow has a **Pause** element, **Resume Event** for the **Pause** element can be the receipt of a platform event message, as shown in the following screenshot:

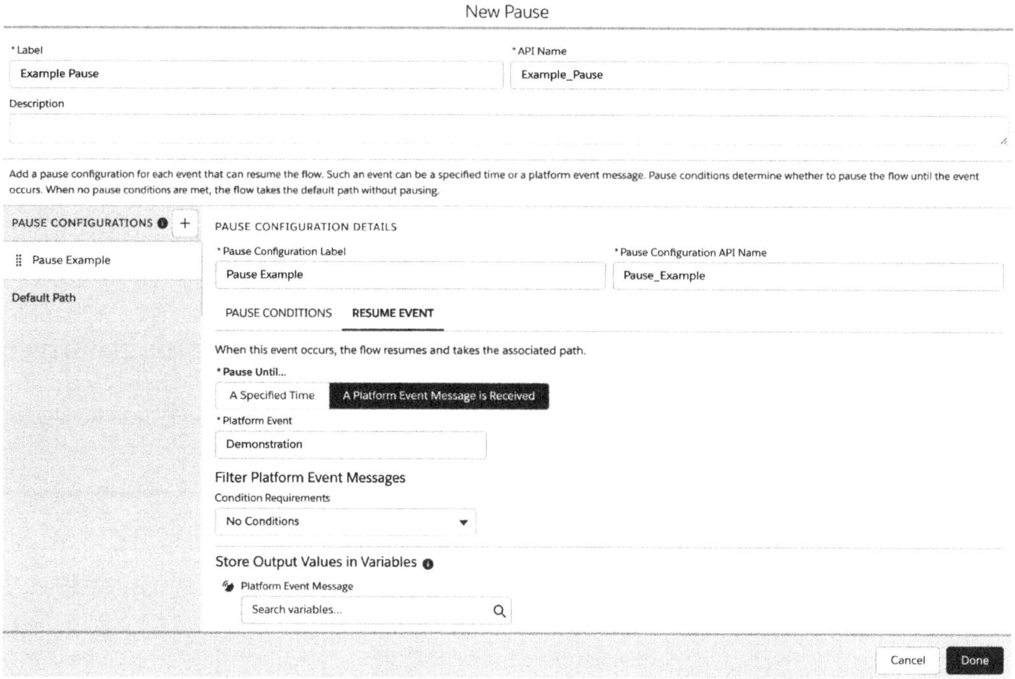

Figure 11.24 – Using a platform event to resume a paused flow

Again, this allows those working with the declarative features of Salesforce and those working with Apex to coordinate the processing of work throughout the system. An example here may be that a flow runs and manipulates a series of records that require some data from an external source. The flow could publish a platform event detailing the information needed (for example, passing the ID of the record to be updated with the information) that is handled by an Apex trigger that makes the callout, updates the record, and publishes a platform event (with the publish on commit option selected) that resumes the paused flow. This is just one of many examples of how, as an Apex developer, you can use platform events to coordinate and work with logic built declaratively on the platform.

We have now seen how to publish and subscribe to platform events using different tools, both declaratively and programmatically. Before we move on to discussing testing, I want to briefly touch on how another feature, **Change Data Capture**, is related to platform events and can be used similarly.

Change Data Capture and platform events

Salesforce Change Data Capture is a solution designed to allow developers to act based upon changes in records within the Salesforce database. Typically, this is to aid in data replication or synchronization from Salesforce to an external system. If an external system requires a synchronized copy of a set of Salesforce data, **Change Data Capture** provides a way of ensuring that relevant changes are synchronized and the external system is notified.

Typically, any replication or synchronization of data to an external third-party system will require a one-time replication of the entire dataset, followed by ongoing synchronization of changes between the two systems. **Change Data Capture** helps with this ongoing synchronization.

The **Change Data Capture** system is based upon platform events and creates change events for selected objects that follow the naming convention `ObjectChangeEvent`. For the `Account` standard object, the events would be of type `AccountChangeEvent`, and for a custom `Job__c` object, the events would be of type `Job__ChangeEvent`.

Because **Change Data Capture** is based on the platform event infrastructure, we can subscribe to change events using either an Apex trigger or through the use of the CometD protocol.

Change event triggers are similar to our platform event triggers in definition, in that they are only available in the `after insert` trigger context.

We can define a change event trigger in the same way that we define any other trigger apart from this choice of a single context:

```
trigger AccountChangeEventTrigger on AccountChangeEvent(after
insert) {

}
```

A change event has a number of pre-defined fields on the event that contain data about the change that has occurred. Firstly, the `changeEventHeader` field contains an instance of the `ChangeEventHeader` Apex class that contains all of the details about the changes within the event. For example, the following code snippet will capture the IDs of the records that were changed in the event before we process the accounts:

```
trigger AccountChangeEventTrigger on AccountChangeEvent(after
insert) {
    Set<Id> changedRecordIds = new Set<Id>();
    for(AccountChangeEvent evt : Trigger.new) {
        List<String> ids = evt.ChangeEventHeader.
```

```
getRecordIds();
        changedRecordIds.addAll(ids);
    }


    //Process accounts using changedRecordIds to retrieve data
}
```

As we can see from the preceding code snippets, working with **Change Data Capture** events is similar to working with platform events, the primary difference being that change events have a pre-determined structure from Salesforce and cannot have custom data fields added.

So far in this chapter, we have seen how to define, publish, and subscribe to platform events as well as how the **Change Data Capture** framework relates to platform events. Now that we have our Apex code written to publish and subscribe to platform events, we need to test the code to verify that it works, so we can deploy it to production.

Testing platform events

When working with platform events in Apex, there are two potential scenarios that we will need to test and validate: when we are publishing platform events and when we are consuming platform events.

Testing whether platform events are publishing

Earlier in the chapter, we defined a DemonstrationEventPublisher class as follows:

```
public with sharing class DemonstrationEventPublisher {

    public static void publishEventWithMessage(String message)
    {
        Demonstration__e demo = new Demonstration__e();
        demo.Message__c = message;
        Database.SaveResult result = Eventbus.publish(demo);
        System.debug('The publish event was a success: ' +
        result.isSuccess());
    }
}
```

We are going to update our class to the flooring code, primarily to make it easier to test but also to enable the calling Apex code to receive some indication that the platform event was published:

```
public with sharing class DemonstrationEventPublisher {

    public static Boolean publishEventWithMessage(String
    message) {
        Demonstration__e demo = new Demonstration__e();
        demo.Message__c = message;
        Database.SaveResult result = Eventbus.publish(demo);
        System.debug('The publish event was a success: ' +
        result.isSuccess());
            return result.isSuccess();
    }
}
```

When testing the publishing of platform events in Apex, we need to consider the following two things:

- We must enclose our `Eventbus.publish` method call within the `Test.startTest()` and `Test.stopTest()` methods. As with all asynchronous Apex, the call of the `Test.stopTest()` method will cause the asynchronous Apex to run synchronously.

- To test that an event has been published, we should assert on the return value of the `isSuccess()` method of the returned `Database.SaveResult` object. In our unit test, we are only validating that the event was published, not that it was processed, which we may validate separately for the associated Apex trigger.

For our preceding `DemonstrationEventPublisher` class, the test is relatively straightforward, as we see in the following snippet:

```
@isTest
private with sharing class DemonstrationEventPublisher_Test {

    @isTest
    private static void testPublishEventWithMessage() {
        Test.startTest();
        Boolean success = DemonstrationEventPublisher.
        publishEventWithMessage('test');
```

```
        Test.stopTest();
        System.assert(success, 'Event was not published
        successfully');
    }
}
```

We have now tested our events being published, so what about testing that they are being consumed appropriately?

Testing the consumption of platform events

As we have previously defined, the following is the trigger for handling our Demonstration__e events:

```
trigger DemonstrationTrigger on Demonstration__e (after insert)
{
    Integer iterations = 0;
    for(Demonstration__e demo : (List<Demonstration__e>)
    Trigger.new) {
        System.debug(demo.Message__c);
        EventBus.TriggerContext.currentContext().
        setResumeCheckpoint(demo.ReplayId);
        iterations++;
        if(iterations == 299) {
            break;
        }
    }
}
```

While useful for debugging our messages when demonstrating how events work, the trigger is not very useful for anything else. Let's update the code as follows so that for each event, we create a Task record with the value of the event's Message__c field being used to populate the Subject field on the Task instance, as shown in the following code snippet:

```
trigger DemonstrationTrigger on Demonstration__e (after insert)
{
    List<Task> tasks = new List<Task>();
    for(Demonstration__e demo : (List<Demonstration__e>)
    Trigger.new) {
```

```
            Task tsk = new Task();
            tsk.Priority = 'High';
            tsk.Subject = demo.Message__c;
            tasks.add(tsk);
        }
    insert tasks;
}
```

We can test this trigger by again using the Test.startTest() and Test.
stopTest() methods to publish our platform event synchronously so that our trigger
may fire. The following test code will test our trigger for us:

```
@isTest
private with sharing class DemonstrationTrigger_Test {

    @isTest
    private static void testCreateTasks() {
        Demonstration__e demo = new Demonstration__e();
        demo.Message__c = 'Test task creation';
        Test.startTest();
        Database.SaveResult result = Eventbus.publish(demo);
        Test.stopTest();
        System.assert(result.isSuccess(), 'Event failed to
        publish correctly');
        List<Task> tasks = [SELECT Id FROM Task WHERE Subject =
        'Test task creation'];
        System.assertEquals(2, tasks.size(), 'Incorrect number
        of tasks created');
    }
}
```

Note that we assert that the two tasks have been created in our final assertion, rather than
one, as we might expect when looking at our trigger code. Why is this? Recall that earlier
in the chapter, in the *Publishing platform events through Flow* section, we built a flow
that subscribes to our platform event and also produces a Task record where the value
of Message__c is used in the Subject field. Therefore, when the event is published,
two records are created. We must always remember when testing our Apex to be aware of
other declarative features that may be operating as well and take them into account for any
validations.

We also have the ability to choose when events are delivered within a test using the `Test.getEventBus().deliver()` method between our calls to `Test.startTest()` and `Test.stopTest()`. This allows us to test code where we are either sending multiple platform events or throwing `EventBus.RetryableException`.

For example, take the following trigger, which subscribes to an event called `UpdateAccount__e`. This event has a field for the `Name` value of an `Account` record called `Account_Name__c` and a corresponding value to populate the `Account` record's `AccontNumber` field, which is `called Account_Number__c`. The trigger will retrieve all the `Account` records to update and throw an instance of `Eventbus.RetryableException` if it cannot find a matching `Account` instance. An example scenario here is when the `AccountNumber` value is being populated by a third-party billing service and the new `Account` record is being created via a long-running asynchronous process. The code for the trigger is as follows:

```
trigger UpdateAccountEventTrigger on UpdateAccount__e (after
insert) {
    Set<String> names = new Set<String>();
    for(UpdateAccount__e evt : Trigger.new) {
        names.add(evt.Account_Name__c);
    }

    Map<String, Account> accountsByName = new Map<String,
    Account>();
    for(Account acc : [SELECT Name, AccountNumber FROM Account
    WHERE Name in :names]) {
        accountsByName.put(acc.Name, acc);
    }

    for(UpdateAccount__e evt : Trigger.new) {
        if(accountsByName.containsKey(evt.Account_Name__c)) {
            accountsByName.get(evt.Account_Name__c).
            AccountNumber = evt.Account_Number__c;
        } else {
            throw new Eventbus.RetryableException('No account
            exists for Name currently');
        }
    }
}
```

```
    update accountsByName.values();
}
```

To test this code, we can use `Test.getEventBus().deliver()` to deliver the event multiple times, both before and after the `Account` record exists, to verify the functionality. A test class to do this is provided as follows:

```
@isTest
private with sharing class UpdateAccountEventTrigger_Test {
    @isTest
    private static void testPublishAndRetry() {
        String accName = 'HM Bonding Ltd';
        Test.startTest();
        UpdateAccount__e evt = new UpdateAccount__e ();
        evt.Account_Name__c = accName;
        evt.Account_Number__c = '007';
        EventBus.publish(evt);

        Test.getEventBus().deliver();
        EventBusSubscriber[] subscribers = [SELECT Name, Type,
        Position, Retries, LastError FROM EventBusSubscriber
        WHERE Topic='UpdateAccount__e'];

        for (EventBusSubscriber sub : subscribers) {
            if (sub.Name == 'UpdateAccountEventTrigger') {
                System.assertEquals(1, sub.Retries);
            }
        }

        Account acc = new Account();
        acc.Name = accName;
        insert acc;

        Test.getEventBus().deliver();
        Test.stopTest();

        acc = [SELECT AccountNumber FROM Account WHERE Id =
        :acc.Id LIMIT 1];
```

```
        System.assertEquals('007', acc.AccountNumber,
        'Incorrect Account Number set');
    }
}
```

In our test method, we create and publish our `UpdateAccount__e` and call `Test.getEventBus().deliver()` to deliver the event before the `Account` record for HM Bonding Ltd exists. We then retry and verify that the `EventBusSubscriber` record associated to our `UpdateAccountEventTrigger` has its `Retries` property set to 1.

Following this, we then insert the required `Account` record and call `Test.getEventBus().deliver()` to deliver the record a second time, when it will be correctly processed. Our test ends with the retrieval of the updated `Account` record and an assertion that the update has occurred as expected.

This concludes our section on testing the consumption of platform events within Apex, in which we have seen how we can test both the consumption of events but also how we can work with retry logic should an error occur. The final section in this chapter before we conclude is a discussion on the consumption of events on external systems using the CometD protocol.

A discussion of the CometD protocol and handling events externally

One of the key benefits of the platform event framework is the ability to consume platform events as a subscriber off-platform. To consume platform events, you need to connect and subscribe to an event channel using the CometD protocol.

It is outside the scope of this book to discuss connecting using CometD; however, you can use the streaming tool available through Salesforce Workbench at `https://workbench.developerforce.com/streaming.php` to subscribe to the channel and see events as an external service. To do this, select the **Generic Subscriptions** option and enter `/event/eventName` in the **Subscription** box, and then press the **Subscribe** button.

For example, in the following screenshot, I have subscribed to the `UpdateAccount__e` event channel. If you then publish an event using **Execute Anonymous**, you will see the event consumed as shown in the following screenshot:

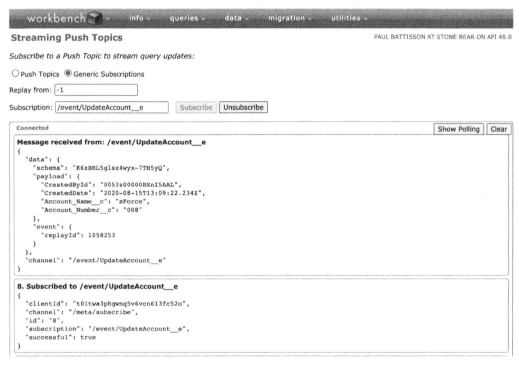

Figure 11.25 – Subscribing to an event channel and consuming an event in Workbench

If you wish to subscribe to a channel in an external application, I recommend using one of the pre-built libraries for integrating with Salesforce, which will make this much easier. For example, I have a blog at `https://paulbattisson.com/blog/2017/consuming-platform-events-in-10-lines-of-javascript/` that details how to consume platform events in JavaScript using 10 lines of code. Platform events are a powerful integration feature that can allow us to communicate with an external solution as needed. This concludes this chapter by showing the final way in which we can consume the events we have published.

Summary

In this chapter, we have covered platform events in detail and discussed a number of ways in which we can both publish and consume them. We began the chapter by discussing what is meant by the term **event-driven architecture** and described how an event bus allows us to both publish and consume events and has an operating model that can be thought of as being analogous to how Twitter operates.

The next section then discussed the key use cases for platform events and how we can use platform events to decouple applications to make them easier to scale and grow. We also discussed how we can connect to external systems in a simpler fashion through the use of platform events.

With our understanding of these use cases in place, we then moved on to how we define a platform event and how a platform event is defined as metadata within Salesforce. We then looked at a number of ways of publishing events through the use of Apex, Process Builder, flows, and the Salesforce REST API. We noted how for all of these methods bar Apex, we were simply creating a record against a database using the same structures as we would to create new custom or standard object records.

Following this, we reviewed the ways in which we can subscribe to, consume, and handle platform events on the platform using Apex, Process Builder, and Flow. We also touched on how we can use platform events to allow us to restart paused flows to allow us to work more closely with administrators in building connected solutions.

We then looked at how the **Change Data Capture** functionality is based upon the platform events framework and how this means that we can handle change events in Apex in a similar manner to how we handle platform events, through the use of a trigger. We also looked at how the change events defined for an object have pre-defined properties to allow us to see the changes made to a record.

The penultimate section of the chapter focused on how we can test our code that works with platform events. We firstly looked at how we can test code that is publishing events and how we can verify that an event has been published using the returned `Database.SaveResult` instance. Following this, we discussed ways of testing Apex code that consumes platform events, including code that throws an instance of `EventBus.RetryableException`.

We ended the chapter by discussing how to consume events off-platform using CometD and how we can see the format of events using the Workbench tool.

In the next chapter, we will look at another way of integrating with Salesforce through the use of custom-defined Apex REST APIs, exploring how they work, how we define them, and how we test them.

12
Apex REST and Custom Web Services

With this chapter, we are going to finish this section of the book by discussing how we can expose Apex classes as RESTful web services. In the previous chapters, we have seen a variety of different asynchronous Apex options and how we can utilize them to build more scalable solutions. A common use case for these options was making callouts to external services to integrate them with Salesforce from the Salesforce side. This is referred to as an *outbound integration* as we are making a call from Salesforce *out* to an external system. In *Chapter 11, Using Platform Events*, we discussed the use of platform events and how they can be utilized to provide bidirectional communication, which is both an outbound integration through the external consumption of events, but also an inbound integration by having external services publish platform events to be consumed on platform.

This chapter focuses on another method of providing inbound integration options, Apex REST, that is, custom RESTful endpoints developed in Apex. In this chapter, we will cover the following topics:

- An overview of the REST paradigm and what it means
- When to use custom endpoints developed in Apex

- How to define a custom endpoint

- Exposing custom endpoints for use

- Working with the `URLRewriter` class to provide more user-friendly endpoints

- Handling and working with data in JSON or XML

- Using custom metadata to perform dynamic parsing

- Testing custom endpoints using Workbench

- Testing Apex REST code

Technical requirements

The code for the chapter can be found here:

```
https://github.com/PacktPublishing/Mastering-Apex-Programming/
tree/Chapter-12
```

An overview of REST

REST stands for **REpresentational State Transfer** and is an architectural structure designed to make it simple to connect systems across the internet using existing standards and protocols. The purpose of REST is to help define a uniform set of stateless operations that can be performed between systems. A basic driving principle behind a RESTful API is that it should use the standards that form the basis of the internet, that is, the **HyperText Transfer Protocol** (**HTTP**), to allow for resources to be accessed and data transferred between systems in a simple and repeatable manner.

In general, RESTful APIs require a descriptive **Uniform Resource Locator** (**URL**) to identify the resource we are working with, a standard HTTP method to indicate what action is being performed, and a media type description to describe the format of the data being transferred or the required format for data being returned.

Ideally, the URI for a RESTful API is a *clean* URL, or *user-friendly* URL. This typically means that a URL should follow the format `https://domain.com/noun` (going forward, we will drop the domain and focus only on the endpoint portion of the URL) where `noun` is the resource we are working with, for example:

- `/account`: Resource relating to the account data

- `/user`: User-related data

- `/order`: Order-related information

There is some debate as to whether it is better to use a singular or plural form of the noun. However, we will follow the practice of Salesforce and use the singular form here.

This URL structure then allows us to reference specific resource instances of that noun following another `/`, that is, a sub-resource. The account with the identifier `123` would be located at the URI `/account/123`.

In situations where we have an action that is not specific to a particular resource, then a descriptive verb should be used, such as the following:

- `/convert` for converting currencies
- `/query` for querying

By using descriptive nouns and verbs in such a format, the URLs are simpler to read for developers and explicit in what they are used for. This is one of the strengths of REST; it is easy for developers to work with and helps to make explicit the resource they are accessing, which is also enhanced by the use of the standard HTTP methods in our requests.

HTTP methods

RESTful APIs are built to use the HTTP standards that underpin the internet, including the use of the HTTP methods. The standard HTTP methods and their usage are as follows:

- `GET`: Retrieves the resource at a given location, for example, retrieving an account or set of accounts
- `POST`: Creates a new sub-resource at the resource location, for example, creating an account
- `PUT`: Updates or replaces a resource completely, for example, replacing a document
- `PATCH`: Partially updates a resource, for example, updating a single field on an account
- `DELETE`: Deletes the specified resource

Combining a method with a URL therefore provides a simple way of determining what action is being taken. Examples include the following:

- `GET /account`: Retrieves account records
- `GET /user/123`: Retrieves the user with ID `123`
- `POST /order`: Creates an order with a given set of data

- `PUT /order/xyz`: Replaces the order resource with `Id xyz` with the resource bundle provided

- `PATCH /order/tuv`: Updates the order resource with `Id tuv` with the updated values

- `DELETE /account/abc`: Deletes the account with `Id abc`

- `GET /convert`: Retrieves a conversion for some given currencies

Some of these endpoints will take in data through the request body, that is, a set of data sent by the client to the endpoint. Typically, this is data describing a resource we want to `POST`, `PUT` or `PATCH`. Other endpoints will retrieve parameters via URL parameters. This is most typical for verb-based endpoints. For example, the standard Salesforce REST API query endpoint consumes the query via the URL, for example, the following call queries for all account data:

```
GET https://yourInstance.salesforce.com/services/data/v49.0/
query/?q=SELECT+name+from+Account
```

This covers the basics of what the REST paradigm is and how a RESTful API looks and operates at a high level. As we work through this chapter, we will dive into some of these concepts in more detail. However, we must first ensure we understand when we would want to work with a custom endpoint.

REST and Apex – when to use custom endpoints

Salesforce provides a fully featured REST API as standard and will automatically make an endpoint available for the standard CRUD operations on any new custom objects you define. The API also includes endpoints for standard operations, such as querying, running invocable actions, and describing sObject metadata, alongside a composite endpoint for working on multiple sObjects together. Given all this, why and when might you want to build a custom endpoint? Let's consider a couple of scenarios where it might make sense.

Replacing a legacy integration

Firstly, consider the scenario where you are implementing Salesforce within an organization and a legacy solution exists that is using a pre-existing REST API on the system Salesforce is replacing. It is extremely unlikely that the existing system will have a REST API that matches the standard Salesforce REST API endpoints. So, we are presented with the options of either updating the existing application to call the Salesforce API, or writing a custom API on Salesforce that mirrors the existing endpoints, thereby making replacement easier.

If you do not have the necessary development skills available to update the existing solution's code base, or cannot for other reasons, such as a lack of access or excessive cost, then it would be sensible to mirror the existing series of API endpoints in Salesforce to make the transition easier.

From an architectural perspective as well, this may be considered a *cleaner* solution as it does not explicitly tie the other solution to Salesforce. While the standard Salesforce APIs are fully featured, they do refer to Salesforce-specific API names; for example, field and object names will include the relevant __c suffix for custom objects and fields. This leads us on to the next scenario, where it may be more prudent to create a custom endpoint.

Generic endpoints

As noted in the previous section, the standard Salesforce endpoints require any solution calling them to have an understanding of the data structure of your Salesforce instance. For integrations performed on a single customer instance, this is typically not a problem. However, if you are distributing an application via the AppExchange and wish to make the API more publicly available, this may not be desirable. A custom API endpoint will allow you to abstract away the Salesforce data schema to provide a more generic endpoint.

This is also the case when you wish to provide a single endpoint that may take in data from multiple sources and you need to map this data appropriately. As an example, a client I worked with had two different systems catering orders from customers, one for business retail orders and another for consumer orders. A more generic custom endpoint allowed the customer to take in order data from either system and have Salesforce parse the data into the correct schema. This also made it easier for the organization as they developed and improved their order capture systems. This scenario can also be extended further to form our next use case – having custom logic or a complex endpoint.

Custom logic or complex endpoints

In the previous example for the customer storing both B2B and B2C orders within a single Salesforce environment, logic was needed on the Salesforce side to determine how to map the data provided to the correct metadata items within Salesforce. As an example, orders that were B2C in nature should be stored against person accounts, whereas those that were B2B should be stored against an account and contact combination. You may have a need for other logic to fire off within Salesforce on an API call, such as data aggregation, querying, or DML that is not provided out of the box with Salesforce.

In these instances, a custom Apex REST endpoint is a good option as we can hide the details of the implementation and logic away from the caller of the endpoint and manage this all within Apex appropriately. Similarly, by working with Apex, we can sometimes rationalize multiple calls through the standard API into a single call through a custom endpoint. Salesforce provides a composite API endpoint that allows you to make multiple requests at once; however, the caller must have knowledge of the Salesforce schema to perform this, which again is not always desirable.

With this understanding of some common use cases, let's now look at defining REST endpoints in Apex.

Defining endpoints

All Apex classes exposed as web services need to be defined as global in scope to ensure that they are visible to outside users. To define a class as an Apex REST service, we must annotate the class with the `@RestResource` annotation and provide a URL mapping. The following code snippet shows the definition of an Apex class for the `/Example` endpoint:

```
@RestResource(urlMapping = '/Example/*')
global with sharing class ApexRESTExample {


}
```

Within the class, we must then define methods and annotate them with the appropriate method annotation to expose them as an HTTP method. These methods must be static as they are called without a specific instance of the class instantiated. In the following code block, we can see some basic Apex methods that have all the provided annotations:

```
@RestResource(urlMapping = '/Example/*')
global with sharing class ApexRESTExample {

    @HttpGet
    global static String getExampleResponse() {
        return 'Example';
    }

    @HttpPost
    global static String postExampleResponse(String inputData)
    {
```

```
        return 'You posted ' + inputData;
    }


    @HttpPut
    global static String putExampleResponse(String inputData) {
        return 'You put ' + inputData;
    }


    @HttpPatch
    global static String patchExampleResponse(String inputData)
    {
        return 'You patched ' + inputData;
    }


    @HttpDelete
    global static String deleteExampleResponse() {
        return 'Example delete';
    }
}
```

This class provides an endpoint available at `/services/apexrest/Example` that will operate for all the different HTTP methods and provide responses, as shown in the preceding code block. It is not the most useful of endpoints, but it does provide us with an illustration of how we can expose methods and take in inputs.

In the `postExampleResponse`, `putExampleResponse`, and `patchExampleResponse` methods, we have a parameter in the method definition, a `String` variable with the parameter name `inputData`.

Apex REST methods can take in a variety of input data types, such as the following:

- Apex primitives (excluding the generic sObject type and Blob)
- sObjects
- Lists or maps of Apex primitive types or sObjects (note that the key type in a map must be a `String`)
- User-defined types in Apex where member variables are of the types listed here

To pass values to these parameters, we specify them as values in the request body. In JSON, this would be the following:

```
{'inputData': 'Test'}
```

And in XML, it would be the following:

```
<request>
    <inputData>Test</inputData>
</request>
```

These sets of data are parsed automatically by Apex to populate the parameters in the method signatures. This is one of the helpful pieces of work and automatic mapping that Salesforce does for us within the Apex REST framework. Similarly, response data is automatically parsed into the relevant return data type. However, let's take things a bit further and check an example.

A more detailed example

Let's look at defining a more concrete real-world example. We are going to define a custom Apex REST endpoint for Account records for an organization that works with hospitals and doctors. Instead of the standard /Account endpoint, we want to provide a /hospital endpoint that will automatically filter for Account records with the Hospital record type.

To follow along in your own environment add a record type called Hospital to the Account object.

Let's start by defining a new Apex class for our HospitalRESTService class:

```
@RestResource(urlMapping = '/hospital/*')
global with sharing class HospitalRESTService {


}
```

We will now define the GET method for the endpoint, which will retrieve the details of a hospital using a unique identifier. In the following screenshot, you can see the definition for the custom **Hospital Ref Code** field we will be using as the identifier:

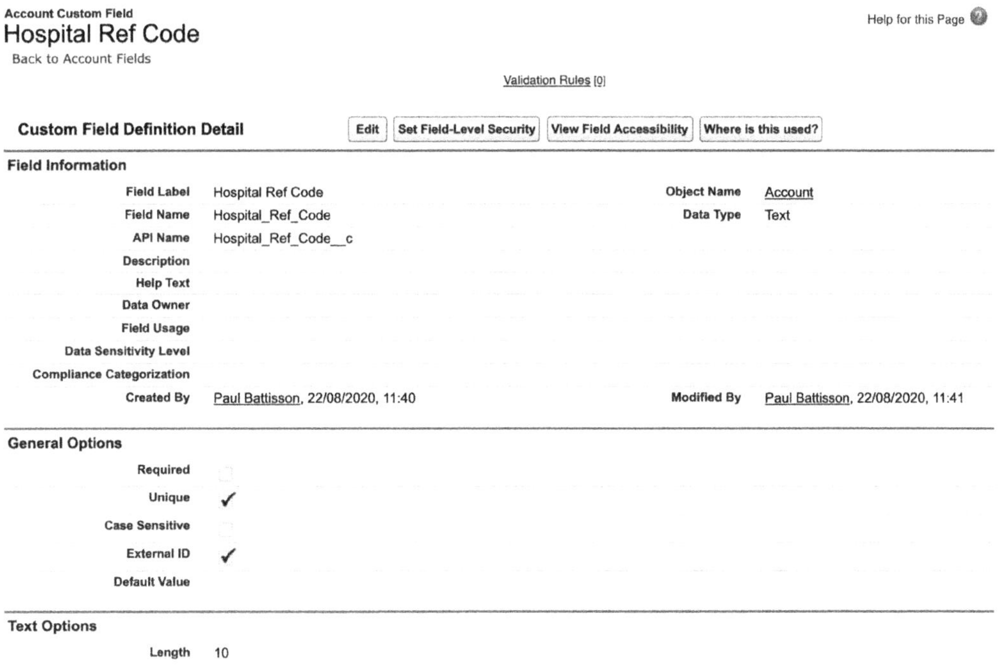

Account Custom Field
Hospital Ref Code
Back to Account Fields

Help for this Page

Validation Rules [0]

Custom Field Definition Detail	Edit	Set Field-Level Security	View Field Accessibility	Where is this used?

Field Information

Field Label	Hospital Ref Code	Object Name	Account
Field Name	Hospital_Ref_Code	Data Type	Text
API Name	Hospital_Ref_Code__c		
Description			
Help Text			
Data Owner			
Field Usage			
Data Sensitivity Level			
Compliance Categorization			
Created By	Paul Battisson, 22/08/2020, 11:40	Modified By	Paul Battisson, 22/08/2020, 11:41

General Options

Required	☐
Unique	✓
Case Sensitive	☐
External ID	✓
Default Value	

Text Options

Length	10

Figure 12.1 – Hospital Ref Code custom field definition

Our method for handling the GET call will require inspection of the URL of the request to retrieve the correct code. For example, if a GET request is made to /hospital/ACME123, we need to find and return the hospital with Hospital Ref Code ACME123. The template for our method is shown in the following snippet:

```
@HttpGet
global static Account doGet() {


}
```

It is a common naming convention in Apex REST classes to specify the methods as doGet, doPost, handleGet, handlePost or some other format where it clearly highlights what the method is undertaking.

We can retrieve the URL of the request by using the `requestURI` on the `RestRequest` instance for the request. We retrieve the instance for the current context using the `RestContext.request` property. This is shown in the following snippet:

```
@HttpGet
global static Account doGet() {
    RestRequest req = RestContext.request;
    String url = req.requestURI;
}
```

We can then manipulate this string as we would any other string, splitting it on the / character to retrieve the identifier, which will be at the end of the string. In the Apex documentation, the `substring` method is used. However, I prefer to use the `split` method as it enables you to handle nested URLs should you need them.

The following code shows how we can retrieve the value from the URL and retrieve the parameter for us to query and return the correct `Account` record:

```
@HttpGet
global static Account doGet() {
    RestRequest req = RestContext.request;
    List<String> splitUrl = req.requestURI.split('/');
    String refCode = splitUrl[splitUrl.size() - 1];
    List<Account> hospitals = [SELECT Name, Hospital_Ref_
    Code__c FROM Account WHERE
    Hospital_Ref_Code__c = :refCode];
    if(hospitals.size() == 1) {
        return hospitals[0];
    }
    return null;
}
```

Note that in this code, we are returning an `Account` instance, which will look something like the following:

```
{
  'attributes' : {
    'type' : 'Account',
    'url' : '/services/data/v49.0/sobjects/
    Account/0013z00002Uf1fQAAR'
```

```
    },
    'Name' : 'Acme Hospital',
    'Hospital_Ref_Code__c' : 'ACME123',
    'Id' : '0013z00002Uf1fQAAR'
}
```

If we want to maintain some agnosticism from the Salesforce schema, we should instead return a custom type that abstracts the schema away. The return we have in the preceding code includes not only Salesforce field API names, but also describes information for the record. This is information we do not wish to expose and so should return a custom data type instead.

Let's create a `HospitalWrapper` class that we will use to return our data in an abstracted format. The following code shows our `HospitalWrapper` class definition:

```
global class HospitalWrapper {
    String Name;
    String Ref_Code;
    public HospitalWrapper(Account acc) {
        if(acc != null) {
            this.Name = acc.Name;
            this.Ref_Code = acc.Hospital_Ref_Code__c;
        }
    }
}
```

We have explicitly declared a constructor to accept an `Account` record instance and map the field values to the member variables of our `HospitalWrapper` class. We can then update our `doGet` method as follows to utilize this class and return the information:

```
@HttpGet
global static HospitalWrapper doGet() {
    RestRequest req = RestContext.request;
    List<String> splitUrl = req.requestURI.split('/');
    String refCode = splitUrl[splitUrl.size() - 1];
    List<Account> hospitals = [SELECT Name, Hospital_Ref_
    Code__c FROM Account WHERE
    Hospital_Ref_Code__c = :refCode];
    if(hospitals.size() == 1) {
        return new HospitalWrapper(hospitals[0]);
```

```
    }
    return null;
}
```

The data returned from this call for the same record as before is now agnostic of the Salesforce database schema, as shown in the following code:

```
{
    'Ref_Code' : 'ACME123',
    'Name' : 'Acme Hospital'
}
```

Salesforce has made working with data through Apex REST easy by automatically serializing and deserializing the data provided to the endpoints in a custom format. If we now define our doPost method, we can take in an instance of the HospitalWrapper class and Salesforce will automatically convert valid JSON input to this format. If we add a doPost method as shown in the following code, then we can create records from the data by passing in a body of data that is formatted to match our HospitalWrapper class:

```
@HttpPost
global static String doPost(HospitalWrapper hospital) {
    Id hospitalRTId = Schema.SObjectType.Account.
    getRecordTypeInfosByDeveloperName().get('Hospital').
    getRecordTypeId();
    Account acc = new Account();
    acc.RecordTypeId = hospitalRTId;
    acc.Name = hospital.Name;
    acc.Hospital_Ref_Code__c = hospital.Ref_Code;
    insert acc;
    return acc.Hospital_Ref_Code__c;
}
```

To populate this, the JSON body would then be like the following:

```
{
    'hospital': {
        'Ref_Code' : 'SPRING12',
        'Name' : 'Palm Springs General Hospital'
    }
}
```

This updated code has abstracted away the Salesforce specifics from our calling system, but before we continue, I want to discuss an alternative way we could have achieved this that may have led to a slightly cleaner implementation from the calling system's perspective.

In this request body, we have a JSON object with a property called `hospital` that then contains an object representation of the hospital instance we are passing in. From the calling system's perspective, this is a slight duplication, as we have already indicated we are creating a new hospital by calling `POST` on the `/hospital` endpoint. The reason we have this `hospital` property within the JSON is because in order for Apex to deserialize the input to our `HospitalWrapper` instance, the keys of the top-level JSON object in the request body must match the names of the parameters within the method signature. In this instance, the `HospitalWrapper instance` we accept in the method signature is named `hospital`, and so in the top level of the method body, we explicitly have a `hospital` property.

It could be argued for a cleaner implementation that we would want our request body to be similar to the following snippet:

```
{
    'Ref_Code' : 'SPRING12',
    'Name' : 'Palm Springs General Hospital'
}
```

How would we update our method signature to do this? As noted, the top-level properties of the JSON object have to match the parameters specified in the method signature, so if we update the `doPut` method to the following:

```
@HttpPost
global static String doPost(String Name, String Ref_Code) {
    Id hospitalRTId = Schema.SObjectType.Account.
    getRecordTypeInfosByDeveloperName().get('Hospital').
    getRecordTypeId();
    Account acc = new Account();
    acc.RecordTypeId = hospitalRTId;
    acc.Name = Name;
    acc.Hospital_Ref_Code__c = Ref_Code;
    insert acc;
    return acc.Hospital_Ref_Code__c;
}
```

Then the JSON body we specified would work as its top-level properties match the parameters in the method signature.

There is no inherently right or wrong answer here. The design of RESTful APIs, like the design of any code, is, to a large degree, personal. If I were writing this specific API, I would probably choose the latter option for my code to keep things cleaner overall. However, this would add some limitations to the way in which I maintain my code going forward. If I add a new field, I now need to add it to all the method signatures and mappings. With the wrapper class, I can add the new property to the wrapper class once and the change will be propagated across the code.

In all the examples we have seen so far, we have known the exact structure of the request body for us to be able to parameterize the method signature for Apex to do the mapping for us. What about in the scenario where we are not sure exactly of which parameters we will be getting or which values we should be populating? Earlier in the chapter, I highlighted a scenario where I had worked with an organization where a single endpoint was provided for orders of different types to be captured. In this scenario, we want our endpoint to be more dynamic to allow us to choose how we are populating data to runtime.

Another common scenario is the need to be able to allow the API to be updated declaratively. One of the benefits of the standard Salesforce API endpoints is that whenever a new field is added to the Salesforce schema, it is available for use within the standard API immediately. With custom endpoints like those we have seen so far, anytime a new field is added, a developer is required to make the necessary changes. This is a particular problem for ISVs offering an API on their application. For example, if my application has a custom API that creates records on an object within my managed package and a subscriber adds a field to the object that they wish to capture, here, rather than rewrite the entire API, I want to have my API be dynamic enough to handle this at runtime through an easy-to-configure system. In the next section, we will see how we can do this using custom metadata types.

Dynamic parsing using custom metadata

In the examples so far, we have let Apex do most of the heavy lifting for us in translating our request body into Apex data types for us to work with. In this section, we will look at how we could do this manually.

We want to be able, at runtime, to determine how we should map the data provided to us to different fields within Salesforce. To do this, we will be using a custom metadata type.

In the following screenshot, you can see the definition for my **API Mapping** custom metadata type. I have added an additional **Target Field** text field on to the metadata type, so we can create records using the `DeveloperName` field to hold the API property, and the `Target_Field__c` field to hold the API name of the field to populate:

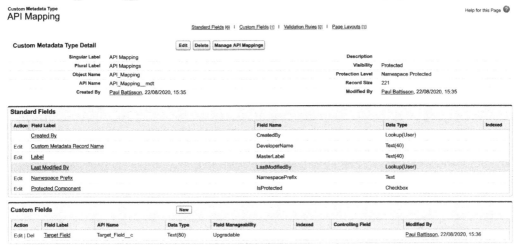

Figure 12.2 – API Mapping custom metadata type definition

Next, I have created two records to allow us to map the fields we were previously working with in our examples. You can see these in the following screenshot:

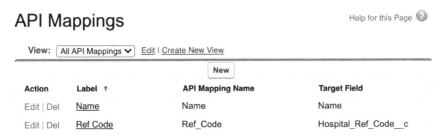

Figure 12.3 – API Mapping records for Name and Hospital_Ref_Code

Let's now update our `doPost` method to utilize these new mappings. Firstly, we need to receive a generic JSON dataset rather than specific named parameters. To do this, we remove the parameters from our method signature and retrieve the body of the request using the same `RestRequest` object we worked with in the `doGet` method. We will also need to retrieve all of our API Mapping records to allow us to process the JSON data. Our updated `POST` method so far then is as follows:

```
@HttpPost
global static String doPost() {
```

```
    Id hospitalRTId = Schema.SObjectType.Account.
    getRecordTypeInfosByDeveloperName().get('Hospital').
    getRecordTypeId();

    List<API_Mapping__mdt> mappings = [SELECT DeveloperName,
    Target_Field__c FROM API_Mapping__mdt];

    Blob requestBody = RestContext.request.requestBody;

    //...
}
```

We are assuming JSON data in this example and will discuss this in more detail in the *Handling request body data* section in terms of how to deal with data of different formats.

For now, we will simply deserialize our request body JSON data into a variable of the Map<String, Object> type for us to work with. For this simple example, this will suffice, but again we will see more information on parsing JSON in the aforementioned section later in this chapter:

```
@HttpPost
global static String doPost() {
    Id hospitalRTId = Schema.SObjectType.Account.
    getRecordTypeInfosByDeveloperName().get('Hospital').
    getRecordTypeId();

    List<API_Mapping__mdt> mappings = [SELECT DeveloperName,
    Target_Field__c FROM API_Mapping__mdt];

    Blob requestBody = RestContext.request.requestBody;

    Map<String, Object> hospitalData = (Map<String, Object>)
    JSON.deserializeUntyped(requestBody.toString());

    //...
}
```

With this work complete, we can now create a new Account record to hold the data for our hospital, assign it the correct record type, and then loop through the API_ Mapping__mdt metadata records to populate the relevant fields on the new record before inserting it into the database. The following snippet shows the final version of our doPut method to do this:

```
@HttpPost
global static String doPost() {
    Id hospitalRTId = Schema.SObjectType.Account.
    getRecordTypeInfosByDeveloperName().get('Hospital').
    getRecordTypeId();
```

```
List<API_Mapping__mdt> mappings = [SELECT DeveloperName,
Target_Field__c FROM API_Mapping__mdt];

Blob requestBody = RestContext.request.requestBody;

Map<String, Object> hospitalData = (Map<String, Object>)
JSON.deserializeUntyped(requestBody.toString());


Account hospital = new Account();

hospital.RecordTypeId = hospitalRTId;

for(API_Mapping__mdt mapping : mappings) {
    if(hospitalData.containsKey(mapping.DeveloperName)) {
        hospital.put(mapping.Target_Field__c, hospitalData.
        get(mapping.DeveloperName));
    }
}

insert hospital;


return hospital.Hospital_Ref_Code__c;
}
```

This structure using custom metadata records enables us to add in new fields quickly and easily in the future and makes our API more flexible. This is particularly useful in those scenarios we highlighted, such as where an ISV wants to enable a customer to extend their API with additional fields readily.

We have spent all of this chapter so far looking at how we define endpoints for use in different ways to allow us to work with data. Let's now look at how we can test these APIs we have created through the Developer Workbench tool.

Testing endpoints using Workbench

In *Chapter 11*, *Using Platform Events*, we saw how we can publish platform events through the Salesforce REST API using the Workbench tool at `https://workbench. developerforce.com/restExplorer.php`. When we define a new Apex REST API, we can access and test the API using the same REST Explorer tool.

Any custom Apex REST endpoint is exposed through the /services/apexrest/ yourURLMapping endpoint. For our hospital endpoint, this is /services/ apexrest/hospital.

In the following screenshot, you can see how I have entered this URL with the ACME123 resource identifier, and run a GET request to retrieve the hospital record with Hospital_ Ref_Code__c set to ACME123:

Figure 12.4 – Running a GET request against a custom endpoint using the Workbench REST Explorer

You can see in the screenshot that the REST Explorer formats the response from the API. However, you can click the **Show Raw Response** link and the raw response from the request will be shown.

In the following screenshot, you can see the output from making a POST request, including the request body and the raw response information:

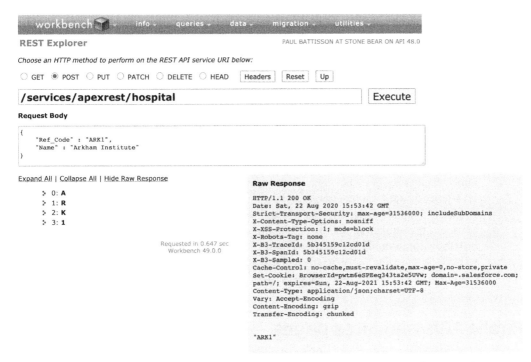

Figure 12.5 – Running a POST request through the Workbench REST explorer and viewing the request body and raw response

Workbench makes it very easy for us to test our APIs as we are building them to validate that they operate as expected. We can test methods of any type and easily view the data we are passing into, and receiving from, the API. Eventually, however, we will want to expose our endpoints out to partners and clients rather than just testing by ourselves. In the next section, we will see how this can be done.

Exposing endpoints

In the previous section, we saw how our new custom API was exposed at the endpoint `/services/apexrest/hospital`. The starting portion of this URL will be the instance for our Salesforce org, for example, `https://um1.salesforce.com`. Our endpoints are therefore accessible through the standard API authentication mechanisms— that is, using OAuth 2.0 or by passing `sessionId` into the request.

Accessing Salesforce APIs in this manner is covered in detail in the REST API Developers Guide and details how we can access APIs using the standard mechanisms. What about the instances where we want to expose an API to the public for use?

> **Note**
>
> In general, we will want our APIs to be authenticated to allow us to ensure that we are controlling the flow of information and keeping data private. There are some instances, however, where we will want to expose data to the public for it to be used. As an example, one organization I worked with maintained a public database of branches and contact details for branches that were exposed on a series of websites, including their own and those of their partners (think similar to a member organization where it would allow you to see member branches, the number of members, key contact details for the branch, and so on). Providing a public API is a great way of exposing data to one or more websites in the same way a headless CMS does. I have also seen this approach used to provide data such as a public product catalogue or news feed.

Public APIs and Sites pages

We can provide public access to an API using the **Sites** pages and **Guest User for Sites**. Using our earlier example `/hospital` endpoint, we can expose the endpoint to allow for any public user to retrieve information about a hospital using **Hospital Ref Code**.

Firstly, we need to define a new site within our **SETUP** menu. In the following screenshot, you can see the definition I have created for a site called **api**. We have accepted most of the default settings and been provided with a URL for us to work with:

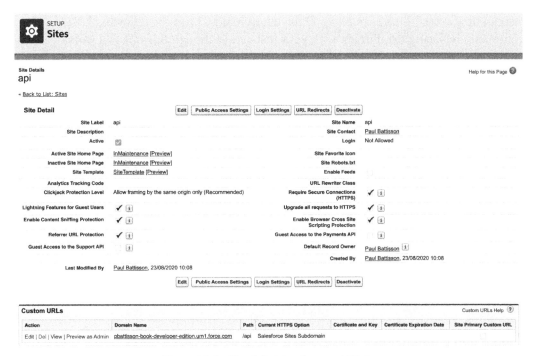

Figure 12.6 – Site definition for our API site

Once your site is defined and activated, using the **Public Access Settings** button, we can access **Profile for the Site Guest User**. This is the profile that is in effect when the site is accessed by an unauthenticated user. For our API to work, we need to provide this profile with **Read**-level access to the `Account` object and add `HospitalRESTService` to the **Enabled Apex Class Access** list. Once this is done, the final tweak for us to make is to update our `HospitalRESTService` class to be **without sharing**.

> **Further information**
>
> In a production environment, we would more likely create discrete sharing rules for the **Guest User** based upon criteria on the record, for example, only sharing those records with a **Publicly Accessible** checkbox marked as true. For the purposes of this example, we will simply assume all `Account` records in the system should be available. Similarly, we would enforce field-level security using the mechanisms highlighted in *Chapter 6, Secure Apex Programming*.

We can now access the API publicly. Open a terminal and run the following URL command; replacing the domain with your instance (although this one will work):

```
curl https://pbattisson-book-developer-edition.um1.force.com/
api/services/apexrest/hospital/ACME123
```

The Apex class runs as anticipated and returns us the correct data.

The use of a site allows us to publicly expose this API endpoint for use. However, we still have the `/services/apexrest` portion of the URL, which is not necessarily ideal. Before we move on to handling different data types in Apex REST classes, I want to briefly discuss an alternative option to Apex REST that uses what we have just seen within the Sites setup to allow us to produce an API endpoint that will have a similar effect.

An alternative using URL Rewriter and Visualforce pages

One of the features available to us within a Salesforce site is the option to use rewrite incoming URLs to the site to allow more user- and SEO-friendly URLs to be used. A typical example is one where if our site was hosting a blog, rather than using the more standard Salesforce URL `/blog?id=1234567890bloghere`, which is not SEO- or user-friendly, we would use `/blog/2020/02/14/why-apex-developers-are-the-best-partners`. We do this using a class that implements the `Site.UrlRewriter` interface.

Sadly, this interface does not work with API endpoints and so cannot be used to redirect our Apex REST APIs. There is a workaround for this though, which is to return our JSON data via a Visualforce page.

> **Note**
> This is a workaround and is not the optimal way of handling these requirements. This will only work for GET requests for JSON data and not the other HTTP methods. I am including it here as it is a known workaround and has some use cases for scenarios such as exposing a blog post as JSON data. I would, however, recommend against using this in general and working with the more standard sites endpoint as discussed.

Let's start by creating a Visualforce page that will render some data and has the JSON `contentType` header. We are also suppressing the standard page sidebar, header, and stylesheets. The following code snippet shows my `HospitalJSON` page:

```
<apex:page controller='HospitalDataController'
contentType='application/json; charset=utf-8'
showHeader='false' standardStylesheets='false' sidebar='false'>
    {!jsonOutput}
</apex:page>
```

Our `HospitalDataController` is defined as follows:

```
public without sharing class HospitalDataController {

    public String jsonOutput {get; private set;}

    public HospitalDataController() {
        String refCode = ApexPages.currentPage().
        getParameters().get('refCode');
        List<Account> hospitals = [SELECT Name, Hospital_Ref_
        Code__c FROM Account WHERE Hospital_Ref_Code__c =
        :refCode];
        if(hospitals.size() == 1) {
            jsonOutput = JSON.serializePretty(new
            HospitalRESTService.HospitalWrapper(hospitals[0]));
        }
    }
}
```

Note that this controller uses `without sharing`. We have used the same code to retrieve the hospital and the `HospitalWrapper` class from `HospitalRESTService`.

Finally, we have our `Site.UrlRewriter` implementation, `HospitalAPIRewriter`, shown in the following code block:

```
global class HospitalAPIRewriter implements Site.UrlRewriter {
    global PageReference mapRequestUrl(PageReference
    friendlyUrl) {
        String url = friendlyUrl.getUrl();
        String matchPattern = '/v1/hospital/';
        if(url.startsWith(matchPattern)) {
```

```
                        String refCode = url.substring(matchPattern.
                        length(), url.length());
                        return new Pagereference('/HospitalJSON?refCode=' +
                        refCode);
                }
            return null;
        }


        global PageReference[] generateUrlFor(PageReference[]
        yourSalesforceUrls) {
            return null;
        }
    }
}
```

The `mapRequestUrl` function takes in a user-friendly URL and maps it to use our `HospitalJSON` page, extracting the `refCode` from the end of the URL and passing it through as a URL parameter.

The final step to using this is to edit the site definition to use `HospitalAPIRewriter` as the `URL Rewriter Class` and add the `HospitalJSON` page to the **Site Visualforce Pages**. The following screenshot shows what the site will look like once both these items are done:

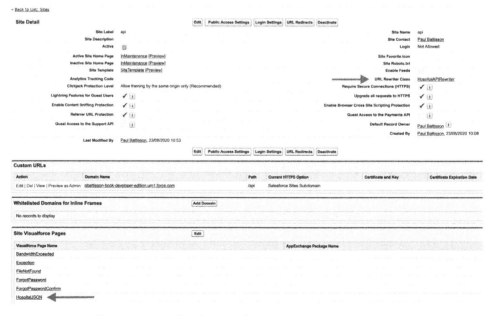

Figure 12.7 – Updated site configuration to use URL Rewriter

Visiting your site URL with `/v1/hospital` as the target location will now return a JSON representation of the data. In the following screenshot, you can see the data returned by the sites URL as well as some example code to retrieve the data as JSON in the console:

Figure 12.8 – Output from using a Visualforce page and URL Rewriter

For simple public endpoints such as blog entries, this can be a very effective way of providing an endpoint that is both user- and SEO-friendly that can return your JSON data.

Throughout this chapter so far, we have focused only on the use of JSON data and have mostly worked with this data using the built-in serialization and deserialization that Salesforce performs for us. In the next section, we will see how we can work with either JSON or XML data within the request body of the API to provide those calling the API with more flexibility.

Handling request body data

When working with Apex REST endpoints, Apex will parse any JSON and XML request bodies and response data automatically, when the method signature for the annotate method contains parameters to be deserialized to. In my experience, this is the easiest and most effective way of working with data in Apex REST and removes the need for data parsing from the endpoint itself. There are some situations, however, where this will not be possible and so it will be necessary for the endpoint to handle the parsing of data itself.

Recall the code we had for the `HospitalRESTService.doPost()` method:

```
@HttpPost
global static String doPost() {
    Id hospitalRTId = Schema.SObjectType.Account.
getRecordTypeInfosByDeveloperName().get('Hospital').
```

```
getRecordTypeId();
    List<API_Mapping__mdt> mappings = [SELECT DeveloperName,
    Target_Field__c FROM API_Mapping__mdt];
    Blob requestBody = RestContext.request.requestBody;
    Map<String, Object> hospitalData = (Map<String, Object>)
    JSON.deserializeUntyped(requestBody.toString());
    Account hospital = new Account();
    hospital.RecordTypeId = hospitalRTId;
    for(API_Mapping__mdt mapping : mappings) {
        if(hospitalData.containsKey(mapping.DeveloperName)) {
            hospital.put(mapping.Target_Field__c, hospitalData.
            get(mapping.DeveloperName));
        }
    }
    insert hospital;
    return hospital.Hospital_Ref_Code__c;
}
```

From the preceding code, we see that if we attempt to pass in XML to this API, we will retrieve an error as we attempt to parse XML data using a JSON parser. To ascertain what type of data we are retrieving, we need to inspect the headers on the request and find the value for the Content-Type header. Then, when making a request containing JSON, this should be set to application/json, and, when working with XML, it should be set to text/xml. We can rewrite our code as follows to allow us to handle this.

To begin with, I have added enum to manage the different data types:

```
private enum DATA_TYPE {XML, JSON}
```

In the following snippet, you can see the updated version of our doPost method that utilizes this enum and delegates to another method to handle the parsing:

```
@HttpPost
global static String doPost() {
    //Retrieve record type and API mapping records
    Id hospitalRTId = Schema.SObjectType.Account.
    getRecordTypeInfosByDeveloperName().get('Hospital').
    getRecordTypeId();
    List<API_Mapping__mdt> mappings = [SELECT DeveloperName,
    Target_Field__c FROM API_Mapping__mdt];
```

```
    Map<String, Object> hospitalData = new Map<String,
    Object>();
     //Determine if we are handling JSON or XML
    if(RestContext.request.headers.get('Content-Type').
    contains('json')) {
        hospitalData = parseData(DATA_TYPE.JSON, RestContext.
        request.requestBody);
    } else if(RestContext.request.headers.get('Content-Type').
    contains('xml')) {
        hospitalData = parseData(DATA_TYPE.XML, RestContext.
request.requestBody);
    }


    //Populate the Account object as before and insert the new
    //record
    Account hospital = new Account();
    hospital.RecordTypeId = hospitalRTId;
    for(API_Mapping__mdt mapping : mappings) {
        if(hospitalData.containsKey(mapping.DeveloperName)) {
            hospital.put(mapping.Target_Field__c, hospitalData.
            get(mapping.DeveloperName));
        }
    }
    insert hospital;
    return hospital.Hospital_Ref_Code__c;
}
```

Then, the `parseData` method will appear as follows:

```
private static Map<String, Object> parseData(DATA_TYPE
requestDataType, Blob data) {
    Map<String, Object> dataMapping = new Map<String,
    Object>();

    switch on requestDataType {
        when JSON {
            //return parsed JSON
        }
```

```
        when XML {
                //return parsed XML
        }
    }
    return dataMapping;
}
```

By extracting the processing code to an external method, we have made it reusable and more easy to test as well more extensible, should an additional data type be needed in the future.

Let's now discuss how we can populate the code to perform the actual parsing dependent on the complexity of the data we have received. We are going to start by reviewing how we can handle JSON data and then switch to manipulating XML.

Handling JSON

There are three ways in which we can effectively deserialize JSON within Apex. These are as follows:

- Through deserialization calls
- Through the use of the `JSONParser` class
- Through the use of a third-party library

The first of these is based upon the idea that an object in JSON is effectively a series of key-value pairs that loosely reflects the structure of maps within Apex. For the data we are receiving in our request, we can simply deserialize into a `Map<String, Object>` data type and cast the generic `Object` values correctly at runtime (this could be an extension of `API_Mapping__mdt` to hold what type of data should be contained for mapping to a field of the appropriate type). For our input, we could use the following code snippet and it will correctly parse our JSON data:

```
when JSON {
    dataMapping = (Map<String,Object>)JSON.
    deserializeUntyped(data.toString());
}
```

This uses the JSON.deserializeUntyped method, which will parse our JSON into a generic data type that we must cast and then can process. We could also deserialize to a more structured type such as our HospitalWrapper class using the JSON.deserialize method and referencing our HospitalWrapper class type as follows:

```
HospitalWrapper wrap = (HospitalWrapper)JSON.deserialize(data.
toString(), HospitalWrapper.class);
```

These options are great for when you are working with a known API that you have a greater degree of control over. What if you were working with a more complex JSON object that you wanted to parse?

This is where the JSONParser class is useful. The JSONParser class allows you to interrogate a JSON string as a collection of tokens and either process or deserialize the data as you read it. This is far more complex that simply deserializing and is typically used when dealing with web service callouts rather than with inbound data as you are in control of the data that is being accepted by the endpoint. Should you be processing a complex JSON object, I have personally found it useful to use option three from our three potential methods and work with a third-party library such as JSONParse (https://github.com/open-force/jsonparse).

This open source library makes it easy to work with complex JSON types and access data in a simpler manner, rather than running repeated deserializations on complex types such as the following:

```
Map<String, Object> root = (Map<String, Object>)JSON.
deserializeUntyped(jsonData);
Map<String, Object> contents = (Map<String, Object>)root.
get('contents');
List<Object> chapters = (List<Object>)contents.get('chapters');
Map<String, Object> chapter1 = (Map<String, Object>)
chapters(0);
String chapterTitle = String.valueOf(secondItem.get('title'));
```

JSONParse allows you to write simpler code, such as the following:

```
new JSONParse(jsonData).get('contents.chapters.[0].title').
getStringValue();
```

This is much easier to read and removes the need for multiple calls within our code that are abstracted away.

For our example code, we are going to simply use the following command:

```
when JSON {
    dataMapping = (Map<String,Object>)JSON.
    deserializeUntyped(data.toString());
}
```

For our scenario, working with our data manually is easily manageable due to its simple nature. In more complex scenarios, using such a library can make it much simpler and easier to work with JSON data, rather than having to manually make many repeated deserialization calls.

Let's now deal with working with XML.

Handling XML

XML does not have the same simple parsing or deserialization engine as JSON because it is a more structured language and can be used to store more complex applications. It is, in itself, a markup language and can be easily translated for display using XSLT processing. It was historically used as a data change format because it could be parsed on multiple platforms, in almost all languages, and, for statically typed languages, can include more details pertaining to metadata.

Within Apex, we can process XML as either a stream or using the **DOM** (short for **Document Object Model**). Streams are more useful when you are processing a set of data from a web service callout or other method and wish to inspect or use only part of the data. If the data you are receiving contains information or events that you want to skip or not process, then the XMLStreamReader class will enable you to process the data effectively.

When working with XML using the DOM, we work on the entire set of data as a tree of nodes that we can navigate and in parts of data, as needed. For example, the XML we would pass in as our request body for the service we have built would be as follows:

```
<request>
    <Name>West Wish Hospital</Name>
    <Ref_Code>WEWISH1</Ref_Code>
</request>
```

The `<request>` tag is the root element we will retrieve once we have created `XMLDocument` from our data. The code to do this is as follows:

```
Dom.Document doc = new Dom.Document();
doc.load(data.toString());
Dom.XMLNode req = doc.getRootElement();
```

For those familiar with navigating the DOM on a web page, it is a similar process to retrieve information from the DOM here. Because we know our data is single layered, we can simply loop through the child nodes of our root element and parse in a similar fashion to before, as shown in the following code:

```
for(Dom.XMLNode childNode : req.getChildElements()) {
    dataMapping.put(childNode.getName(), childNode.getText());
}
```

This allows us an easy way to navigate through the data and retrieve the information we need in order to process the request.

In general, it is more common on the modern web to work with JSON-based payloads than XML, but it is important to either explicitly define that a custom endpoint only works with JSON, or enable the endpoint to parse XML correctly, as shown.

We will now finish the chapter by looking at the correct way to unit test a custom Apex REST endpoint.

Testing Apex REST code

To test Apex REST services, we must explicitly set `RestRequest` for the `RestContext.request` property that the methods will be using. Testing Apex REST methods is actually a very straightforward process in Apex as they are static methods that are globally scoped. For us to test the `doGet` method, we will need to first update the `HospitalWrapper` class to allow the test to view the `Name` and `Ref_Code` properties by annotating them with `@TestVisible`, as shown in the following snippet:

```
global class HospitalWrapper {

    @TestVisible
    String Name;
    @TestVisible
    String Ref_Code;
```

```
    public HospitalWrapper(Account acc) {
        if(acc != null) {
            this.Name = acc.Name;
            this.Ref_Code = acc.Hospital_Ref_Code__c;
        }
    }
}
```

We are only using this wrapper class within our REST service and Salesforce will still show private member variables when serializing an Apex class, so marking as @TestVisible is better for maintaining our encapsulation and avoiding the leaking of data unnecessarily.

In the following code snippet, I have defined a new Apex test class, HospitalRESTService_Test, and created an @TestSetup annotated method to ensure we have a record to retrieve in our tests:

```
@isTest
private with sharing class HospitalRESTService_Test {

    @TestSetup
    static void makeData(){
        Id hospitalRTId = Schema.SObjectType.Account.
        getRecordTypeInfosByDeveloperName().get('Hospital').
        getRecordTypeId();
        Account demoHospital = new Account(Name = 'Demo',
        Hospital_Ref_Code__c = 'DEMO');
        insert demoHospital;
    }

}
```

For our doGet method, we need to test both a request that returns a result and a request that returns null (that is, finds no hospital). In our test, we need to construct a RestRequest instance and populate both the requestURI and httpMethod parameters to the appropriate values for the method to use, and set this request as the value to be retrieved from our RestContext variable.

In the following code, we do this and also finish the test method structure by calling the method under test within our `startTest` and `stopTest` methods, and then assert on the returned value:

```
@isTest
private static void testRetrieveHospital() {
    RestRequest req = new RestRequest();
    req.requestURI = '/hospital/DEMO';
    req.httpMethod = 'GET';
    RestContext.request = req;

    Test.startTest();

    HospitalRESTService.HospitalWrapper hospital =
    HospitalRESTService.doGet();

    Test.stopTest();

    System.assertNotEquals(null, hospital, 'Null value
    returned');
    System.assertEquals('Demo', hospital.Name, 'Incorrect Name
    returned');
}
```

We can also write a similar test to validate the fact that a `null` value is returned when no records are matched, as shown in the following code block:

```
@isTest
private static void testRetrieveNull() {
    RestRequest req = new RestRequest();
    req.requestURI = '/hospital/NO_RESULT';
    req.httpMethod = 'GET';
    RestContext.request = req;

    Test.startTest();

    HospitalRESTService.HospitalWrapper hospital =
    HospitalRESTService.doGet();
```

```
    Test.stopTest();


    System.assertEquals(null, hospital, 'Null value returned');
}
```

Now, the `doGet` method has been tested, so what do we need to do for the `doPost` method?

Firstly, let's review the code for `doPost` and `parseData`, as shown in the following code block:

```
@HttpPost
global static String doPost() {
    Id hospitalRTId = Schema.SObjectType.Account.
    getRecordTypeInfosByDeveloperName().get('Hospital').
    getRecordTypeId();
    List<API_Mapping__mdt> mappings = [SELECT DeveloperName,
    Target_Field__c FROM API_Mapping__mdt];
    Map<String, Object> hospitalData = new Map<String,
    Object>();
    if(RestContext.request.headers.get('Content-Type').
    contains('json')) {
        hospitalData = parseData(DATA_TYPE.JSON, RestContext.
        request.requestBody);
    } else if(RestContext.request.headers.get('Content-Type').
    contains('xml')) {
        hospitalData = parseData(DATA_TYPE.XML, RestContext.
        request.requestBody);
    }


    Account hospital = new Account();
    hospital.RecordTypeId = hospitalRTId;
    for(API_Mapping__mdt mapping : mappings) {
        if(hospitalData.containsKey(mapping.DeveloperName)) {
            hospital.put(mapping.Target_Field__c, hospitalData.
            get(mapping.DeveloperName));
        }
    }
    insert hospital;
    return hospital.Hospital_Ref_Code__c;
```

```
}


private static Map<String, Object> parseData(DATA_TYPE
requestDataType, Blob data) {
    Map<String, Object> dataMapping = new Map<String,
    Object>();


    switch on requestDataType {
        when JSON {
            HospitalWrapper wrap = (HospitalWrapper)JSON.
            deserialize(data.toString(), HospitalWrapper.
            class);
            System.debug(wrap);
            dataMapping = (Map<String,Object>)JSON.
            deserializeUntyped(data.toString());
        }
        when XML {
            Dom.Document doc = new Dom.Document();
            doc.load(data.toString());
            Dom.XMLNode req = doc.getRootElement();


            for(Dom.XMLNode childNode : req.getChildElements())
{
                dataMapping.put(childNode.getName(), childNode.
                getText());
            }
        }
    }
    return dataMapping;
}
```

First, to test appropriately, we will extract the retrieval of the API_Mapping__mdt
records to a utility method so that we can return records for use in a testing context. There
is currently no way of creating custom metadata records in Apex, and so this allows us
to manage the data for testing only. Our updated code for the doPost method is then as
follows:

```
@HttpPost
global static String doPost() {
```

```
    Id hospitalRTId = Schema.SObjectType.Account.
getRecordTypeInfosByDeveloperName().get('Hospital').
getRecordTypeId();
    List<API_Mapping__mdt> mappings =
    retrieveMappingsMetadata();
    Map<String, Object> hospitalData = new Map<String,
    Object>();
    if(RestContext.request.headers.get('Content-Type').
    contains('json')) {
        hospitalData = parseData(DATA_TYPE.JSON, RestContext.
        request.requestBody);
    } else if(RestContext.request.headers.get('Content-Type').
    contains('xml')) {
        hospitalData = parseData(DATA_TYPE.XML, RestContext.
        request.requestBody);
    }


    Account hospital = new Account();
    hospital.RecordTypeId = hospitalRTId;
    for(API_Mapping__mdt mapping : mappings) {
        if(hospitalData.containsKey(mapping.DeveloperName)) {
            hospital.put(mapping.Target_Field__c, hospitalData.
            get(mapping.DeveloperName));
        }
    }
    insert hospital;
    return hospital.Hospital_Ref_Code__c;
}
```

And the `retrieveMappingsMetadata` method is as follows:

```
private static List<API_Mapping__mdt>
retrieveMappingsMetadata() {
    if(Test.isRunningTest()) {
        List<API_Mapping__mdt> testData = new List<API_
        Mapping__mdt>();
        testData.add(new API_Mapping__mdt(DeveloperName =
        'Name', Target_Field__c = 'Name'));
        testData.add(new API_Mapping__mdt(DeveloperName = 'Ref_
```

```
        Code', Target_Field__c = 'Hospital_Ref_Code__c'));
        return testData;
    }


    return [SELECT DeveloperName, Target_Field__c FROM API_
    Mapping__mdt];
}
```

For our first test, we should validate whether a JSON request is processed correctly. We follow the same pattern as before, creating a `RestRequest` instance and populating the values we need on the `headers` and `requestBody` properties, as shown here:

```
@isTest
private static void testPostValidJSON() {
    RestRequest req = new RestRequest();
    req.requestURI = '/hospital/';
    req.httpMethod = 'POST';
    req.addHeader('Content-Type', 'application/json');
    req.requestBody =
    Blob.valueOf('{"Name":"Test Post JSON",
    Ref_Code":"TEST_JSON"}');
    RestContext.request = req;


    Test.startTest();


    String resp = HospitalRESTService.doPost();


    Test.stopTest();


    System.assertEquals('TEST_JSON', resp, 'Incorrect response
    returned');
    List<Account> accounts = [SELECT Id FROM Account WHERE Name
    = 'Test Post JSON'];
    System.assertEquals(1, accounts.size(), 'Account not
    inserted');
}
```

Similarly, we can set the `requestBody` and `Content-Type` headers for the XML instance, as shown in the following code block:

```
@isTest
private static void testPostValidXML() {
    RestRequest req = new RestRequest();
    req.requestURI = '/hospital/';
    req.httpMethod = 'POST';
    req.addHeader('Content-Type', 'text/xml');
    req.requestBody = Blob.valueOf('<request><Name>Test Post
    XML</Name><Ref_Code>TEST_XML</Ref_Code></request>');
    RestContext.request = req;

    Test.startTest();

    String resp = HospitalRESTService.doPost();

    Test.stopTest();

    System.assertEquals('TEST_XML', resp, 'Incorrect response
    returned');
    List<Account> accounts = [SELECT Id FROM Account WHERE Name
    = 'Test Post XML'];
    System.assertEquals(1, accounts.size(), 'Account not
    inserted');
}
```

All of our test methods for our Apex REST class use this same method of creating an example request for the test to use with the parameters required to simulate the request itself and allow us to test our Apex code in a simple repeatable manner.

Summary

In this chapter, we have covered the creation of custom REST endpoints in Apex in detail, beginning with an overview of the REST paradigm and how a RESTful endpoint is structured to utilize the common HTTP methods underpinning the core infrastructure of the internet. We discussed how and when we might use a custom endpoint rather than a standard Salesforce REST endpoint.

The next section of the chapter focused on defining endpoints in both a simple and more complex manner, as well as how we can use custom metadata to help provide a dynamic endpoint that is particularly useful in product development environments. After having built a set of endpoints, we saw how we can utilize the Workbench tool to test them internally to validate behavior.

Following this, we focused on how we can expose an endpoint as a public API using sites, as well as an alternative that utilized both the `URLRewriter` interface and Visualforce pages for more SEO- and user-friendly `GET` requests. For `POST` (and `PUT` and `PATCH`) requests, we looked at the different ways of handling JSON and XML data efficiently to parse different request types and provide a more generic API.

We then completed the chapter with a final section on testing our code and how to create a `RestRequest` instance for use, as well as looking at how to use custom metadata within tests.

This chapter finished the second part of the book on *Asynchronous Apex and Apex REST*, in which we have seen the many asynchronous processing tools available to us within the Apex language to allow the solutions we create to scale and grow, as well as how to integrate these solutions in a scalable manner with external systems. The final section of the book focuses on improving the performance of the Apex code we have written.

Section 3 – Apex Performance

In this final section, we will combine what we have learned so far to help look at how we profile an application and improve its performance. We will also discuss the trade-offs of the different options and wrap things up with a discussion on the impact that architecture has on a solution.

This section covers the following chapters:

- *Chapter 13, Performance and the Salesforce Governor Limits*
- *Chapter 14, Performance Profiling*
- *Chapter 15, Improving Apex Performance*
- *Chapter 16, Performance and Application Architectures*

13
Performance and the Salesforce Governor Limits

In this chapter, we are going to begin our third and final section of the book, where we focus on performance within Apex, how we can profile Apex, and how we can improve the performance of our applications.

Performance as an area of study is something I find fascinating as it contains a number of unique overlaps from both the human and technical sides of software development. Improving performance for the sake of it is likely to lead to code that is much more difficult to maintain and manage going forward. Applications that do not take performance into account will quickly become slow and provide a negative user experience.

For Salesforce applications in particular, code tends to not receive much maintenance after it has been written and deployed, particularly in circumstances where a customer has paid a consultancy to deliver a piece of functionality in a one-off project. I often encounter organizations that contain solutions that are still operating fine, without any changes, after 5 or more years. Because of this fact, we as Salesforce developers have a duty of care to our customers and end users to try and predict the future and optimize a certain amount ahead of time. However, as Donald Knuth famously wrote, *premature optimization is the root of all evil*. We can spend too much time working out an optimization that will have little or no impact and yet cost time and money to produce or maintain.

In this chapter, we are going to begin our journey into the world of Salesforce performance by understanding governor limits. We will be looking at the following:

- Understanding the Salesforce application request lifecycle
- Looking at what multi-tenancy is and the need for governor limits
- Studying governor limits and why we as developers should embrace them
- Looking at how we should begin to think about performance on the Salesforce platform

Let's begin by discussing the Salesforce application request lifecycle.

The Salesforce application request lifecycle

Salesforce at its heart is a transactional database, and the majority of customer use cases today still revolve around working with the core objects at the heart of Sales Cloud or Service Cloud. Over the (at the time of writing) 21 years Salesforce has operated as an entity, they have developed an extremely rich and robust platform for application development, as we have seen throughout this book.

With the majority of use cases still revolving around these core clouds, the majority of Salesforce applications still follow a fairly standard pattern that can be summarized in the following steps:

1. The end user interacts with the screen to request some data or a form.
2. The end user enters some data—either a new record or an update to an existing record—and presses save.
3. Salesforce receives the data over the internet.
4. Salesforce runs some processing on the record.

5. Salesforce saves the record to the database.

6. Updated data is returned and the user is presented an updated or a new view.

I have drawn this process out in the following figure, with the dashed boxes labeled to correspond with the preceding steps:

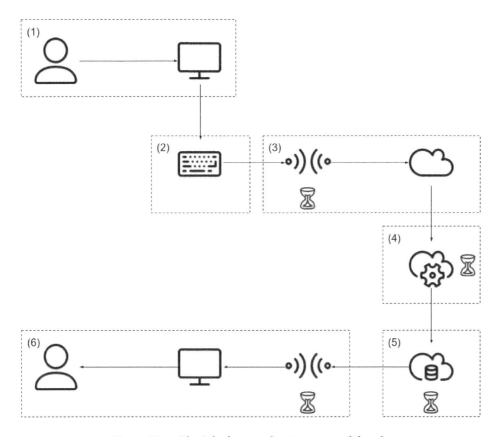

Figure 13.1 – The Salesforce application request lifecycle

I have also added a number of hourglass images to all the points where there is a potential performance implication. We can control the volume of data we are sending over the wire; lowering this will speed up communication in steps 3 and 6. In step 4, if we are performing some processing on some data in Apex prior to it being saved, we are potentially slowing down the responsiveness of the solution. In step 5, when we add automation such as triggers, workflow, processes, and flows, we are again requiring extra work to be done before the end user is returned an update. I have excluded potential hourglasses here on the screen elements that we could also control, as inefficient rendering choices can impact performance there.

The point of this diagram is to illustrate there are a number of points that can impact the responsiveness of an application and therefore the user experience. One of the limits we will discuss is the maximum time for processing on the CPU during a transaction of 10 seconds. 10 seconds is a very short amount of time when we think about it in comparison to a lot of our day-to-day lives; however, the processing time on the CPU is leaving our user waiting for a response. Try to think about how you would react if you pressed a button on a website and you waited for over 10 seconds for a response. You are very unlikely to be happy or to count that as a great user experience.

When working with Apex and reviewing performance, it is therefore important for us to understand what our end goal of performance improvement is and how the piece we are working on fits into the bigger picture of the application. With this in mind, let's now look a bit deeper under the hood of Salesforce and its multi-tenant architecture, and what this means for our performance.

Multi-tenancy and performance

Salesforce is a multi-tenant platform, that is, multiple customers (tenants) rent space or pay for resources on a single Salesforce server. This is largely abstracted away from end users, but is still a critical architectural consideration. It is this key design decision that partly necessitates Salesforce to be a metadata-driven platform—we define all objects, fields, relationships, page layouts, automation, and logic as metadata for a particular instance rather than hard-set values for the instance as we would with other platforms.

The standard analogy for describing a multi-tenant environment is an apartment block, where utilities and service infrastructure is shared. To ensure that this works well, everyone has to abide by an agreed set of standards around managing certain shared areas and constrained resources. For example, in many apartment blocks there is a shared set of washing machines and driers. No single tenant can use all of these at once, otherwise it blocks any other tenants from using these resources. In the same way, if a Salesforce instance (which has multiple orgs running on it) has a limited amount of CPU space, RAM, or other hardware, then no single org can or should be able to monopolize these resources, blocking other tenants.

We can extend this analogy of our laundry machines and other services, such as electricity, to think about how this will impact the notion of performance. The Salesforce platform, similar to these services, takes a minimum baseline view of performance. Salesforce provides a baseline level of performance that is unknown to us; we as developers and customers on the platform do not know how powerful the hardware underpinning the platform is, but we can be sure that it will provide a consistent level of performance for all tenants.

What does this mean for us as developers in terms of performance? Firstly, it means when we are dealing with performance, we have to accept and understand that we are hardware constrained. Typically, this is not something that's dealt with by web developers as you can always purchase a bigger server. For Salesforce developers, there is no bigger or faster server; instead, you are running on a preset platform outside your control to the largest extent and so must keep that in mind.

Secondly, we have to be clear on where our process can be optimized and the impact this optimization will have. It is very rare that we can optimize for one aspect of a process and not impact others, for example, trading CPU cycles for memory. While it may be easy for us to optimize for a single constraint, such as the number of database queries, doing so will inevitably lead to an increase in usage of another resource, such as memory or CPU. The ideal outcome for our work is where we find a global minimum for this multivariable problem, but more likely we will have to accept that we are going to find the least bad option or best compromise given the set of resources we have. This is a real balancing act and one that will not be easy, but it also brings me on to the final big impact multi-tenancy has on performance considerations for developers—you must think ahead.

At the start of this chapter, I quoted Donald Knuth as having said *premature optimization is the root of all evil*, so am I now contradicting this maxim? The full quote from Knuth is shown as follows (with our excerpt highlighted):

> *"Programmers waste enormous amounts of time thinking about, or worrying about, the speed of noncritical parts of their programs, and these attempts at efficiency actually have a strong negative impact when debugging and maintenance are considered. We should forget about small efficiencies, say about 97% of the time:* **premature optimization is the root of all evil***. Yet we should not pass up our opportunities in that critical 3%."*

As developers on a multi-tenant platform, we have to think ahead about how our system will be used—different platforms, different data volumes, and the interplay of areas of the system can all have a major impact on the performance of our application. For Salesforce developers, a small set of practices (many of which have been highlighted in this book already) can allow us to write clean code, which performs in a way that precludes concern. This is the 97% Knuth is referring to; most of our code will simply become harder to manage, maintain, read, and work with if we spend too much time working on detailed optimizations. We should only look to optimize when we are in those strange 3% scenarios.

Salesforce helps to maintain a baseline level of performance for all users by enforcing governor limits on the platform that restrict the monopolization of a resource by a single developer and help to ensure that, for requests made, there is a good and consistent baseline performance in the way in which the application runs. Let's now look at what governor limits are and why we as developers should embrace them.

Governor limits and why we should embrace them

We are not going to list all the various governor limits in this section, as there is little value in this and Salesforce provides an easily accessible list in the Apex developers guide, which is regularly updated. We are, however, going to discuss what governor limits are in principle and why we should embrace them.

Salesforce governor limits are thresholds that restrict developers from monopolizing resources in a way that would detriment the performance of the Salesforce application for all users of the platform. Each governor limit imposes a maximum available utilization for each tenant to ensure that the operations of one tenant do not adversely affect the other tenants. For example, take the limit for the number of queries in a transaction. When working with any platform, database tuning and query performance are key areas of concern to ensure that an application can grow and scale effectively.

Salesforce enforces a limit on the number of queries a developer can make for two reasons; firstly, to ensure that a single tenant does not consume too great a proportion of CPU and database resources through repeated queries. The Force.com Query Optimizer is a very effective tool at parsing SOQL into SQL for running against the underlying database, but making many repeated calls to the database would slow down the experience for other users (including your own users and colleagues) and tenants. The limit is therefore in place to protect against this.

Secondly, the limits are in place to maintain a baseline experience for an end user. Salesforce has to ensure that its customers receive a level of service on the platform that matches their expectations. However, if another developer writes some code or develops a solution that is slow and inefficient, most end users are likely to just say *Salesforce is slow*, without an understanding that it is not necessarily the fault of Salesforce. From a brand perspective, this is not good for Salesforce as people will negatively associate their platform with poor performance.

To help ensure that their customers have a performant and acceptable user experience that is not too slow, Salesforce enforces governor limits to provide a maximum threshold on the amount of work that can be done in a single transaction and thus the time a request takes. It is important therefore that we recognize that the limits are in place not to frustrate good developers, but to help protect against bad development practices.

It is for this second reason that I think that we as developers should embrace the governor limits that have been put in place. These limits provide developers with a framework that they must adhere to, and boundaries they must stay within to successfully run their code. These limits ensure that we cannot do anything that would severely impact the performance of the system to provide a slower experience for any end users, either internal or external to our organization.

The limits also force Salesforce developers to think ahead to a small degree and learn some best practices to avoid exceeding the governor limits. Exceeding a governor limit causes an exception to be thrown that cannot be caught and handled by a developer; the entire execution simply halts and all changes are rolled back. It is imperative therefore that we avoid exceeding any governor limits and ensure that our code stays within the thresholds to avoid any issues.

There are a number of common reasons for governor limits being exceeded, which can be thought of as falling into one of three categories:

- **Bad implementations (typically in Apex)**: The most common are some of the bad practices we discussed at the beginning of the book, such as queries and DML statements within loops. These are common errors and are also easy to resolve.

- **Mixed implementations where too many tools are being utilized together**: A prime example is having a mixture of workflow, process builder processes, flows, and Apex together on an object that all consume resources and interact in an unintended manner to either cause unnecessary loops or to simply consume more resources than required if all of them are delivered in a single tool. These errors are time-consuming to fix but it's doable through a combination of refactoring and maintenance.

- **External factors such as managed packages and external systems interacting with our code and solutions to produce unintended results**: This is particularly true in larger environments where there are multiple large managed packages or external systems operating in a manner that can lead to issues with shared limits such as the CPU time. In these instances, work must be done in the host org to try and mitigate these issues.

Part of the process to help us avoid exceeding these limits will be thorough testing of our code using standard Apex tests. As discussed in *Chapter 5, Testing Apex Code*, all code should be tested for positive, negative, and bulk cases to ensure that we are avoiding any unnecessary errors. There will be instances where we will need to do more detailed performance profiling and analysis though, which we will discuss in detail in *Chapter 14, Performance Profiling*. Before we move onto this, let's finish this chapter by discussing how we should think about performance and what performance means.

Thinking about performance

For Salesforce developers, there are therefore two ways in which we can think about performance:

- Ensuring that we stay within the governor limits
- Improving application responsiveness and resource usage

It is important to understand the difference between these two ways of thinking when we deal with performance. In the first instance, our focus is solely on ensuring that we have tested the application to ensure that resources throttled by governor limits are not exceeded so that the application can proceed. This would be the default view for testing when developing a trigger on an object that is primarily created record by record in the user interface, for example. We want to ensure that our trigger can handle bulk instances such as when a data load occurs, but our predominant use case is for single record execution. We want to test that we are not going to exceed governor limits in that bulk case, but it is not to enhance the overall solution. This is typically done during initial development and testing.

In the second instance, we are actively trying to improve performance for some noticeable benefit. For example, we may have some existing code that operates on multiple records and has an inefficient query or a new process added, which means we are noticing slower performance that we wish to improve, or we could be reaching a governor limit that would negatively impact user experience. This can occur either before a piece of work is deployed or during its support and maintenance lifecycle.

It can be helpful to think of these two reasons as the proverbial carrot (improving performance for end user benefit and better resource usage as per the second instance) and the stick (ensuring we do not break governor limits, as in the first instance). It is important that we are aware of these two different reasons as they will help us to answer the key questions we need to ask when reviewing performance, which are as follows:

- What are we trying to improve?

- Why are we trying to improve it?

- What do we need to measure?

These three questions, as we will see in the following chapters, play an integral role in helping us profile our solutions appropriately so that we may improve performance. They will also allow us to explain to business users the rationale behind the work we are doing, and why we are focusing on this, rather than a new feature. It is often difficult for business users, who are typically sponsoring the work, to understand why time and resources should be invested in performance work, especially when the benefits may be intangible to them.

For example, let's say we have an existing process to which a new automation step has been added. This new step is causing another save operation and therefore invoking the save order of execution again within the transaction and consuming resources. We want to validate that the system is using resources appropriately and that this update is not going to slow the system down for users (remember that the user is waiting during this save order of execution), which will require us to run some performance profiling, then identify if there is an issue, before we decide to act on this and update the solution. We will dive into this model in more information in *Chapter 14, Performance Profiling*, but it allows us to discuss the rationale with our business user, as follows:

- *What are we trying to improve?* We are trying to improve the resource usage of the overall process given this additional step we have added.

- *Why are we trying to improve it?* We want to ensure we are not at risk of exceeding governor limits and are not providing the end user with a sub-optimal experience through long loading times.

- *What do we need to measure?* We need to measure the resource usage under a variety of different scenarios to determine whether we are near this governor threshold and what the typical experience for an end user will be. For example, we may wish to push any remaining updates to an asynchronous processing method if we are approaching a governor limit, but should inform the user that this is happening and that the update will not be instant.

Providing information in this format makes it much easier for a business user to understand the rationale and can provide a useful communication framework for building the base of a business case. Working to improve performance should not be done without a valid business case and some analysis to ensure that the work is necessary and will have a positive impact. With that in mind, we will now summarize what we have discussed in this chapter so that we can move on to discussing how we profile our work to determine this in the next chapter.

Summary

In this chapter, we began by discussing the lifecycle of a request for a Salesforce application and how that is impacted by the Apex code we write. We saw how important it is for developers to remember that any code we write in Apex that is run on the server may block the user's application from being responsive and create a negative user experience. From this, we discussed, when looking at how we determine how to improve performance, that we must understand the structure of the Salesforce platform and what that means in terms of resource management—namely that resources are shared and that a baseline of performance must be guaranteed by having a limit to the resources that a single operation can use.

These limits are the governor limits, and we saw how they provide a guaranteed level of performance for end users across the platform. We also discussed why we as developers should embrace the governor limits to help us ensure that our application will avoid producing poor user experiences. We then discussed how we should think about performance on the platform, in particular when it comes to working with the governor limits. As developers on the platform, we have both the carrot of faster and improved user experiences and the stick of governor limit exceptions to help ensure we do not monopolize resources and that the Apex code we write fits within a band of acceptable performance.

We finished the chapter by extending this to start the discussion on how we think about communicating the need to improve performance to a business stakeholder and the key questions we should ask ourselves. To reiterate the sentiment of the full Donald Knuth quote we shared, we must ensure that we do not optimize prematurely or focus on the wrong areas of our application, but instead work on the areas of the application where improvement will have the greatest impact and therefore add the most business value.

Now that we have an understanding of the governor limits and how we should think about performance in general, we will move onto the next chapter, where we can begin to discuss how to profile our applications to measure both whether improvements are needed and the impact of the changes we make.

14
Performance Profiling

In *Chapter 13*, *Performance and the Salesforce Governor Limits*, we discussed performance at a high level and how it relates to the Salesforce governor limits. We also spoke about how we should begin to think about performance with respect to this model.

In this chapter, we are going to start looking at how we actually go about working on improving the performance of our applications through profiling. We are going to focus on Apex, as this is the core topic of the book, but we will also discuss how we can begin to profile both Visualforce and Lightning Web Components performance as well, to illustrate how the entire life cycle of user interaction needs to be considered.

In this chapter, we will cover the following topics:

- The need for performance profiling and measurement
- The OODA methodology and how it will allow us to have a framework for success
- Big O notation and magnitude analysis
- How to profile Apex performance
- Using the `Limits` class
- Profiling Visualforce page performance
- Profiling Lightning Web Components performance

Let's begin by looking at why we want to profile our application and the importance of measuring the resource usage of our system. Note that whenever I refer to performance throughout this chapter and the remainder of the book, I may be referring to either improved resource utilization, or improved time to respond/return data for the user. The two are interchangeable for a lot of the instances that we will be discussing, and so for brevity and consistency, we will use the single term *performance* here.

Technical Requirements

The code for the chapter can be found here: `https://github.com/PacktPublishing/Mastering-Apex-Programming/tree/Chapter-14`

Measure twice, cut once

In order for us to begin understanding how we can improve our application's performance, we must first know how it is performing and what resources are being utilized by the application. This can be summed up in the following quote:

> *If you cannot measure it, you cannot improve it*

This quote is attributed to many individuals (Lord Kelvin and Peter Drucker, to name two), but regardless of who said it, it captures the essence of how we should think about performance testing and analysis. Before we can make any reasonable assertion that we want to improve the performance of some code, we need to measure and understand what the code is doing and how resources are being utilized. Without this measurement step, we will have no true understanding of whether the work we have undertaken has improved the performance of our code or whether it has had no significant impact at all.

I have titled this section *Measure twice, cut once*, as this is another important maxim that we must keep in mind when we start to consider performance analysis. It comes from more practical skills such as woodworking, where you want to measure the wood you are about to cut twice, and then make the cut once. Only after measuring twice can you be confident that the measurement you are making is accurate, as you cannot uncut your wood.

If we take a single measurement, can we be certain that it is an accurate representation of how the system operates? What would be the outcome if, for example, the single measurement we took indicated that there were no performance issues within the solution? It could be that this is completely accurate, and we have no work to do. However, it could be the case that this is a false negative, that is, we do have performance issues, but we are not exercising the code in a way that would highlight them appropriately. We should therefore ensure that we take multiple measurements to observe the behavior of the system under different loads and validate that we actually understand what is happening. We should measure multiple times, and then make the changes to the system once.

How do we go about deciding how to make these changes? Once we have made our measurements, what is the process we should follow? This is where I recommend using the OODA methodology, which we will discuss next.

The OODA methodology

The **OODA** (short for **Observe, Orient, Decide, Act**) loop and OODA methodology was first coined by US military strategist Colonel John Boyd and was applied to help make improved decisions during combat operations. It has since become widely used within different industries and operations, and I have found it to be an extremely effective way of working with performance testing, although it has been used within software circles by a variety of individuals for a long time.

The OODA loop comprises four steps, which form its acronym. These steps are shown in the following diagram:

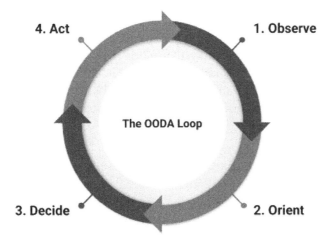

Figure 14.1 – The OODA loop

We can use this same loop to define a methodology that will allow us to test the performance of our applications and determine whether to take action. Let's look at these steps in more detail and how they specifically relate to the process of performance analysis.

Observe

In this first step, we take our measurements for our system and observe its current state. This is the first part of the profiling stage, where we gather information on what resources are being used and how the system is operating. Note that for our purposes we may decide to observe all the governor-limited resources and their usage for the solution or only some, depending on what our aim is. If, for example, we have received a governor limit exception, we may wish to focus on that particular resource.

Orient

Once we have taken our measurements, we need to orient ourselves on the situation. This is where our analysis takes place. How much of this resource are we using? How does this scale? What is the magnitude of the issue? What do our previous experiences with the solution tell us about this? At the end of this step, we should ensure that we sufficiently understand the system's behavior and usage of the resources in question to allow us to proceed.

Decide

The next step is to decide on what action to take. The first thing we need to do is determine, based upon the analysis we have undertaken in the orient step, whether we want to take any action at all (doing nothing is, in itself, an action and can be considered the null hypothesis outcome). If we want to take action, we need to determine what action that is and what outcome we expect from that action. For example, we may choose to refactor a set of code to reduce the number of queries being made. Our hypothesis is that this refactoring will reduce the number of queries by 50%. It is important that we have a hypothesis that is testable and verifiable before we take the next step, which is to act.

Act

The final step in an iteration of the loop is to act, that is, to implement the changes we have identified in our code as a potential solution. Once we have taken the action, we should verify that it has produced the outcome we expect by testing our hypothesis. In the previous example, this would be verifying that the number of queries made has reduced by 50%. The outcome of this test then feeds back into the next cycle of the loop. If the changes had the impact we expected, we can test them more thoroughly in the system as part of a regression test, using the same OODA loop, and then move on to another problem. If the changes did not have the impact we imagined, we can begin observing again to ascertain why that is and make further changes if appropriate.

By following a methodology such as this, we can ensure that we have a well-structured and testable way of improving the performance of our application that also enables us to document the different steps undertaken and decisions made. In the orient step, we need to ensure that we are analyzing the situation correctly and understand the magnitude of the problem. A common way of doing this is through the use of big O notation as part of our magnitude analysis. Before we begin looking at how we capture data and measurements within Apex, let's finish our conceptual understanding by reviewing what big O notation is and how magnitude analysis works.

Big O notation and magnitude analysis

Big O notation is a way in which we can analyze the amount of complexity there is within an operation (typically time complexity) to help understand the magnitude or scale of the operation under consideration. The O here stands for *Order*, and big O notation follows the convention of writing O and then the complexity (in terms of number of operations) in brackets after, such as $O(1)$, $O(n)$, and $O(n^2)$. In this notation, n denotes the size or number of items inputted. Let's see some examples to understand how we can use this notation.

The following code snippet, given a list of any size, simply outputs its length to the debug logs:

```
public static void printSize(List<Account> accounts) {
    System.debug('There are ' + accounts.size() + ' accounts
    in the list');
}
```

If we pass in a list of 1 account or a list of 100 accounts, the number of operations run will stay the same, a fixed constant, and so we denote this as having complexity O(1), that is, the number of operations is always fixed and constant. This is the most optimal of solutions as the system scales infinitely. Another example would be the following code snippet:

```
public static List<Account> getAccounts(List<Id> accountIds) {
    return [SELECT Name FROM Account WHERE Id IN :accountIds];
}
```

This code, by itself, scales constantly in terms of queries, running a single query no matter how many items we pass in to the method. This is the ideal situation for any snippet of code.

Next imagine we had the following code snippet that accepts a list of accounts and debugs their names individually:

```
public static void printNames(List<Account> accounts) {
    for(Account acc : accounts) {
        System.debug('This account has the name ' + acc.
        Name);
    }
}
```

In order to analyze what order of magnitude this snippet is, we have to consider what happens as our function receives larger lists. For a list of one item, we have an extremely quick loop that runs once and debugs once. For a list of two items, we have two `debug` statements, and for 10 items, the loop runs 10 times and prints 10 items to the `debug` logs. So, if we have a list of some arbitrary size n, the loop will run n times, and so we would denote this code as being O(n). Such scaling is linear, that is, as the number of items we operate on increases, the code we have written scales linearly.

Typically, this is a good solution. However, we must be aware when our use of resources that are governor constrained scale in a linear fashion, as this can still lead to exceptions as we reach larger data volumes. For example, in the following code snippet, we run a query per item:

```
public static void getAccountsAndPrintNames(List<Id>
accountIds) {
    for(Id accId : accountIds) {
        Account acc = [SELECT Name FROM Account WHERE Id =
        :accId];
        System.debug('This account has the name ' + acc.
        Name);
    }
}
```

In this scenario, our code also scales linearly, and has complexity O(n). However, the number of queries we may issue is a constrained resource with a governor limit. If we have 101 items in the `accountIds` list, we will hit a governor limit. We would therefore still need to refactor this code. You may, in fact, recognize such a bad practice being part of the *Bulkification* section from *Chapter 1, Common Apex Mistakes*.

Ideally, we want to have code that scales either linearly or is constant, as in the preceding example. However, we may have situations where we find code that scales in a quadratic, cubic, or even exponential fashion. Let's take the following code:

```
public static Boolean checkForDuplicates(List<Account> accs) {
    Boolean hasDuplicates = false;

    for(Integer i = 0; i < accs.size(); i++) {
        for(Integer j = 0; j < accs.size(); j++) {
            if(i == j) {
                continue;
            }

            if(accs[i].Name == accs[j].Name) {
                hasDuplicates = true;
            }
        }
    }

    return hasDuplicates;
}
```

The preceding code is a basic set of code for determining whether we have duplicate accounts in the list using the account's name for matching. How does this code scale? For every item in the list, we loop through the list again to allow us to check for duplicates. If the list contains a single record, we loop through once, for two records, the outer loop runs twice and the inner loop runs twice for each iteration, so a total of four iterations. For a list of five items, the outer loop runs five times and the inner loop runs five times per outer loop iteration, so 25 times in total (5 inner iterations for 5 outer iterations—5 × 5 = 25). We can see that this code is scaling quadratically, that is, the number of iterations is the square of the list size. As the size of the list doubles, the number of iterations quadruples, which is denoted as $O(n^2)$.

Note

If you are having trouble visualizing this, try updating the code as follows:

```
public static Boolean checkForDuplicates(List<Account> accs) {
        Boolean hasDuplicates = false;
        Integer count = 0;

        for(Integer i = 0; i < accs.size(); i++) {
                for(Integer j = 0; j < accs.size(); j++) {

                        count++;
                        if(i == j) {
                                continue;
                        }

                        if(accs[i].Name == accs[j].Name) {
                                hasDuplicates = true;
                        }
                }
        }
        System.debug(count);
        return hasDuplicates;
}
```

You can then run the code with lists of varying sizes to see how it causes the count variable to always be the square of the list size. When running an analysis, a simple counter like this can be an extremely handy tool. You can simply run it for a series of numbers, record the results, and plot them in a spreadsheet tool to see the scaling effect.

Any code that scales in a power series like this, whether $O(n^2)$ (quadratically), $O(n^3)$ (cubically), or above must be analyzed and, wherever possible, should be refactored to remove such scaling. In the worst-case scenarios, code may have a complexity of $O(x^n)$, that is, the code scales exponentially for some factor, x. An example would be attempting to find all possible subsets of a set of items, such as all possible combinations of different products. If you had no products, then you have a single subset/combination that is zero products. If you have a single product, you have two combinations—that of no products or one product. For two products, you have four combinations, for three you have eight, and so on. We can see this in the following diagram:

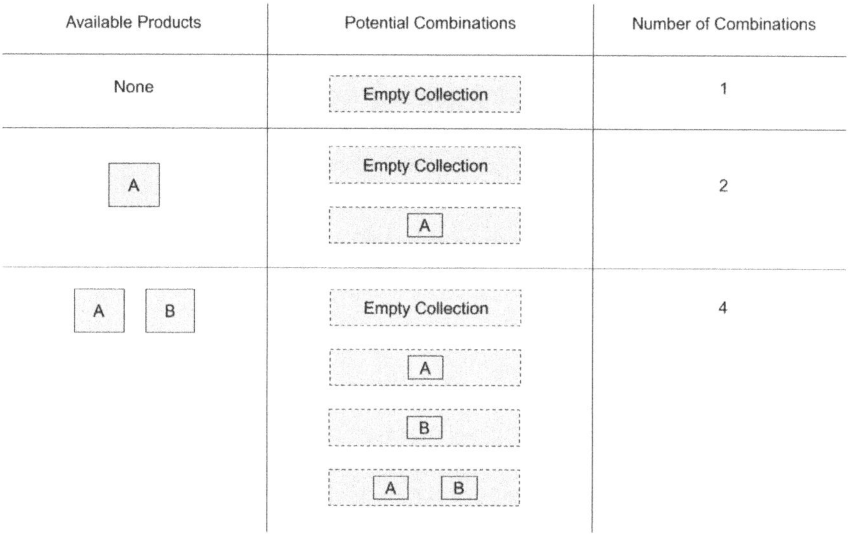

Available Products	Potential Combinations	Number of Combinations
None	Empty Collection	1
A	Empty Collection A	2
A B	Empty Collection A B A B	4

Figure 14.2 – Potential product combinations and exponential scaling

This would scale exponentially. The pattern here is that for n products, there are 2^n possible combinations. This number gets large rapidly (2^{20} is 1,048,576) and will quickly make our solution inefficient to run.

In Apex, we are unlikely to encounter exponential growth problems, but our code can easily fall into a trap of becoming quadratic in nature, a common example being making loops with loops to retrieve or process data on parent-child relationships. If our preceding code had been executed by a trigger containing 200 records, then 40,000 iterations would have occurred. For a modern processor, this is more than easy for it to handle quickly and efficiently. However, again we must be aware of the resources we have available to us.

Performing this analysis allows us to understand the magnitude of our problem and undertake the orient portion of the OODA loop effectively. Now that we have figured out how we can analyze the data we capture, let's move on to the next section, where we are going to discuss how we can profile our Apex.

Profiling Apex performance

In order to profile our Apex code, we need to take a series of measurements as to what governor resources have been utilized at multiple steps within the code's execution path. The reason to take multiple recordings is so that we can ensure that we can identify where within the code the resources are being utilized.

Unlike other platforms, which allow the inspection of code, including memory usage, for different portions of the code, there is no such feature in Salesforce. We must perform our profiling manually and then run our analysis to determine what action to take. The way in which we will do this is through the use of the Limits class.

The Limits class

If you review a debug log generated by Salesforce when a process runs, you will see at the end of the log a long list of information that details the resource usage for the different namespaces that were invoked during the transaction. An example of this information is shown in the following screenshot:

```
13:37:42.128 (128542604)|LIMIT_USAGE_FOR_NS|(default)|
   Number of SOQL queries: 0 out of 200
   Number of query rows: 0 out of 50000
   Number of SOSL queries: 0 out of 20
   Number of DML statements: 0 out of 150
   Number of DML rows: 0 out of 10000
   Maximum CPU time: 0 out of 60000
   Maximum heap size: 0 out of 12000000
   Number of callouts: 0 out of 100
   Number of Email Invocations: 0 out of 10
   Number of future calls: 0 out of 50
   Number of queueable jobs added to the queue: 0 out of 1
   Number of Mobile Apex push calls: 0 out of 10
```

Figure 14.3 – Resource usage information at the end of a debug log

This information profiles the resource usage for the transaction overall, and allows us to see how our resources are being used. While this information is helpful at a transaction-level perspective, for us to profile and analyze which areas of our Apex need improvement, we need to be able to retrieve similar statistics at multiple steps throughout the transaction.

To retrieve this data, we will need to use the `Limits` system class. The `Limits` class provides a series of methods in one of two formats; `getResourceName`, which returns the current usage of the resource, and `getLimitResourceName`, which returns the limit for the resource, where `ResourceName` is the name of the resource we are profiling. All of these methods are `public` and `static` and so can be called from anywhere within our Apex code, as follows:

```
public static Boolean checkForDuplicates(List<Account accs) {
    Boolean hasDuplicates = false;
    System.debug('Method start CPU usage:' + Limits.
    getCpuTime());
    for(Integer i = 0; i < accs.size(); i++) {
        for(Integer j = 0; j < accs.size(); j++) {
            if(i == j) {
                continue;
            }

            if(accs[i].Name == accs[j].Name) {
                hasDuplicates = true;
            }
        }
    }
    System.debug('Method end CPU usage:' + Limits.
    getCpuTime());
    return hasDuplicates;
}
```

If we run the preceding code, then it will debug the CPU usage at the start and end of the method as it is executed. This is helpful, but requires us to do the calculation on how much of the CPU time was used between the two calls. More typically, we would write our code as follows, to perform the calculation for us:

```
public static Boolean checkForDuplicates(List<Account accs) {
    Boolean hasDuplicates = false;
    Integer startCpuTime = Limits.getCpuTime();
    for(Integer i = 0; i < accs.size(); i++) {
        for(Integer j = 0; j < accs.size(); j++) {
            if(i == j) {
                continue;
```

```
                }

            if(accs[i].Name == accs[j].Name) {
                hasDuplicates = true;
            }
        }
    }
    Integer totalUsage = Limits.getCpuTime() - startCpuTime;
    System.debug('Method CPU usage:' + totalUsage);
    return hasDuplicates;
}
```

This same approach can work for any of the limits that we may want to profile, including SOQL queries, return query rows, and other limits. It works extremely well for situations where we want to hone in and focus on a single resource in detail in a single method. It becomes more cumbersome to work with as we try to do more detailed profiling across a transaction, and is more commonly extracted to a useful utility class for reuse. Let's now look at how such a utility class may be structured.

A utility class to profile Apex

Before we begin to write our profiling utility, let's think about what output we expect from this utility class. When it comes to profiling information, we can have the information output to the debug log for us to inspect, making the information transient, that is, it will only exist for the transaction and will not persist. There may also be a need for the output to be logged to a data store or collected by a third party for it to be used long term or allow aggregation for analytics. We may also want this profiling utility to persist within our code so that we can turn it on and off in the future to allow us to debug errors that are due to governor limit exceptions. This could allow the utility to operate in tandem with the Logger utility we discussed in *Chapter 4, Exceptions and Exception Handling*. We may also want the utility to allow us to check at runtime whether we are going to surpass a governor limit and block the action from occurring if so.

These are all valid use cases and are raised here to highlight the many ways in which such a utility could be used. We are going to build out the first use case, recording information to the debug log in a transient fashion to allow us to analyze what is occurring. When considering how best to manage a system long term, however, you should consider how you can reuse this utility for the different use cases.

Additionally, we want to be able to measure the usage of a specific governor resource for a specific method or block of code. This way, we can profile multiple methods or code blocks within the application quickly and easily to determine where the majority of our resources are being utilized. We also want to be able to profile specific resources rather than always profile all resources, as this will help to reduce the noise in the data and make it much easier for us to review.

To begin, let's define a new class called `ProfilingUtility` and add `private static Map<String, Integer>` for us to utilize in recording for multiple different methods or blocks, as shown in the following code block:

```
public with sharing class ProfilingUtility {
    private static Map<String, Integer> recordings;
}
```

There are a limited and fixed set of items we can record limits for, so we want to ensure we have a restricted and preset list, which is a perfect use case for enum. Let's add an enum to the class called `Resource`, as shown in the following code snippet:

```
public enum Resource {
    AGGREGATE_QUERIES, ASYNC_CALLS, CALLOUTS, CPU_TIME, DML_
    ROWS,
    DML_STATEMENTS, EMAIL_INVOCATIONS, FUTURE_CALLS, HEAP_SIZE,
    MOBILE_PUSH_CALLS, QUERIES, QUERY_LOCATOR_ROWS, QUERY_ROWS,
    QUEUEABLE_JOBS, SOSL_QUERIES
}
```

To make a recording, we need to know what we are naming the recording (this could be a method name or a custom string) and the resource we want to record for using the `Resource` enum.

Firstly, let's create a `private` method that returns the current usage of a given resource using the `Resource` enum, as we will use this to get values when both starting and stopping recordings. Our `getResourceValue` method to do this is shown in the following code snippet:

```
private static Integer getResourceValue(Resource governor) {
    Integer value = 0;
    switch on governor {
        when AGGREGATE_QUERIES{
            value = Limits.getAggregateQueries();
```

```
        }
    when ASYNC_CALLS{
        value = Limits.getAsyncCalls();
    }
    when CALLOUTS{
        value = Limits.getCallouts();
    }
    when CPU_TIME{
        value = Limits.getCpuTime();
    }
    when DML_ROWS{
        value = Limits.getDmlRows();
    }
    when DML_STATEMENTS{
        value = Limits.getDmlStatements();
    }
    when EMAIL_INVOCATIONS{
        value = Limits.getEmailInvocations();
    }
    when FUTURE_CALLS{
        value = Limits.getFutureCalls();
    }
    when HEAP_SIZE{
        value = Limits.getHeapSize();
    }
    when MOBILE_PUSH_CALLS{
        value = Limits.getMobilePushApexCalls();
    }
    when QUERIES{
        value = Limits.getQueries();
    }
    when QUERY_LOCATOR_ROWS{
        value = Limits.getQueryLocatorRows();
    }
    when QUERY_ROWS{
        value = Limits.getQueryRows();
```

```
        }
        when QUEUEABLE_JOBS{
            value = Limits.getQueueableJobs();
        }
        when SOSL_QUERIES{
            value = Limits.getSoslQueries();
        }
    }
    return value;

}
```

Using this method, we can build our method to begin recording for a given resource with a name. We will call this method startRecording and, in the method, will store the data we retrieve from getResourceValue in our recordings map, as we can see in the following code block:

```
public static void startRecording(String recordingName,
Resource governor) {
    if(recordings == null) {
        recordings = new Map<String, Integer>();
    }
    recordings.put(recordingName, getResourceValue(governor));
}
```

This method will take the first recording. We now need a stopRecording method that will take a second recording and calculate a total usage before debugging, again using the getResourceValue method, as can be seen in the following code block:

```
public static void stopRecording(String recordingName, Resource
governor) {
    Integer value = getResourceValue(governor);
    Integer total = value - recordings.get(recordingName);
    System.debug('Total usage of resource ' + governor.name() +
    ' for recording ' + recordingName + ' was: ' + total);
}
```

We can now use this utility class within our code to take a recording of governor resource usage on arbitrary code blocks or methods. The best use of this class in my experience is to utilize it within a testing framework.

As we have discussed a number of times within this book, a rigorous and robust testing framework allows us to have confidence in the code we have written and the outcomes that code provides. We should be testing positive, negative, and bulk use cases within the tests we write, and we can now include this utility class in those tests to verify behavior and allow us to analyze in a repeatable manner how our code is behaving. Whenever we are profiling performances, we should take multiple readings of the same experiment to validate that the data we receive is accurate and not just subject to a one-off issue.

For example, let's take our earlier checkForDuplicates method, which we believed was scaling quadratically, as a reminder that the code for this method was as follows:

```
public static Boolean checkForDuplicates(List<Account> accs) {
    Boolean hasDuplicates = false;

    for(Integer i = 0; i < accs.size(); i++) {
        for(Integer j = 0; j < accs.size(); j++) {
            if(i == j) {
                continue;
            }

            if(accs[i].Name == accs[j].Name) {
                hasDuplicates = true;
            }
        }
    }

    return hasDuplicates;
}
```

I have placed this in a class called CodeToProfile for the example here. We can write a test method that is configurable to run with a varying number of accounts and use our ProfilingUtility class to record CPU usage. An example test structure to do this is shown in the following code block:

```
@isTest
private with sharing class CodeToProfile_Test {

    private static final Integer NUM_ACCOUNTS = 5;
    private static final Boolean INCLUDE_DUPLICATE = true;
```

```
@isTest
private static void testProfileCheckForDuplicates() {

    List<Account> testAccounts = new List<Account>();
    for(Integer i = 0; i < NUM_ACCOUNTS; i++) {
        if(i == NUM_ACCOUNTS - 1 && INCLUDE_DUPLICATE) {
            testAccounts.add(new Account(Name = 'Account
            0'));
        } else {
            testAccounts.add(new Account(Name = 'Account '
            + i));
        }
    }

    Test.startTest();
    ProfilingUtility.startRecording('checkForDuplicates' +
    NUM_ACCOUNTS, ProfilingUtility.Resource.CPU_TIME);
    Boolean containsDuplicates = CodeToProfile.
    checkForDuplicates(testAccounts);
    ProfilingUtility.stopRecording('checkForDuplicates' +
    NUM_ACCOUNTS, ProfilingUtility.Resource.CPU_TIME);
    Test.stopTest();

    System.assertEquals(INCLUDE_DUPLICATE,
    containsDuplicates);
}

}
```

I have run the tests for sizes of 5, 10, 25, 50, 100, 250, and 500 records and plotted them on the graph shown in the following diagram:

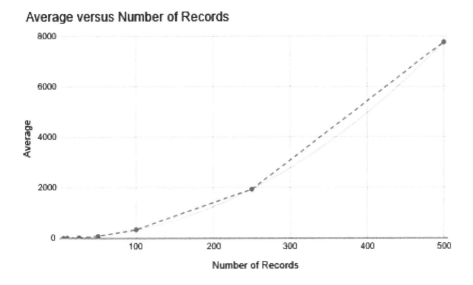

Figure 14.4 – Performance data from testing

The dashed line on this graph is the plot line between our actual data points, which are highlighted. I took the average of four runs of the data to get these points as an illustrative sample. The curved line is a trend line that matches the quadratic function, scaled to fit the graph. In a real-world performance test, I would expect to validate the data at more increments, say every 50 records, to get a clearer line before looking at trend data. However, in just this simple run, we could look at the trend line and see that we would expect a test with 400 records to use about 5,000 ms of CPU time. If we were to run the test with 400 records, we could see the result we retrieve, which for me, after running the code four times, came out at 5,014 ms.

The important analysis we can now do from this data is see where we think the limit of our code is. A quadratic law such as this infers that doubling the number of records quadruples the resource usage. Looking through the data we have, we would anticipate that somewhere between 550 and 600 records, we would surpass the CPU time. Again, a quick run for 550 records returns 9,860 ms, which is near our total limit.

With this information, we can now decide how we want to proceed: do we either enforce a limit on our code to only work with under 550 records (or being sensible, a limit of 500 to provide extra headway), or do we refactor the code? This information we have allows us to present these options back to the business we are working with and understand how we should handle these scenarios to take the appropriate action.

As a final note on running these tests, you may find that you can run this code with a size of 600 and actually receive a valid return over 10,000 ms, that is, above the governor limit. I was able to run for 600 records and profile using over 11,000 ms of CPU time. How is this possible? CPU time is a soft governor limit unlike, for example, the number of SOQL queries. This is because the time to run can vary and is also dependent upon the instance load. I ran these tests on a developer instance early on a Saturday morning UK time, a quiet period for Salesforce. If I were running the same test at 3 p.m. on a Monday, I would expect it to error.

The Apex system has the right to terminate long-running processes, but will not necessarily enforce that limit if the resource load on the instance is not high. My advice is to always work and aim for below 10,000 ms in testing to ensure that you can be comfortable and safe in a production environment. While this is not officially documented behavior, a good write-up can be found on the Salesforce StackExchange discussion board at `https://salesforce.stackexchange.com/questions/48648/maximum-cpu-time-limit-allowed-to-be-exceeded-in-sandbox/49351#49351` for those interested in reading further.

Now that we have seen how to profile our Apex code, let's discuss the other code-based areas of the application we may wish to profile the performance of, starting with Visualforce.

Profiling Visualforce performance

Over the past few years, there has been a shift within Salesforce development away from the use of Visualforce toward the use of first Aura, and more recently the Lightning Web Components framework. While this has meant that the number of new Visualforce pages being created has dropped significantly, for those working with an existing environment, which is rich with Visualforce pages, a good measure is to simply update the pages to work within Lightning Experience to help maximize Lightning adoption and provide a short- to medium-term solution.

When undertaking this work, it can also be a useful process to work to improve the performance of existing Visualforce pages to help improve your application's overall performance. There are still instances where new Visualforce pages are being built and deployed, notably for some custom communities and sites pages, where page performance is an important measure.

Visualforce is a server-side framework, and as such maintains the state between transactions through the view state. The view state is a bundle of data that contains information about the state of the controller for the page to enable communication of information between transactions. This is extremely helpful for allowing developers to build interactive pages that can work with information across requests.

To view the view state of a Visualforce page, you should enable both **Development Mode** and **Show View State in Development Mode** on your user profile, as shown in the following screenshot. This will then allow you, when working with a Visualforce page, to see the development mode toolbar and view state for the page:

Figure 14.5 – Enabling the development mode and view state display

I have generated the following simple Visualforce page and controller to allow us to see how the view state for a page is presented. The following code snippet shows the simple controller we are using:

```
public with sharing class ViewStateController {
    public transient String transientString { get; set; }
    public String nonTransientString { get; set; }


    public ViewStateController() {
        transientString = 'This is a transient string';
        nonTransientString = 'This is a non-transient string';
    }


    public PageReference refresh() {
        return null;
    }
}
```

The controller has a pair of properties, one of which is marked as `transient` and therefore will not be contained within the view state. I am outputting these strings on a simple Visualforce page, the code for which is shown in the following code snippet:

```
<apex:page controller="ViewStateController">
    <apex:form>
```

```
            <p>{!nontransientString}</p>
            <p>{!transientString}</p>
            <apex:commandButton value="Refresh" action="{!refresh}"
    />
        </apex:form>
    </apex:page>
```

This simple example highlights one of the key parts of Visualforce performance tuning, namely, knowing how to correctly manage the view state. The smaller the view state of the page, the less data is sent between transactions and needs to be reinstated within the Apex controller, providing a double performance benefit.

In the following screenshot, I have expanded the view state information for this page to show how only the `nontransientString` variable is stored in the view state:

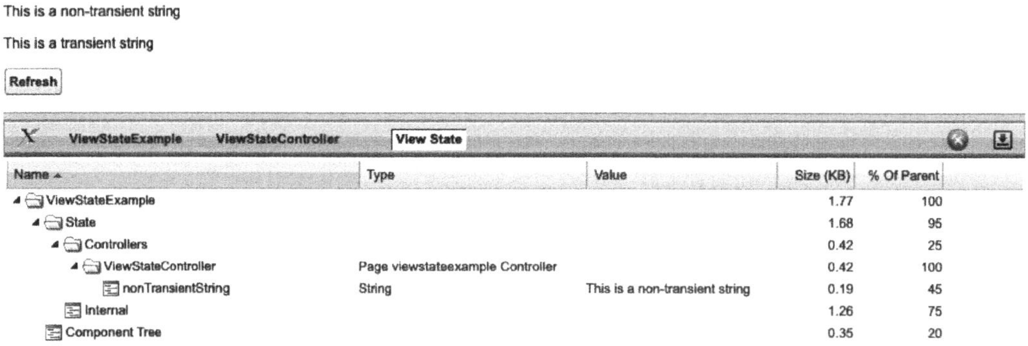

This is a non-transient string

This is a transient string

Refresh

Name ▲	Type	Value	Size (KB)	% Of Parent
▲ ViewStateExample			1.77	100
▲ State			1.68	95
▲ Controllers			0.42	25
▲ ViewStateController	Page viewstateexample Controller		0.42	100
nonTransientString	String	This is a non-transient string	0.19	45
Internal			1.26	75
Component Tree			0.35	20

Figure 14.6 – Viewing the view state for a simple page

When it comes to improving the performance of Visualforce pages, the two main areas of focus for a developer are to improve performance through view state management and reduction, and through general Apex code performance improvement. Reducing the view state will allow us to improve page load times by reducing the data to be spent between the client and the server for each interaction, as well as making the conversion of the view state into Apex more efficient. Otherwise, general Apex performance improvements apply to simply improve the responsiveness of the application.

It was a common practice to move to a tool such as Visualforce Remote Objects to help improve page performance by reducing the amount the server is required to render and switching to a more modern page approach. However, this has now been deprecated as a practice, so if you intend to rewrite a Visualforce page for improvement, I would highly recommend you do so in the Lightning Web Components framework, the profiling of which we will now discuss.

Profiling Lightning Web Components performance

Lightning Web Components is the newest frontend development framework for the Salesforce platform and is built using modern HTML and JavaScript to provide the best possible performance and web standards compliance. The fact that the framework is built using these standard technologies allows Lightning Web Components to be analyzed in a way that is much closer to an analysis of regular web pages and other JavaScript frameworks.

The main way therefore of profiling Lightning Web Components is through the use of standard web tools such as the Chrome Developer tools. The full use of these tools is outside the scope of this book, but Google provides a large amount of training free of charge for these tools. Salesforce has also released an extension for Google Chrome to enhance the developer tools with the Salesforce Lightning Inspector Chrome extension, which can be obtained from the Chrome extensions library.

After installing this tool, you can record the performance of a page containing components to produce a graph like the one shown in the following screenshot:

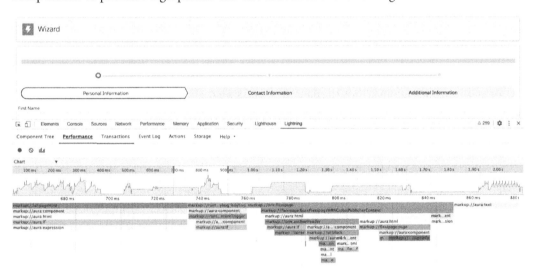

Figure 14.7 – Viewing the Performance tab of the Salesforce Lightning Inspector Chrome extension

This view shows details of how the page was loaded and the code that each component ran within the call stack. Other tabs also detail the various network traffic and calls making up the Salesforce servers, all of which will impact the performance of the components in rendering or interacting with the page. Again, best practices around lazy landing, caching results, and minimizing data transfer can help dramatically improve the performance of Lightning Web Components.

Just as with Visualforce, it is important to also bear in mind the impact that our Apex code running has on the performance of our pages, both in the loading cycle and when making our components interactive. Writing and providing more efficient Apex code will help improve the performance of any interactions with the Salesforce servers and provide a better user experience overall.

We have now seen how we can profile the performance of both Visualforce pages and Lightning Web Components at a high level. If you are having particular problems in performance in the case of either of these user interface frameworks, I highly recommend looking through some of the various blog posts that both Salesforce and the wider community have shared over the years. You should always keep in mind the impact your Apex code is having on this, and work to improve your Apex performance to help keep the user interface responsive. While reviewing performance profiling for these frameworks in detail is beyond the scope of this book, as we saw in *Chapter 13, Performance and the Salesforce Governor Limits* , in *The Salesforce application request life cycle* section, Apex code and its performance will always impact the way in which the overall request runs and so must be considered. With an understanding of how we profile our Apex, let's now summarize what we have learned in this chapter before we look at concrete ways in which we can improve performance.

Summary

We began this chapter by understanding the mindset we should have when profiling performance in our applications to make decisions, that of *measure twice, cut once*, to ensure that we had sufficient data before we acted. From this we looked into a structured methodology, OODA, to help us make informed decisions in profiling and understanding the performance of our Apex code.

We looked at the four steps of OODA individually and how they fit into a broader whole to help us profile, analyze, decide, and act on our code as part of a performance analysis system. From this, we looked into more details of how we perform the analysis required in the orient phase using big O notation and magnitude analysis. Although this involved some basic algebra and mathematics, it provided us with a simple way of reviewing and understanding how to quantify and communicate the impact of the specific processes we had implemented.

ith this tool available to us, we saw specifically how we can profile the different resources utilized by Apex through the use of the Limits class and then generated a utility class for us to utilize in logging out our performance metrics. The code we generated can easily be extended to store and provide these analytics externally if required, but also enables us to run performance analysis within a testing framework to obtain repeatable results. As we saw, it is best to average the results of some of these outputs to obtain a value we can be more confident in for analysis purposes. We brought this all together to run some tests at differing volumes on some code we expected to scale in a particular fashion and verified that it behaved as we had expected in our static analysis. Gathering these metrics will allow us to make effective recommendations and decisions on how best to improve the code going forward, and is a key component of performance analysis.

We finished the chapter by looking briefly at how we profile both Visualforce pages and Lightning Web Components, the two main user interface frameworks on the platform. While a detailed look into performance profiling is outside the scope of this book, we saw at a high level how to profile the areas of these frameworks that are accessible to the client side, and discussed how we must remember that the Apex we write will always impact the performance of any rendering speeds when requests to the server are made.

With an understanding of how to profile Apex and analyze the performance we are seeing, let's now move on to some concrete ways of improving performance for different governor resources in the next chapter.

15
Improving Apex Performance

In the previous chapters of this section, we have focused on the practices involved in profiling the performance of our application to ensure that we can take measurements that will allow us to correctly analyze the performance of the system, as well as how to undertake that analysis.

In this chapter, we are going to focus on practical ways in which you can improve the performance of your code. This list is not a comprehensive list of every possible performance optimization you can make, but rather is a set of optimizations that can help in most instances without being specific to the exact underlying code. Again, performance will be dictated by what your code needs to do, so some of these methods may not apply, but as general patterns and principles, they should assist in improving your code performance overall.

In this chapter, we will cover the following topics:

- Improving CPU time

- Heap size

- Query selectivity

- Number of queries

- Platform cache

- Understanding when to make improvements

Technical Requirements

The code for the chapter can be found here: `https://github.com/ PacktPublishing/Mastering-Apex-Programming/tree/Chapter-15`

Improving CPU time

CPU time is the amount of time spent running our Apex code during a transaction. It is difficult to pin down exactly, as many factors can come into play that determine how much time is spent running a piece of code; however, in general, there are two ways to improve the CPU usage:

- Work on a smaller amount of data (that is, do less work).

- Operate on the data in a more efficient manner.

It is always important to consider whether the first option is possible. Can we make our query more selective (refer to the *Improving query selectivity* section ahead) or simply reduce the amount of work we are doing to speed up the system? A standard synchronous transaction has 10,000 ms of CPU time available. If we are processing 10,000 records, that means 1 ms each. For 1,000 records, that means 10 ms each, again not a lot of time. Anything we can do, therefore, to reduce the scope of the data we are working on will be beneficial in improving our overall performance.

This is not always practical though, and often we will need to find ways of improving the performance of our code through writing it more efficiently. Given the preceding discussion about reducing data size, the next step when working to improve our CPU time will be to consider how we can improve the speed of our loops.

Faster for loops

There are three main ways in which we can structure `for` loops within Apex:

- The iterable `for` loop—`for(Object item : List<Object>)`, commonly used for iteration over query results as `for(Account acc : [SELECT Id, Name FROM Account])`

- The batched SOQL `for` loop, which allows us to handle records in batches of 200 from a query, which is actually written as two loops, an outer loop, `for(List<Account> accs : [SELECT Id, Name FROM Account])`, and an inner loop, `for(Account acc : accs)`

- A more standard loop using an iterator variable—`for(Integer i = 0; i < someTotal; i++)`

All three of these options have their benefits and drawbacks, but more importantly for us, all three perform differently and therefore can consume different amounts of CPU time.

In the following code snippet, I have written a test class, `LoopPerformance_Test`, which has four tests that run these various loop types (there is a duplicate to test declaration of the value of `someTotal` both inside and outside the loop declaration for completeness).

Firstly, we have a method to create the necessary data for our tests, `makeData`:

```
@TestSetup
static void makeData(){
    List<Account> accounts = new List<Account>();
    for(Integer i = 0; i < 5000; i++) {
        accounts.add(new Account(Name = 'Test ' + i));
    }

    insert accounts;
}
```

Our first test uses the SOQL `for` loop format to loop through the account records we have created and print their names to the debug log. The test takes a reading of `CPUTime` before and after our loop runs so we can then output the difference (that is, the time spent executing) through a failing test assertion. We will use this same setup for all our tests and simply change the format of the `for` loop. Our first test is then as follows:

```
@isTest
private static void testSOQLFor() {
```

```
        Integer start = Limits.getCpuTime();


        for(Account acc : [SELECT Name FROM Account]) {
            System.debug(acc.Name);
        }


        Integer stop = Limits.getCpuTime();
        Integer total = stop - start;
        System.assert(false, 'SOQL For Loop Total = ' + total);
    }
```

The second test does the same thing, but uses the batched SOQL `for` loop format:

```
@isTest
private static void testSOQLBatchedFor() {
    Integer start = Limits.getCpuTime();


    for(List<Account> accs : [SELECT Name FROM Account]) {
        for(Account acc : accs) {
            System.debug(acc.Name);
        }
    }


    Integer stop = Limits.getCpuTime();
    Integer total = stop - start;
    System.assert(false, 'Batched SOQL For Loop Total = ' +
    total);
}
```

For our third test, we use a traditional iterator-style `for` loop with the upper maximum/limit defined external to the loop:

```
@isTest
private static void testIteratorExternalMax() {
    Integer start = Limits.getCpuTime();


    List<Account> accs = [SELECT Name FROM Account];
    Integer max = accs.size();
```

```
    for(Integer i = 0; i < max; i++) {
        System.debug(accs[i].Name);
    }

    Integer stop = Limits.getCpuTime();
    Integer total = stop - start;
    System.assert(false, 'Iterator External Max Total = ' +
    total);
}
```

Our final test uses the iterator format, but with the maximum defined in the loop statement itself:

```
@isTest
private static void testIteratorInlineMax() {
    Integer start = Limits.getCpuTime();

    List<Account> accs = [SELECT Name FROM Account];

    for(Integer i = 0; i < accs.size(); i++) {
        System.debug(accs[i].Name);
    }

    Integer stop = Limits.getCpuTime();
    Integer total = stop - start;
    System.assert(false, 'Iterator Inline Max Total = ' +
    total);
}
```

All of these tests will fail on purpose to provide us with a simple way of outputting the CPU time used in looping over 5,000 records.

An example run of this class shows the following:

- The SOQL `for` loop took 218 ms.
- The batched SOQL `for` loop took 569 ms.

- The iterator example with the maximum defined external to the `for` loop took 64 ms.

- The corresponding `for` loop with the maximum defined inline took 68 ms.

As you can see from these numbers, the iterator examples run in about 30% of the time it takes to run the SOQL `for` loop, which itself takes about 40% of the batch SOQL example.

In general then, if we are going to be processing a very large number of records, we should use the iterator format for best performance in CPU time, although, as we will see later on, the impact of other operations will likely be much greater than this loop setup. In general, I would not say you should switch all your loops over to the iterator method, for example, while we get an improvement in CPU time, we do use a lot more heap size; 245,088 bytes in the iterator, instead of 1,250 bytes in the SOQL loop. We will discuss managing the heap size limit shortly. However, this is an important example that highlights the fact that when optimizing for one governor limit, we will often impact another. In the situation where we are concerned with reducing CPU time, this style of loop will help improve our code's performance, but for other situations, the simpler readability of the iterable `for` loop will outlay the performance improvement here at lower volumes. We will discuss how we can also improve the heap size later.

This code will improve the overall speed of our loops; however, as suggested, a good practice is to try and remove the need for a loop altogether where possible. One way of achieving this is typically through the use of a map.

Using maps to remove and reduce looping

A common use case for loops is to organize the results of a query into a map for use later. The simplest use case is when retrieving a list of records from a query and then putting them into a map so that you can retrieve a record using its ID. You can do this by simply passing the query into the constructor of a map with the `Map<Id, sObject>` type, as can be seen in the following code snippet:

```
Map<Id, Account> accsById = new Map<Id, Account>([SELECT Id,
Name FROM Account]);


Account myAccount = accsById.get(myAccountId);
```

Although this is a standard feature of the platform, I have found that there is still a significant portion of developers who have not discovered this handy feature and instead have been looping through records returned for a query to create the same structure.

What about an instance where you wish to search for a record in a set using a custom identifier such as an external ID? In this case, it is not uncommon to see the code that loops through the records to search to find this individual key. For example, I once integrated with a billing system that had a standard Salesforce integration that would delete and replace certain records when they were updated. In Salesforce, I had to reconnect these records to existing Salesforce records using a unique combination of two fields—in this case, the ID of the related contact and the name of a related product. One way of doing this is to loop through both lists of records to find the matches and pair them, as shown in the following code snippet:

```
List<New_Record__c> newRecords; //Our newly generated records
we need to match
List<Match_Record__c> matchRecords; //The data we wish to match
to

for(Integer i = 0; i < newRecords.size(); i++) {
    String matchKey = newRecord[i].Contact__c + '-' +
    newRecord[i].Product__c;
     for(Integer j = 0; j < matchRecords.size(); j++} {
            if(matchKey == matchRecords[j].Custom_Key__c) {
                matchRecord[j].Parent__c = newRecords[i].Id;
                //Populate lookup relationship
                break;
            }
     }
}
```

Although this works, it is a very computationally expensive way of doing so, as again we run a number of statements proportional to i × j. Instead, we could replace our inner loop with a map, as shown in the following code block:

```
List<New_Record__c> newRecords; //Our newly generated records
                                //we need to match
List<Match_Record__c> matchRecords; //The data we wish
                                //to match to

Map<String, Id> newRecordIdsByCustomKey = new Map<String,
Id>();

for(Integer i = 0; i < newRecords.size(); i++) {
```

```
    String matchKey = newRecord[i].Contact__c + '-' +
    newRecord[i].Product__c;

    newRecordIdsByCustomKey(matchKey, newRecord.Id);
}


for(Integer j = 0; j < matchRecords.size(); j++} {
    matchRecord[j].Parent__c = newRecordIdsByCustomKey.
    get(matchRecords[j].Custom_Key__c);
}
```

This code reduces the size of our loops (that is, the number of iterations) and hence CPU time, from proportional to i × j to being proportional to i + j. If i and j are both 100, this is changing from 10,000 iterations to 200, saving 98% of the iterations. Working with maps to organize your data can help you significantly reduce the number of iterations you are running in your code and should be considered a best practice wherever possible.

What we are doing in this instance is effectively taking one data format (a list) that it is not easy to retrieve our desired data from, and parsing it into another format (a map), which makes this easier. This has reduced the number of operations we need to perform and so saved us (potentially) a significant amount of work, as we can see from the simple preceding example. The final way of reducing CPU time that we are going to discuss is an extension of this idea, and is the process of reducing the use of expensive operations wherever possible.

Reducing the use of expensive operations

Within Apex, we have a wide variety of operations available to us, from simple arithmetical ones through to system classes that allow us to retrieve information about the org we are working on dynamically. All of these operations vary in terms of the amount of CPU time they consume. In general, operations that are interrogating the system dynamically are more expensive than operations that operate on static data.

For example, if we wanted to retrieve the Name field of our account record and assign its value to the output variable, we could do it in one of two ways. We could either call the Name field using a static reference or call the get method on the record, passing in the field name. Both options are shown in the following code snippet:

```
String staticOutput = acc.Name;
String dynamicOutput = (String)acc.get('Name');
```

The dynamic variant of this is slower and more CPU intensive than the `static` variant.
As an example, I ran the following code in my org:

```
Account acc = new Account(Name = 'test');
String output1;
String output2;

Integer mark1 = Limits.getCPUTime();

for(Integer i = 0; i < 100000; i++) {
    output1 = acc.Name;
}

Integer mark2 = Limits.getCPUTime();

for(Integer i = 0; i < 100000; i++) {
    output2 = (String)acc.get('Name');
}

Integer mark3 = Limits.getCPUTime();

Integer total1 = mark2 - mark1;
Integer total2 = mark3 - mark2;

System.debug('static: ' + total1);
System.debug('dynamic: ' + total2);
```

This code performs two large loops to help us determine the difference in CPU time for
accessing the Name field directly or through a dynamic reference. Running this code,
we find that the average time after five runs for the different variants is 1,141 ms for the
static option, and 3,030 ms for the dynamic version. The dynamic version is therefore
three times the cost (approximately) of the static version. While each statement is
using a minimal amount of resources (approximately 0.01 ms per statement for the
static variant, and 0.03 ms for the dynamic variant), when coding, we should be aware
of this additional overhead. The example here is a simple one and Salesforce's inbuilt
caching may also come into effect to help improve the process. Wherever possible, we
should attempt to work with static references to fields.

This is not an issue for most developers, but is a concern for ISVs. Another commonly used dynamic call is to the `Schema` class to retrieve information about metadata within the org. Take the following code snippet:

```
Integer mark1 = Limits.getCPUTime();


Map<String, Schema.SObjectType> describeInfo = Schema.
getGlobalDescribe();


Integer mark2 = Limits.getCPUTime();
Integer total1 = mark2 - mark1;


System.debug('CPU Time: ' + total1);
System.debug('Number of items: ' + describeInfo.keySet().
size());
```

I ran this code in two different orgs. In the first, there were 742 items that the describe information returned and the statement took around 70 ms to run. In a separate org with 1,010 metadata items returned by the describe call, the same statement took 85 ms to run. As the size of the org grows, so will the time to make this call.

The simplest way to handle these situations is to cache values locally in variables for reuse. If you are making repeated calls to any of the describe information, you should work to cache these results in a local variable outside the loop, which will remove the need to make repeated calls and reduce your CPU time overall.

Storing items in local variables for caching and improving CPU performance can impact other governor limits, namely, heap size, as more data is stored on the heap for easy access. Let's now look at some ways in which we can reduce heap size usage.

Reducing heap size usage

The heap size is the amount of memory being used to store the various objects, variables, and state of the Apex transaction in memory as it is being processed. For synchronous operations, this is capped at 6 MB and is doubled to 12 MB for asynchronous processes.

Put simply, the way to improve usage of the heap size is to hold less information in memory. Heap size is an interesting governor limit as it has little impact on visible performance to the end user. The end user will never be aware of some code taking 1 MB or 5 MB of heap up, unlike CPU time, where they will perceive the delay in responsiveness. Should you be working with larger datasets, the heap size can start to grow and a number of actions can be taken to reduce it. For the first of these, let's return to `for` loops.

Batched for loops

When discussing `for` loops in the preceding examples, we noted how storing the records we wish to iterate through in a variable to improve CPU time leads, in turn, to an increase in the heap size. In the examples we looked at, this increased the heap size significantly, but not to a level where we might have concerns (245,088 bytes is 0.235 megabytes, or 5% of our heap size). There are situations, however, where we will be retrieving records with a lot of data (the example we used had account records with a single field), such as rich or long text areas or even child records. In these situations, we will have to improve our heap size and for that we should look to use the batched `for` loop we discussed previously.

This loop format actually involves making two loops, making it more expensive in terms of CPU time, but with a lower impact on the heap size. A good example of when to use this format is when processing large volumes of records with many fields retrieved, particularly if those fields are text areas, long text areas, or rich text areas. In those situations, a batched `for` loop can help reduce the heap size implications.

What about more general practices that are not focused on loops? One of the other actions we should take is to ensure that the code we write has been correctly scoped.

Using scoping

When I first started writing software as a full-time profession, I was guided by a senior developer to try and break up the code I was writing into discrete methods, each of which could fit onto a single screen (or around 50 lines at that point). This was one of the best pieces of advice I was given as it made my code easier to read and also easier to test. The human brain has a limited capacity in terms of what it can hold in its short-term memory, and breaking the code into more manageable chunks makes it easier for you to hold the mental model of your code in your head. You can focus on a single method and what it is doing, and do not need to hold the inner workings of what any called methods or processes are doing — the internals of these other methods — in your memory concurrently.

This short-term memory is analogous to the heap for an application. Whenever we break an application up into a set of smaller self-contained methods, it makes it easier for the application to hold data in memory and reduces the amount stored on the heap. In the same way that you, as a human, can ignore the contents of a called method and focus on just the method you are reviewing, Apex does this through scoping.

We can either declare variables at a class level or within a code block (a method, loop, and so on) within Apex. Declaring a class-level variable means that the variable will be available in memory for the lifetime of the instance of that class, while variables declared in a code block will only be available for the scope of that block.

Structuring your code well into discrete functions with limited scope will help to ensure that your code avoids the heap size limit by allowing the Apex memory manager to handle memory effectively. There may be some instances, however, where you need to manage the memory yourself and remove unwanted items from the heap, which we will now discuss.

Removing unwanted items

A common way of hitting the heap size limit is when working with Blob data, that is, data typically from a document. In these scenarios, you may be uploading a file and handling the upload in Apex with little control over what size the uploaded file is. Examples include handling a file upload to share the file with a number of users or handling the upload to forward the file on to a third-party storage service such as S3 on Amazon Web Services.

While Apex has a very robust memory management system, it can sometimes be effective for us to manually free up memory to reduce the heap size.

In the following code snippet, I have taken one of the loops we had earlier that increased our heap size and adapted it to measure the heap size being used:

```
@isTest
private static void testIteratorExternalMax() {
    Integer start = Limits.getCpuTime();


    List<Account> accs = [SELECT Name FROM Account];
    Integer max = accs.size();


    for(Integer i = 0; i < max; i++) {
        System.debug(accs[i].Name);
    }
```

```
    Integer heap = Limits.getHeapSize();
    System.assert(false, 'Heap = ' + heap);
}
```

Again, this test will fail and show us how much of the heap is being utilized, with the majority of this space being used by the accs variable holding our list of account records. We can free up this memory after our loop has run by setting the value of the accs variable to null.

In the following code snippet, you can see an updated version of this test, which shows the difference in heap size through doing this:

```
@isTest
private static void testIteratorExternalMax() {
    Integer start = Limits.getCpuTime();

    List<Account> accs = [SELECT Name FROM Account];
    Integer max = accs.size();

    for(Integer i = 0; i < max; i++) {
        System.debug(accs[i].Name);
    }
    Integer oldHeap = Limits.getHeapSize();

    accs = null;

    Integer newHeap = Limits.getHeapSize();
    System.assert(false, 'Old Heap = ' + oldHeap + ', New Heap
= ' + newHeap);
}
```

Running this code, we will find that this simple action reduces the heap size we are consuming. For example, a single run I performed showed the following:

```
Old Heap = 245033, New Heap = 1147
```

It can be useful therefore to remove any unwanted items from memory manually if you are working with large sets of data or the `Blob` data type and wish to free space to ensure that you do not hit the heap size limit. Combining this with scoping, as we discussed in the previous section, will help you ensure that the memory of your applications is well managed and, in most instances, you will have no concerns with the heap size limit.

As part of our heap size management, we discussed the use of batched `for` loops to help in managing the volume of data passing through a loop. Another way of improving our code is through improving the performance of our queries to make them run faster by selecting fewer records or performing fewer queries. This will also reduce the amount of work we have to do in terms of looping through data, thereby improving our performance further. Let's review how we might do this by looking into improving the selectivity of our queries.

Improving query selectivity

When we run a SOQL query in Salesforce, the `Force.com` query optimizer processes the query and uses a set of statistics calculated in an ongoing fashion to determine the most efficient way to run the query against the underlying database. In order to achieve the best performance possible, we want to make our query as selective as possible to reduce the number of records returned. This has a number of beneficial effects on our performance. Firstly, the query will run faster than it would do if not selective, which will reduce the running time perceived by our end user. Secondly, it will reduce the amount of data returned for us to process or display, thereby improving the performance of the rest of our code. Thirdly, it will mean we have retrieved a smaller number of rows contributing to the query rows governor limit.

So, what makes a query selective? The first thing that indicates selectivity is whether the field is indexed. The following types of field are indexed:

- Standard primary keys (`Id`, `Name`, `OwnerId`)
- Foreign key fields (`CreatedById`, `LastModifiedById`, lookup relationships, master-detail relationships)
- Audit fields (`CreatedDate`, `SystemModstamp`)
- Custom fields marked as unique or `External Id`

If a field is indexed, it will be considered for optimization. Following this, the optimizer then determines how many records are returned using that index. The following calculation is made to determine whether the number of records selected is below the following thresholds:

- For standard indexes, 30 percent of the first million targeted records and 15 percent of the remaining records. The threshold is 1 million records.

- For custom indexes, 10 percent of the first million targeted records and 5 percent of the remaining records. The threshold is 333,333 records.

If the indexed field meets these thresholds, it is considered selective and will be considered for optimization.

Instead of manually calculating this each time, Salesforce provides developers with the **Query Plan** tool in the Developer Console that will provide detailed information on whether a query is selective or not. To enable this in the Developer Console, open the **Preferences** menu and select the **Enable Query Plan** option, as shown in the following screenshot:

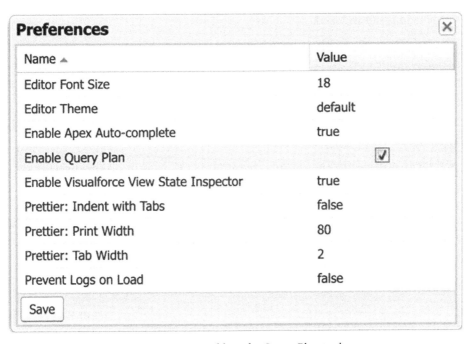

Figure 15.1 – Enabling the Query Plan tool

Once you have selected this option and saved, using the **Query Editor** pane, you can enter a query and use the **Query Plan** button to view metrics on the selectivity of a query. For example, say the following query is run:

```
SELECT Name FROM Account
```

Then the **Query Plan** tool returns the results shown in the following screenshot:

Cardinality	Fields	Leading Operation Type	Cost	sObject Cardinality	sObject Type
125		TableScan	2.72435897435...	125	Account

Figure 15.2 – Query Plan results for a query that is not selective

The statistics returned here inform us of which filter would be used (if any) and why. The columns presented have the following information:

- **Cardinality**: The number of records returned by this operation.

- **Fields**: The indexed fields used by the optimizer in this operation. This will be `null` if the field is not indexed.

- **Leading Operation Type**: The primary operation used by the optimizer to optimize the query, one of either `Index` for an indexed field, `Sharing` for sharing rule-based control, `TableScan` if a full search of the object occurs, and `Other` if an internal Salesforce optimization is used.

- **Cost**: This is a cost score for running the query. Any value over 1 is considered non-selective.

- **sObject Cardinality**: The approximate, number of records on the object.

- **sObject Type**: The object we are querying.

In the preceding example, we can see that no indexed field is available and so a full table scan occurs, which is an expensive operation with a cost of 2.7. We should always aim to have a query with a cost of 1 or less.

Let's consider the following query:

```
SELECT Name FROM Account WHERE Id in ('0013z00002PNSXkAAP',
'0013z00002Uf22NAAR')
```

Running this query through the **Query Plan** tool returns the following information, which shows there are two potential operations, both of which are more selective than our first query by a considerable amount:

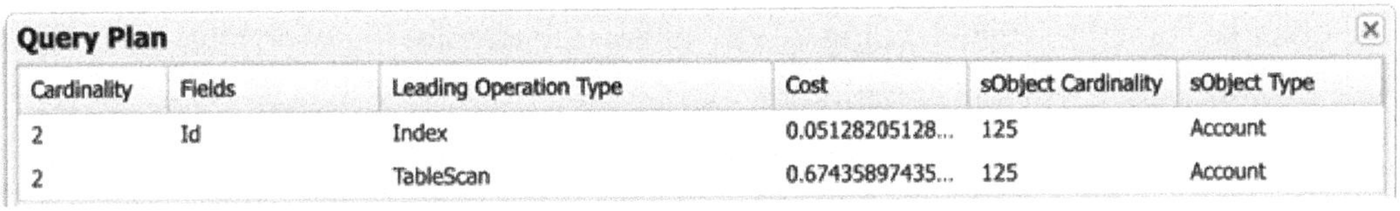

Query Plan   [x]

Cardinality	Fields	Leading Operation Type	Cost	sObject Cardinality	sObject Type
2	Id	Index	0.05128205128...	125	Account
2		TableScan	0.67435897435...	125	Account

Figure 15.3 – A more selective query example

In these results, we can see our cardinality is much lower and both potential operations have a greatly reduced cost, but that our use of an indexed field, the **Id** field, has the most selective query with a cost of 0.05.

It is a good practice to firstly ensure that every query you run has either a WHERE clause or a LIMIT clause to reduce the data returned, but in almost all circumstances, you will find a WHERE clause is required. You should then work to ensure that you have made your query as selective as possible by using an indexed field in the WHERE clause to help in optimizing the query to return data.

You should note that even if you add multiple filters to a WHERE clause, if none of them are indexed, your query is likely to still not be selective. For example, say you are running the following query:

```
SELECT Name FROM Account WHERE Type = 'Customer - Channel' OR
Industry = 'Education'
```

Even on a small dataset (as we have seen, I have 125 **Account** records in this org), this query is not selective, as we can see in the **Query Plan** results in the following screenshot:

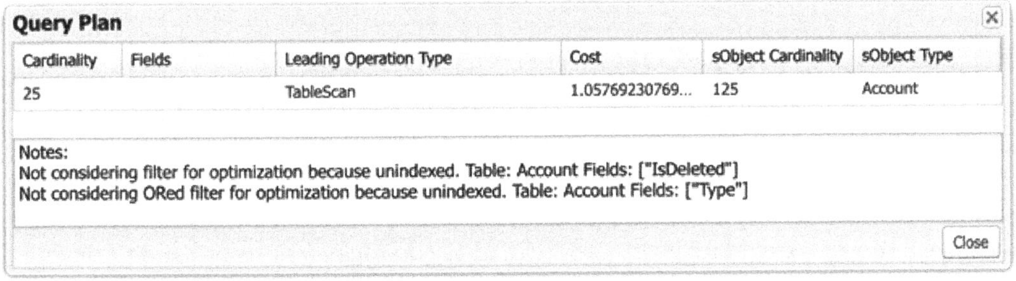

Query Plan   [x]

Cardinality	Fields	Leading Operation Type	Cost	sObject Cardinality	sObject Type
25		TableScan	1.05769230769...	125	Account

Notes:
Not considering filter for optimization because unindexed. Table: Account Fields: ["IsDeleted"]
Not considering ORed filter for optimization because unindexed. Table: Account Fields: ["Type"]

[Close]

Figure 15.4 – A query with multiple WHERE filters that is not selective

Note as well at the bottom of this screenshot that the tool informs us which fields are not being considered for selectivity because they are not indexed.

The other key practice when defining WHERE filters is to attempt to use positive/inclusion operations (IN, =) rather than negative/exclusion operators (NOT, !=) as these exclusion operations are not optimizable, except when using != null and != boolean. It is a good practice therefore to ensure wherever possible that you use positive/inclusion operations to improve optimization chances.

Whenever developing, it is a good practice to run the **Query Plan** tool against your queries if they are using non-indexed fields. It may still be helpful to run the tool even on queries using indexed fields to simply ensure that they are as selective as you anticipate and that you are not hampered by poor query performance.

The other way to improve our code performance related to querying is to reduce the number of queries we are making, which we will review the options around now.

Number of queries

Each query we run takes a small amount of time to run against the database and retrieve data. Although SOQL does not count against CPU time, the time taken can still be perceived by the user. For example, we can run up to 100 queries. If each takes 10 ms, this is an additional second of processing that occurs before our user can interact.

In *Chapter 1, Common Apex Mistakes*, we discussed why bulkification was important and you should not run triggers within loops. There are also a couple of simple ways in which you can reduce the number of queries you are running, which will help to reduce the amount of additional querying and processing, which we will discuss next.

Retrieving child records with a sub query

If retrieving a record and you require child records, consider using a sub query where appropriate to help retrieve all the necessary data at once. This is not always necessarily a good practice; for example, when determining the Batch Apex scope, it is more performant to select the parent records in the batch scope and retrieve the child records in each batch. If you are working with a selective query on the parent record and retrieving a small set of data for each returned record, then this can help avoid additional loops, mapping, and queries.

In general, consider using the **Query Plan** tool on the sub query with an indicative filter (`WHERE Id IN ('ParentId1', 'ParentId2',...)`) to determine whether that query would be considered selective or expensive on its own. As an example, `Account` typically has a limited number of `Contacts` associated with it, thereby reducing the size of the returned dataset and improving selectivity. `Account` may have a much larger volume of `Tasks` associated with it, which would lower the selectivity of the query to retrieve them.

Cache results

Back in *Chapter 1*, *Common Apex Mistakes*, we discussed the use of a singleton to cache results we had retrieved if the data was not expected to change during the transaction. This is an extremely effective tool when retrieving setup-related objects (`Profile`, `Holiday`, `Role`) or custom metadata or custom settings. None of these items should change during the course of a transaction and are slow-moving data, making them comfortably cacheable for the duration of the transaction.

This is what I consider to be a custom transaction cache, which you, as a developer, have added to help remove the need for retrieval of data multiple times during a transaction. If you have such data that is commonly used across an application, you may want to consider using Salesforce's Platform Cache feature, which we will discuss next.

Platform Cache

Salesforce's Platform Cache feature is a feature that allows a developer to designate cache partitions tied to either a user's session or the entire org, which holds data that is often retrieved but changes infrequently (slow-moving data). Examples may include exchange rates in an org cache or a user's current location in a session cache.

To manage data within Platform Cache, it is best practice to use a partition to ensure that you can distribute cache space effectively and ensure that the data is not overwritten incorrectly.

In the following screenshot, you can see a partition I have defined in the cache for storing FX (Foreign eXchange) rates for us to use:

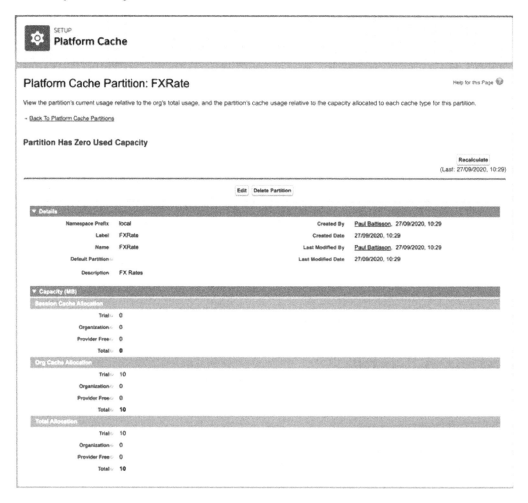

Figure 15.5 – Declaring a Platform Cache partition

For the purpose of this example, let's assume that we want to get a near-live feed of exchange rates with the rate expiring and needing to be refreshed every 15 minutes. We will assume for this example as well that we have a static utility method, FXRateRetriever.getCurrentRate, which takes in a foreign exchange code, for example, GBPUSD, as a string, and retrieves the live exchange rate for this currency pairing from a web service. For the example here, I am using the following mock implementation:

```
public with sharing class FXRateRetriever {
    public static Double getCurrentRate(String ratePairing) {
```

```
        //this is a mocked impementation which simply returns a
random number
        return Math.random();
    }
}
```

To store a value on the cache, we need to call put on the correct partition, specifying a key and a value. We can also specify a **time to live** (**TTL**) in seconds for the value, which must have a minimum of 300 seconds (5 minutes) and a maximum of 172,800 seconds (48 hours). We will set the value to 900 seconds (15 minutes). When specifying a partition, we must designate a namespace if applicable or use the local namespace if not pointing to the cache of a specific managed package.

The following code snippet shows an example of a utility class to store and retrieve a rate pairing from the cache we defined previously:

```
public with sharing class CacheExamples {

    public static void cacheFXRate(Double rate, String pairing)
    {
        Cache.Org.put('local.FXRate.' + pairing, rate, 900);
    }

    public static Double retrieveFXRate(String pairing) {
        return (Double)Cache.Org.get('local.FXRate.' +
        pairing);
    }

}
```

This code is simple and allows us to add and remove items from the cache with our 15 minute TTL value. In order to verify this code, I have used the following test class:

```
@isTest
private with sharing class CacheExamples_Test {

    @isTest
    private static void testSetAndRetrieve() {
        String pairing = 'GBPUSD';
        Double rate = FXRateRetriever.getCurrentRate(pairing);
```

```
      CacheExamples.cacheFXRate(rate, pairing);

      Test.startTest();
      Double returnedRate = CacheExamples.
      retrieveFXRate(pairing);
      Test.stopTest();

      System.assertEquals(rate, returnedRate, 'Incorrect rate
      returned from cache');
   }


}
```

This code works well and allows us to add commonly retrieved values to and from a cache in order to save repeated callouts or queries. What about the following test?

```
@isTest
private static void testSetAndRetrieveNoValueSet() {
    String pairing = 'GBPUSD';

    Test.startTest();
    Double returnedRate = CacheExamples.
    retrieveFXRate(pairing);
    Test.stopTest();

    System.assertNotEquals(null, returnedRate, 'Incorrect rate
    returned from cache');
}
```

This test will fail as a `null` value will be returned when we attempt to retrieve a cached value that does not exist. We have two options to deal with this; either handling things manually by validating for a `null` value and managing ourselves, or by providing an inner class that implements the `Cache.CacheBuilder` interface. This interface includes a single method, `doLoad`, which will populate the value of the cache if it does not exist.

In the following code snippet, we can see a new FXCache class I have defined that implements this interface:

```
public with sharing class FXCache implements Cache.CacheBuilder
{
    public Object doLoad(String pairing) {
        return FXRateRetriever.getCurrentRate(pairing);
    }
}
```

We can now update our second test to use this interface and have a value populated and returned when no value originally exists, as shown in the following code block:

```
@isTest
private static void testSetAndRetrieveNoValueSet() {
    String pairing = 'GBPUSD';

    Test.startTest();
    Cache.OrgPartition orgPart = Cache.Org.getPartition('local.
    FXRate');
    Double returnedRate = (Double)orgPart.get(FXCache.class,
    pairing);
    Test.stopTest();

    System.assertNotEquals(null, returnedRate, 'Incorrect rate
    returned from cache');
}
```

Note that in our updated test, we have retrieved the OrgPartition instance we wish to retrieve the value from first before calling our new get method. This will ensure that the FXCache class instance runs against the correct partition. In our other test, this was specified in our key value, local.FXRate.

Platform Cache is a powerful feature that can enhance the performance of applications when working at scale and requiring data to be retrieved in a regular fashion, but that does not change regularly. A free allocation of 10 MB of cache is provided for Enterprise Edition orgs, and 30 MB for Unlimited and Performance Edition, with a greater allowance available for purchase. If you are working in an environment where there is a set of data that is retrieved regularly but does not change, and you have available a Platform Cache allocation, then I recommend you consider it as a possible enhancement to help improve your system's performance.

We have now seen a number of different ways in which to improve the performance of our Apex code for common issues we may encounter. Before we finish and summarize the chapter, I want to briefly discuss how and when you should choose to make these enhancements.

Understanding when to make some of these improvements

It should be fairly obvious from reading through this chapter that for every improvement we make for one governor-constrained resource, we negatively impact another governor restrained resource. A prime example is that without `for` loops, we were able to dramatically improve CPU time usage, but also increased our heap size usage. So when should we make these improvements and implement some of the items we have seen?

The short answer is *it depends*. I would strongly suggest you avoid blanket implementation of all these improvements as they often clash and it will not typically lead to an optimal solution. The correct thing to do is to write your code with these options in mind and implement these improvements as necessary after testing or during development when it is obvious.

Using the `for` loops as an example, when coding day to day, I tend to use standard SOQL `for` loops as they are more readable and it is a nice piece of syntactical sugar for the code to make it easier to maintain going forward. My first consideration is almost always about maintenance and ease of updating in the future. Good code should be self-documenting, and syntax such as the SOQL `for` loop makes that self-documentation easier. If I am working on a high-volume solution (such as a large Batch Apex solution), then I may switch to the faster `for` loop style. For a Dreamforce presentation one year, I built a machine learning system in Apex that processed mathematical matrices and required lots of `for` loops and only basic data to be stored. This was a prime use case for the faster `for` loop option.

The best advice therefore is to test your code thoroughly and profile it under the best- and worst-case scenarios to see where improvements may need to be made. Some of the improvements here are general good coding practices (not retrieving data multiple times, improving query selectivity, and so on). However, to refer back to the quote from Donald Knuth in *Chapter 13, Performance and the Salesforce Governor Limits*, *premature optimization is the root of all evil*, and we should therefore be careful about making improvements we do not need or that damage us in the long run.

Summary

In this chapter, we have covered a number of ways in which we can improve the performance of our code related to specific governor-constrained resources. We started by looking into improving our CPU time through improved `for` loops, using maps, and reducing the number of expensive operations we are undertaking. This led us to see how we could improve the performance for one resource, but increase the usage of another inadvertently, which we built on in the next section, on heap size.

In the section discussing heap size, we referred back to the looping code and how we can improve heap size utilization in our loops, but again to the detriment of our CPU time. This also led to a discussion around their difference, with some of these limits being perceived by users (time to run) and others just being internal limits (heap size and memory usage). We also discussed the use of scoping to help keep the heap size down, as well as manually clearing memory by setting variables containing large datasets to `null` when they are no longer needed.

Following this, we looked at improving the selectivity of our SOQL queries and the use of the **Query Plan** tool to determine whether an item was selective. To reiterate, a query should always have a `WHERE` clause with an indexed filter wherever possible. We then discussed how, after making our queries more selective, we should also look to reduce their number by retrieving child records alongside using nested queries or through the caching of results in a local variable or singleton instance.

We then wrapped up the concept of caching to discuss caching more broadly across a session of our entire org using the Platform Cache feature. This clever feature makes the caching of data quick and easy and allows slow-moving data to be stored in a readily accessible format for use. We also looked at how we can deal with `null` values being returned from the cache and the use of the `CacheBuilder` interface to help in both populating and retrieving values.

In the next chapter of the book, we are going to discuss performance and architectural considerations, and how they can interplay together to both enhance and degrade performance, as well as some tooling to help in writing your code to be more performant overall.

16
Performance and Application Architectures

In the past few chapters, we have seen how the different implementation options we have in writing our code have varying impacts on the resources our code consumes. All the examples we have seen have been focused at a very fine level of detail, discussing specific ways of looping or improving our queries. These are all decisions that are made by developers during development, but the overall performance of a system is also impacted by the architectural decisions made for the application. In this chapter, we will discuss some of those decisions and the impact they have on the solution, as well as more discuss in broader terms the topic of performance management in relation to maintainability and ease of development.

When it comes to the performance of an application, if the application itself can never be updated and cannot be easily maintained, then developer productivity will be greatly impacted as a consequence. In this chapter, we will also discuss some of the architectural considerations pertaining to developer performance that will impact overall system performance.

In this chapter, we will cover the following topics:

- Using clicks with code
- Code structure and linting
- Object-oriented programming in Apex
- Common Salesforce architectural trade-offs
- Long-term performance management

Using clicks with code

Within Salesforce circles, it is common to hear debates of *clicks versus code* or *clicks before code*. Salesforce is a powerful low-code development platform that has a variety of different tools to enable administrators and those without coding skills to create powerful automated processes. For the remainder of this discussion, I will refer to any individual creating solutions in non-code-based tools exclusively as an *administrator*, eschewing terms such as *citizen developer* or other terminology to try and keep things simple. I will also refer to everything that is not programming involving Apex, Visualforce, Aura, or Lightning Web Components on the platform to be one of the *declarative tools*, and for solutions built using these tools to be built using *clicks*. This includes formula fields, validation rules, workflow, roll-up summary fields, Process Builder, approval processes, Flows, and reports.

Firstly, anyone building a solution on Salesforce should never consider only low-code tools or only code-based tools. To do so is to limit yourself and the scope of the solution you can deliver to your end users. I am also, in a book about Apex, going to state categorically that Apex is not the definitive tool for automation on the platform—there are many situations where it is the wrong tool entirely. In determining the correct tool, there are many key questions regarding context that are critical.

Whether to use clicks or code

When determining how best to deliver a piece of functionality, there are a number of key things to keep in mind when deciding whether to use clicks or code:

- Can this be done (with relative ease) using the declarative tools? How about using programmatic tools?

- What declarative and programmatic automation do we already have in place around this object or business process?

- Will this change to the existing logic make our logic less maintainable?

- Are we following best practices in delivering the solution?

- Who is going to support this solution in the short, medium, and long term?

We should always start by deciding how easy it is to actually build this solution using any of the tools if we had knowledge of how to use all the tools. I recommend that, as an Apex developer, if you are not already very familiar with how the declarative tools work, you would be well advised to spend time familiarizing yourself with them. In general though, we will find many situations where something is possible using both declarative or programmatic tools, but is markedly simpler in one or the other; for example, relating records or updating related information upon saving. If the record to be updated is on a parent or child of the updated record, this can be done fairly simply using Process Builder or Flows. If the record is not directly related or is multiple relationships away, this can become more cumbersome and would be a lot easier in Apex.

This leads on to the second thing to consider: what automation is already in place around that object or business process. In my experience, Salesforce applications tend to be built in a modular fashion around particular objects or a single business process due to the transactional nature of most of the work performed on the platform. For example, you may see automation around a set of objects for a case management process, or around a single object for defaulting behavior or integration with an external solution. When looking to add new automation logic, we should bear in mind what existing automation there is when determining which toolset to use. If we have an existing setup using point and click tools, we should look toward using the same tools, and should make a similar judgement if we are using Apex.

Tied into that is our third consideration: how much easier will this update make the system to maintain? If there is no existing automation that exists in this process or on this object, then this will, of course, make the system harder to maintain in general, but the functionality will all be contained in a single tool. For an existing automation setup, adding in new automation to existing automation can make a solution more brittle and unwieldy. This is particularly true of the declarative toolset as opposed to Apex. Programming languages are more able to be manipulated and organized into the set of classes, functions, interfaces, and so on, that best make sense for the job in hand. With declarative tools, what often starts off as a simple set of logic can quickly balloon into something unwieldy by virtue of the tools being less flexible. This is the nature of any tool that is abstracting code; it will not be as flexible in its design as the same solution written in code. I once worked with an organization where they had been guided to only use the declarative tools and not use code for maintainability. This led to over 100 Process Builder processes and some Flows with over 50 nodes. The solution was extremely brittle and difficult to understand, with updates to one area causing others to fail as no explicit ordering is available on these tools. Eventually, all of this automation was replaced by code and the errors and ordering issues were removed.

This is an example of our fourth consideration coming into play—are we following best practices? Taking Process Builder as an example, it is a best practice to have a single process per object as this is the only way you can guarantee the order of execution for the steps in the process. I would personally say that I am not a fan of a flow ever having more than 25 steps in it. This is not to say that one of these steps could not be a sub-flow and that the overall process far exceed this value, but a large flow quickly becomes difficult to manage and understand (similar to the advice I highlighted in *Chapter 15, Improving Apex Performance*, around restricting method sizes to around 50 lines). If, in delivering a solution using a particular tool, we find ourselves breaking best practice guidelines, then we should consider whether this tool is the most appropriate. This may lead to some uncomfortable moments where we realize that we have a very complex set of declarative automation that needs to be refactored into a code-based solution, but as a system evolves, this often becomes more likely.

With that system evolution in mind, we must also therefore consider who will support the solution in the short, medium, and long term. If the solution will be supported by a business user, we must take extra steps to ensure that the process is robust and that we have confidence in its ability to run and scale. In an organization with administrator resources, the use of declarative options will allow them to self-service their support, and in larger organizations, it is not uncommon to have a team including a variety of resources who can also support code. You should be aware of this, as well as what your contractual support terms are to ensure that the client is not left in trouble should there be a problem in the future.

In general, I think of the Salesforce automation tools as being on a spectrum, with simpler tools such as formula fields, validation rules, and roll-up summaries at the end of the scale with the least complexity, Workflow, and then Process Builder moving along the scale, through to Flows and then into Apex. We need to be aware of how we combine these different tools to ensure that we don't cause further issues through additional complexity that is hard to map out, and from a performance perspective, that we are avoiding extra cycles through the save order of execution. So, let's see how these work out.

Clicks, code, and performance implications

When it comes to performance, in general code will be faster than clicks all things considered due to a reduction in abstractions and the fact that you can be more exact in actions. In many instances, this difference will be imperceptible to the end user; however, it is typically the case when clicks and code are combined that unintended consequences can occur and performance can suffer. In *Chapter 3*, *Triggers and Managing Trigger Execution*, we discussed how Salesforce saves order of execution fires and how any additional saves within this transaction can cause the save order of execution to run again. This is a common problem when Apex, Process Builder, and Flows are all combined as multiple operations occur and cause the order of execution to fire repeatedly.

I have found it to be a general best practice to try and avoid the use of Process Builder and automated Flows on an object when I have an Apex trigger on that object. This allows me to be consistent in my use of tooling, ensure that I am minimizing work wherever possible, and avoiding repeated DML actions from these different tools. This is not always possible and it may require existing declarative work to be rewritten into code, but it will provide a greater level of consistency and more consistent performance than having multiple tools operating and overlapping in ways that can produce unintended consequences.

Note that I am excluding some of the simpler declarative tools, such as formulas, roll-up summary fields, and validation rules, here because they can considerably enhance and complement a code-based solution to reduce the amount of work needed (although they still must be considered carefully as a validation rule, for example, could readily stop a trigger from operating).

In summary, the same *it depends* rule applies as we discussed at the end of *Chapter 15, Improving Apex Performance*. However, because of how much the functionality of Process Builder, Flows, and Apex overlaps when deciding the best set of tools for building a solution, you should ensure that you are being consistent in order to stop unintended consequences. Overlapping solutions can lead not only to errors, but will also be detrimental to performance as multiple iterations of the save order of execution occur. The time taken as a developer to piece together multiple solutions and how they interact also has a significant impact on a developer's productivity and how they must both deliver and test a solution.

With this in mind, and given the focus of this book is squarely on Apex, let's now look at how we can work to improve our code's structure to enhance the performance of both our code and its developer.

Code structure and linting

When it comes to removing errors within an application, the earlier you can do this the better. One of the most useful tools for assisting a developer in doing this is to use a linter to help in reviewing your code to make suggestions around common bad practices or issues. For Apex developers, the open source Apex PMD library is my go-to tool to use for this and has a community created plugin for Visual Studio Code available to allow it to integrate nicely with the SFDX plugins for Visual Studio Code.

The use of a linter such as Apex PMD will allow you to catch common errors and enforce best practices in your code, and is particularly useful in a team setting to provide a baseline of agreed standards. Many deployment tools also include it as a step prior to deployment between environments to help verify the quality of the code being deployed before deploying it.

I have found a linting tool to be a helpful way of nudging myself and others in a development team to avoid any bad practices that may creep in during development, as well enabling the developer to get a view of the state of the code they will be working on before they begin updating it.

I would therefore recommend that if you are not already using a linting tool in your development, you add one in to help make you aware of any best practices you may be missing. Following these practices will help improve the structure of your code overall and lower the chances of you receiving errors going forward. With that said though, considering more generally as to how you can best use the object-oriented features of the Apex language can ensure that you can successfully test and scale your application, which we will discuss in more detail now.

Object-oriented programming in Apex

Apex is a fully featured object-oriented programming language that enables developers to utilize features such as inheritance, polymorphism, abstraction, and encapsulation in order to develop applications in a way that is easy to manage, scale, and test. It is often the case that the first introduction to Apex that many developers get is through a trigger, which, by nature, is a very linear structure for organizing code. A trigger will run from the first line to the last in order and does not have any of the standard OOP capabilities; triggers cannot implement an interface or extend any classes. Although it is a best practice to extract the logic within a trigger to a set of classes and methods, as we saw in *Chapter 3, Triggers and Managing Trigger Execution*, it is not a requirement to do so, and many triggers are still written that do not follow this best practice.

Many developers do not start to work with the object-oriented capabilities of Apex until they are dealing with a more complex scenario. Working with these Apex features can help increase your ability to test, debug, and scale the application throughout its life cycle.

We saw in *Chapter 15, Improving Apex Performance*, how separating your code can help you to lower the heap size through allowing variables and other in-memory items to go out of scope. Correctly splitting your code into smaller more discrete functions can also assist in making it much easier to test and profile the performance of your code using the set of tools we discussed in *Chapter 14, Performance Profiling*. Profiling smaller blocks of code will make it much easier for you to have confidence in any changes you make to increase performance in general. This also enables you to adhere more readily to principles such as the single responsibility principle, that is, that every class or function within some code should be responsible for a single part of the overall program's functionality. Following this principle will also aid you in more readily applying other object-oriented principles.

The correct application of more general object-oriented principles can also help in increasing developer productivity and improving the flexibility of your application to changes going forward. It is a common maxim that you should code to interfaces not implementations. This is not as readily possible for Salesforce due to the overheads that can come into play through taking a purely interface-driven approach. However, I advise developers to actively look at how they can better implement their Apex code to utilize object-oriented patterns and reuse code.

We have seen examples in this book, such as the trigger handler framework in *Chapter 3, Triggers and Managing Trigger Execution*, the test data factory in *Chapter 5, Testing Apex Code*, and combining custom metadata with Batch Apex in *Chapter 8, Working with Batch Apex*, to highlight a few examples. If you read through these pieces of code again with a view to notice how they evolved out of an idea and took shape through a simple iterative process, it will become more evident that a large portion of the code that we write can use these principles to make it more scalable and easy to work with.

Need to add a new trigger on an object with the correct routing logic? Using the trigger handler framework highlighting this becomes quick and easy. As a developer, having a robust set of well-structured frameworks such as these will make handling future updates much easier and make testing of these updates much simpler. It will also enable you to focus on ensuring that your code meets these best practices and standards. There will always be points at which decisions have to be made in designs that have trade-offs that can impact an application's performance and scalability, which we will cover next.

Common Salesforce architectural trade-offs

As you implement a solution programmatically in Salesforce you will be faced with a number of choices that will impact the performance—real, perceived, and possible, of your application. In this section, we will cover four of the most common architectural trade-offs that you may encounter when deciding how to structure your code-based solution.

Synchronous versus asynchronous

As we discussed in the second section of this book, there are a number of asynchronous programming options available to us on the Salesforce platform for a variety of use cases. When designing a solution in Apex, you will sometimes need to determine whether you should move toward using an asynchronous processing option instead of attempting to run the process synchronously.

We have already covered in chapters 7 to 11 some of the different use cases and options available. However, to reiterate, working in an asynchronous context will allow you to process a much higher volume of data than if you operated in a purely synchronous context. This can help to improve the perceived performance of your application by hiding the time taken to process the work from the user, as well as enabling you to deal with a much higher volume of items to process. You must be careful to consider any timing implications of the processing, irrespective of whether the user may expect the job to have been completed too early or not. Switching to an asynchronous setup such as this can lower the perceived performance of the application as they have to wait a small period of time for the asynchronous transaction to complete. Synchronous processes, on the other hand, will not be able to process as large a volume of transactions, but do enable a more instantaneous response to the end user.

The perceived performance is something we must be aware of as developers to ensure that we do not negatively impact the end user's experience and, in turn, negate the overall opinion of the solution that has been built. One way in which we can help manage this in certain instances is through the chunking of work in the user interface through a wizard.

Wizards to help chunk

When working with larger sets of data and processes that require greater amounts of data, it is worth reviewing whether the process can be chunked into a wizard through the user interface. This not only allows you to perform smaller chunks of work that can occur synchronously and therefore provide instant feedback, but also allows you to modularize your code more readily.

An example may be a process in a telesales scenario where a customer may call in to register. As part of this process, we need to do the following:

1. Capture their unique identifiers (name, email, phone number).
2. Check for duplicates against the existing database.
3. Capture their address using a postcode lookup tool.
4. Select an offer from a set of available products.
5. Generate a subscription in a third-party subscription management system.
6. Save and register the sale within Salesforce as a case or an opportunity.

Running these steps together all at once would likely cause either an extremely slow experience or a governor exception, as well as some duplication of effort. This is a perfect scenario where a wizard can help to chunk this work up into discrete steps with smaller bundles of work to process. We will not need to make multiple callouts at once and we can ensure that the application is more responsive for the agent on the phone and therefore easier for the customer calling.

While this is a useful method in this situation, we must also be aware that again this method can decrease perceived performance in other situations, for example, if applied to a sales person who is entering the information on a desktop or mobile app and not on the phone. Again, here we must balance the implications of improving real performance against any changes in perceived performance.

Client versus server processing of data

Building upon the idea of processing data using a wizard, the introduction of the Lightning Web Component framework allows developers to process more data locally rather than on the server in Apex. This can be a useful way of improving performance by passing data to the client for processing in the browser.

There is a fine balance to be struck here (as with all options); whether it is faster to process the data on the server and reduce the data to a smaller set to transfer, or whether the necessary data structure is more custom. In this case, it may be best manipulated on the client side and ensures that we do not tightly couple the server-side logic to a specific client-side implementation.

For example, consider the situation where we have a component with a custom chart that is rendering data using a charting library requiring a specific data structure, using data we are retrieving from a SOQL query in an Apex class. In this situation, it may be more prudent to return the raw data from the SOQL query to the client for processing into the correct format than processing into the desired format in Apex for a couple of reasons.

Firstly, from a long-term management perspective, this allows us to replace the specific charting library, or offer variants using other libraries, which all process the same data locally. Secondly, the processing of the data may be quicker on the client machine than in Apex, as it can be processed directly into the format needed for the library yet still may require an intermediary format in Apex. Thirdly, there is a consideration to be taken in terms of whether there is a significant difference in the volume of data being transferred, which can cause delays. Typically, in a scenario such as this, the data should be pre-aggregated through the use of the Analytics API or an aggregate query, and so should be relatively small to transfer and negligible in size difference compared to the client required format. However, in scenarios where the data needs to be aggregated, it may be better to do this in Apex and then transfer the smaller bundle.

As we have already noted, a large portion of performance choices are not a simple answer and fall very much into the *it depends* discussion. The use of client-side or server-side processing with Salesforce is another one of these situations where we must consider the entire flow of data throughout the life cycle as well as long-term flexibility (such as within changing a charting framework) to help determine the right decision. This flexibility to change is something we want to try and maintain within our application code, but can become harder as the solution grows or as we implement more patterns, as we will discuss in our next trade-off.

Enterprise patterns versus flexibility

Salesforce is used by many large enterprise organizations throughout the world and has many enterprise-scale applications built on it for the AppExchange by **Independent Software Vendors (ISVs)**. We have mentioned patterns a few times throughout this book, but mainly in relation to specific code implementations instead of more generic architectural patterns that you can implement across the entire application.

As an application grows in size and scope, the use of enterprise patterns can assist in keeping code well-structured and organized, which, in turn, assists in developer productivity and in reducing the likelihood of issues. Additionally, the use of these patterns can assist in enabling you to introduce new features using interfaces and work at removing dependencies between components within an application. For example, using a dependency injection framework enables you to decouple applications by passing any dependencies into the class itself rather than explicitly coupling the class to an implementation. This makes it easier to add new implementations going forward to work with.

There are a number of great libraries and books available on the use of enterprise patterns on the platform that I recommend you spend time reading and reviewing. However, it should be noted that in some instances, these will be overkill and may, in fact, hamper your flexibility, lower your development performance, or lower your application's performance.

For example, when starting out on a green field implementation, I tend to utilize my standard trigger handler and test data factory patterns to assist in managing triggers and writing appropriate unit tests. When working with a web service returning JSON, I will also use the `JSONParse` library I referenced in *Chapter 12, Apex REST and Custom Web Services*. Aside from these, I will not typically set up any larger dependencies for my project or the application as they tend to add overhead and are an example of premature optimization.

While I do not expect that many developers would start a brand-new project with a large series of dependencies, I want to highlight that when you are making decisions around which patterns you are looking to implement, you should be aware of both the overhead of adding these patterns to solve a particular problem and consider how often they will be used. Any code that you add to your application is code that you have to manage and maintain in the future. If the application you are working on is going to be part of a suite of applications for a multinational organization with 20,000 users, then consistency and the use of these patterns will help to provide stability throughout the application. Alternatively, if you are aiming to deliver a smaller or more discrete piece of functionality, then the use of such patterns may be premature.

Remember that code should be dynamic and constantly revisited and updated to help you more as your application grows and scales. Managing the performance of an application over the long term requires you to keep a number of different concepts in mind, which we will discuss now in the final section of this chapter.

Managing long-term performance of an application

Throughout this book, we have covered a number of different patterns, practices, and pieces of functionality to help you build better Salesforce applications that will scale as the use of your application scales over time. We started looking at how we can remove common Apex mistakes, and worked through trigger patterns, exceptions, testing, and secure programming, before diving into the many asynchronous options that were available to us in Apex to help the application scale. After understanding our toolset, we then reviewed how to correctly profile our applications and some of the various methods we can employ to improve our use of resources.

All of these items, along with the discussions we have had in this chapter, come together to culminate in helping us understand how we should think about managing the performance of an application in the long term. Very few applications start off with a high volume of data, but over time almost all get there. This does not mean just a high volume of data created every day, just that over time, the data stored within a Salesforce organization will grow and can have performance implications if the application is not designed to cope with it.

A prime example of this is when querying, including very selective filters to help reduce the data retrieved or searched. One organization I worked with asked for assistance as they had a piece of code that had suddenly started failing and nobody knew why. After a very brief investigation, I spotted that they had a query that was selecting using statuses and not a more selective filter. A small update to the code to use a set of IDs to filter, and everything was running again and performance improved from what it had been from the outset.

This story is not to proclaim some genius level insight. I would expect that most developers would have been able to figure out where the offending query was, nor is it to blame the previous developer; they may have been told the assumption that data would be deleted, or that extra records would not grow was a safe one. I once similarly worked with a company that sold 5 products, which overall created 10 bundles/price points. Fast-forward 5 years and their marketing team had created another 300 bundles/price points for various marketing campaigns and promotions and the solution I had designed was not working. The issue was a combination of changed requirements, a miscommunication (or lack of transfer) of training to the newer marketing team members, and a lack of maintenance.

If you are involved in the active day-to-day management or maintenance of an org as a customer or end user, then I strongly advise you to create some form of performance testing framework as described in *Chapter 14, Performance Profiling*, and start a habit of regularly running it and reviewing the results. Be sure to document your application and identify any potential bottlenecks and assumptions that are in place. What will happen if we grow our customer base by 20% year on year? Will every area still operate as expected? Will we have enough data storage? What parts of our application work with volumes of data that may have issues over time? Thinking proactively of your environment, and working to have a regular schedule of maintenance and improvement as regards the solution, will ensure that you can have confidence going forward.

For consultants who are engaged in short- to medium-term projects, you should aim to always get every assumption you have documented verified. Code defensively, limiting the data returned and always acting as if you have to work with large data volumes. This will help you to ensure that you can deliver a solution that will scale over the long term, but can also provide additional value to the client by handing this documentation over. If the client has existing patterns and standards such as those we have discussed throughout the book, work with them and improve them. If they do not, again try to introduce good practices such as trigger frameworks into their environment to set a good precedent for future developers and work.

To summarize, to successfully manage the performance of a Salesforce application long term will require you to review, maintain, and update the application over time to use newer tools and standards as they become available. It is a powerful feature of the Salesforce platform that so many historical versions of the API are supported. However, you should work to ensure that over time, you update these and the application in general to use the newer features that are available to keep technical debt low. You should also work hard to ensure that you are regularly testing and profiling your application to ensure that it will satisfy ongoing demands and take appropriate action where necessary.

Summary

In this chapter, we have covered a number of the different architectural decisions that will impact the performance of your application, both in terms of resource usage and developer productivity. We started by discussing the impacts of using licks or code in our application and how to determine the best solution at the time. Following this, we moved on to discuss code structure and linting to help ensure that common bugs or performance issues were caught early.

This led into a more general discussion of the use of object-oriented patterns in Apex and how they can help make it easier to test and profile our code for scale, as well as ensure that we can modularize our code for increased developer performance as we make changes in the future. From here we dove into specific architectural trade-offs that you need to consider when designing different types of solutions using Apex.

Finally, we finished the chapter with a discussion on managing the performance of an application over the long term and the actions we should take to help set the owner of the application up for success. This was the culmination of all the items we have covered in the book, helping us to truly understand how to master the Apex language to build applications that are both scalable and robust.

Other Books You May Enjoy

If you enjoyed this book, you may be interested in these other books by Packt:

Hands-On Low-Code Application Development with Salesforce

Enrico Murru

ISBN: 978-1-80020-977-0

- Get to grips with the fundamentals of data modeling to enhance data quality
- Deliver dynamic configuration capabilities using custom settings and metadata types
- Secure your data by implementing the Salesforce security model
- Customize Salesforce applications with Lightning App Builder
- Create impressive pages for your community using Experience Builder
- Use Data Loader to import and export data without writing any code
- Embrace the Salesforce Ohana culture to share knowledge and learn from the global Salesforce community

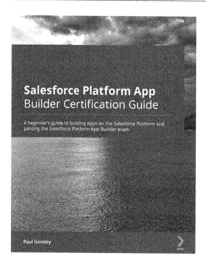

Salesforce Platform App Builder Certification Guide

Paul Goodey

ISBN: 978-1-80020-643-4

- Explore the core features of the Lightning Platform
- Design and build an appropriate data model for a given scenario
- Identify the Lightning Platform's features and capabilities
- Customize the Salesforce Lightning Experience UI
- Implement business logic and process automation
- Identify the capabilities of declarative customization

Leave a review - let other readers know what you think

Please share your thoughts on this book with others by leaving a review on the site that you bought it from. If you purchased the book from Amazon, please leave us an honest review on this book's Amazon page. This is vital so that other potential readers can see and use your unbiased opinion to make purchasing decisions, we can understand what our customers think about our products, and our authors can see your feedback on the title that they have worked with Packt to create. It will only take a few minutes of your time, but is valuable to other potential customers, our authors, and Packt. Thank you!

Index

A

Apex
  object-oriented programming 329, 330
  used, for sharing records 95-98
Apex class
  Apex Scheduler, using 168-171
  job limits, scheduling 178, 179
  scheduled job, monitoring 176-178
  scheduling 167, 168
  suicidal scheduling 176
  System.schedule method, using 171-174
  System.schedule method, versus
    System.scheduleBatch for
    Batch Apex classes 174, 175
Apex class security 102
Apex Interactive Debugger
  about 30
  ISV Customer Debugger 30
Apex performance
  Limits class 281, 282
  profiling 281
  utility class 283-290
Apex Replay Debugger
  using, for debugging 26-29
Apex REST code
  testing 249-256

Apex Scheduler
  using 168-171
Apex testing
  best practices 85, 86
  need for 72, 73
Apex triggers
  used, for handling platform
    events 200-202
application
  long-term performance,
    managing 334-336
application performance
  profiling 272, 273
application programming
    interface (API) 16, 84

B

base interface, Batch Apex class
  callout-enabled batch classes 133, 134
  stateful batch implementations 131-133
Batch Apex
  asynchronous queue processing 128
  batch classes, scheduling 138
  chaining batches 142

complex logical manipulation
  processes 127
custom metadata 139-141
exception handling 148, 149
high-volume web service callouts 127
invoking 137
invoking, with Database.
  executeBatch 138
Iterable, versus QueryLocator 134-137
large data volumes scenario 126
managed sharing recalculations 129
monitoring 146-148
multiple batches, executing
  in parallel 142-146
platform events 148, 149
scheduled class 139-141
testing 149, 150
updates, scheduling to records 128
using 126
versus Queueable Apex 155
Batch Apex class
  base interface 130, 131
  defining 130
Batch Apex classes
  System.schedule methods, versus
    System.scheduleBatch for 174, 175
big O notation 275-280
bulkification
  about 8
  DML, performing within loops 14, 15
  querying, for data within loops 11-13

C

cache
  results 315
central processing unit (CPU) 13
Change Data Capture system 209

child records
  retrieving, with sub query 314
clicks
  using 325, 326
  using, with code 324
code
  using 325, 326
code structure
  and linting 328
cold data 8, 9
CometD protocol 216
comma-separated values (CSV) 80
complex endpoints 223
configuration data
  retrieving, in bulkified way 8
continuous integration (CI) 17
CPU time, improving
  about 298
  faster, for loops 299-302
  maps, using 302-304
  usage of expensive operations,
    reducing 304-306
Create, Read, Edit, and Delete (CRED) 91
custom endpoints
  using 222
custom exception types
  using 69
custom metadata
  using, for dynamic parsing 232-235

D

data
  creating, with test data factory 73-78
  retrieving, throughout transaction 9, 10
  sharing, throughout transaction 9, 10
Database.executeBatch
  Batch Apex, invoking 138

Data Manipulation Language (DML) 8, 81
Document Object Model (DOM) 248
dynamic parsing
    with custom metadata 232-235

E

endpoints
    defining 224-226
    example 226-232
    exposing 237, 238
    testing, with Workbench 235, 236
errors
    catching 58-60
event bus 184-186
event-driven architecture 184, 185
events
    handling, externally 216
    publishing, with Process
        Builder 193-195
exception logging framework 62-66
exceptions
    expected exceptions 56
    types 56
    unexpected exceptions 56
    unknown exceptions 57

F

field permissions
    enforcing 98-102
finally block
    using 60, 61
Flow
    platform events, publishing 195-198
future method invocations
    execution, monitoring of 120, 121

future method, mixed DML error
    large callouts 113
    slow callouts 113
future methods
    calling 119, 120
    data, coordinating 116-119
    defining 114-116
    mixed DML error 112
    need for 112
    state, passing 116-119
    testing 121-124
    use cases for 113, 114

G

GACK
    about 57
    dealing with 57
generic endpoints 223
governor limits 266-268

H

hardcoding 15-17
heap size usage, reducing
    about 306
    batched for loops 307
    scoping, using 307
    unwanted items, removing 308-310
hot data 8, 9
HTTP methods
    about 221, 222
    DELETE 221
    GET 221
    PATCH 221
    POST 221
    PUT 221

HyperText Transfer Protocol
    (HTTP) 82, 220

I

Independent Software Vendor (ISV)
    Custom Debugger 30
integrated development
    environment (IDE) 73

J

Java Virtual Machine (JVM) 4
JSON
  handling 246-248

L

legacy integration
  replacing 222
Lightning Web Component performance
  profiling 293, 294
Limits class 281, 282
log levels
  used, for generating debug logs 21-23

M

magnitude analysis 275-280
multi-tenancy 264

N

null pointer exceptions
  about 4
  on object instances 5
  using, when working with maps 6, 7

O

object
  enforcing 98-102
object-oriented (OO) 11
object-oriented programming
  in Apex 329, 330
Observe, Orient, Decide, Act (OODA)
  about 273
  act 275
  decide 274
  observe 274
  orient 274

P

performance 265-270
Platform Cache 315-319
platform events
  consumption, testing 212-216
  defining 188-191
  handling 200
  handling, with Apex triggers 200-202
  publishing 188-191
  publishing, through Flow 195-198
  subscribing to 200
  testing 210, 211
platform events, in Apex
  working with 191, 192
platform events, in Process Builder
  subscribing to 203-208
platform events, use cases
  about 186
  asynchronous processes 186
  decoupling applications 188
  external connections 187

Process Builder
  used, for publishing events 193-195
Public APIs 238-240

Q

query selectivity 310-314
Queueable Apex
  about 152-154
  callouts 157
  callouts, allowing 160
  chained processes 157
  child/chained jobs, enqueuing 161, 162
  complex processes 156, 157
  extensive processes 156, 157
  implementations, defining 158, 159
  invoking 160, 161
  need for 156
  testing 162, 163
  versus Batch Apex 155
  versus future methods 154, 155

R

REpresentational State Transfer
    (REST) 220
request body data
  handling 243-246
REST API
  events, publishing 198, 199
RESTful web services
  testing, with static resources 81-85

S

Salesforce
  debugging on 20

Salesforce application request
    lifecycle 262-264
Salesforce, architectural trade-offs
  about 330
  client, versus server processing
    of data 332, 333
  enterprise patterns, versus
    flexibility 333, 334
  synchronous, versus
    asynchronous 330, 331
  wizards, for chunk 331, 332
Salesforce Developer Experience (SDF)
  using 23-26
Salesforce Object Query
    Language (SOQL) 12
Salesforce Order of Execution
  about 34, 35
  example scenario 35, 36
  save order of execution 36-38
Salesforce platform
  clicks, versus code 38, 39
  permissions, working on 90, 91
  sharing and permissions 91
  sharing, working on 90, 91
scheduled Apex class
  testing 179-182
scheduled Apex jobs
  need for 166
  one-off execution 166
  repeating jobs 167
  testing 179-182
setup objects 112
sharing framework
  enforcing 92-95
singleton class
  versus static class 11
Sites pages 238-240

software development
  precautions 20
SOQL
  permissions and security,
      enforcing within 103, 104
SOQL injection
  vulnerabilities, avoiding 104-106
state
  capturing 66-69
static resources
  used, for testing RESTful
      web services 81-85
streaming logs
  using 23-26
sub query
  child records, retrieving 314
System.schedule method
  using 171-174
  versus System.scheduleBatch, for
      Batch Apex classes 174, 175

T

testability 129
test data factory
  loading, with Test.loadData 79-81
  using, to create data 73-78
Test-Driven Development (TDD) 21
Test.startTest
  using 85
Test.stopTest
  using 85
time to live (TTL) 317
tools
  selecting 30, 31
trigger
  architecture 39-41

trigger execution
  controlling 49-52
trigger handler frameworks
  using 41-49

U

unexpected exceptions 56
Uniform Resource Locator
      (URL) 220, 221
unknown exceptions 57
URL Rewriter
  using 240
user interface (UI) 72
utility class 283-290

V

Visualforce pages
  creating 241, 242
  using 240
Visualforce performance
  profiling 290-292

W

Workbench
  endpoints, testing 235, 236
  URL 235

X

XML
  handling 248, 249

Made in the USA
Las Vegas, NV
19 December 2020